AUTHENTICALLY BLACK AND TRULY CATHOLIC

Authentically Black and Truly Catholic

The Rise of Black Catholicism in the Great Migration

Matthew J. Cressler

NEW YORK UNIVERSITY PRESS
New York

NEW YORK UNIVERSITY PRESS
New York
www.nyupress.org

© 2017 by New York University
All rights reserved

References to Internet websites (URLs) were accurate at the time of writing. Neither the author nor New York University Press is responsible for URLs that may have expired or changed since the manuscript was prepared.

ISBN: 978-1-4798-4132-5 (hardback)
ISBN: 978-1-4798-8096-6 (paperback)

For Library of Congress Cataloging-in-Publication data, please contact the Library of Congress.

New York University Press books are printed on acid-free paper, and their binding materials are chosen for strength and durability. We strive to use environmentally responsible suppliers and materials to the greatest extent possible in publishing our books.

Manufactured in the United States of America

10 9 8 7 6 5 4 3 2 1

Also available as an ebook

To Mary Dolores Gadpaille, Father George Clements, and all the Black people who made and continue to make Catholic Chicago

And to Mary Ellen, always

CONTENTS

Acknowledgments	ix
Introduction	1
1. Migrants and Missionaries: "Foreign Missions" on the South Side of Chicago	19
2. Becoming Catholic: Education, Evangelization, and Conversion	49
3. The Living Stations of the Cross: Black Catholic Difference in the Black Metropolis	83
4. Black Catholics and Black Power: Concerned Black Catholics and the Struggle for Self-Determination	116
5. Becoming Black Catholics: The Black Catholic Movement and the Rise of Black Catholicism	152
Conclusion	195
Notes	203
Bibliography	239
Index	253
About the Author	263

ACKNOWLEDGMENTS

This book began, in a very real sense, with gifts. A long time ago my father bought me Cyprian Davis's classic *History of Black Catholics*, not knowing all of what it was. My mentor gave me a used copy of Lawrence Lucas's *Black Priest/White Church* some years later, introducing me to the story that sparked this project. I could not have imagined where these gifts would lead me.

This book is born of the grace and generosity of the Black Catholic Chicagoans who welcomed me into their homes and invited me to their parishes. Special thanks goes to the women and men who opened their lives to me in interviews (and introduced me to more and more people to talk to): Adrienne Curry, Mary Howard, Delores Williams, Dr. C. Vanessa White, Dr. Sheila Adams, Dr. Kimberly Lymore, Dr. Timone Davis, Cheryl Cattledge, and the parishioners at St. Malachy and Corpus Christi. My research would not have been possible without the willingness of priests and sisters serving in Black parishes to provide access to untapped sources and share their own sense of the city's history. Thank you Fr. Richard Andrus, Fr. Matthew Eyerman, Fr. Robert Miller, Fr. Freddy Washington, Fr. Andrew Smith, Sr. Marita Zeller, Sr. Mary Lou Bigler, and the Sisters of St. Francis in Dubuque, Iowa. Cardinal Francis George spoke with me not long before he passed away, recalling his childhood pilgrimage to Corpus Christi's Living Stations of the Cross with his mother. Archbishop Wilton D. Gregory graciously granted me an interview in which he reflected on the Church's "moments of glory and moments of shame" when it came to its Black brothers and sisters. Andrew Lyke aided in the beginning and end of my research, first as director of Chicago's Office for Black Catholics and later in sharing stories of his uncle, the late Archbishop James P. Lyke. Sr. Jamie Phelps and Fr. Maurice Nutt have both been far more supportive than I deserve, not only sharing their experiences and expertise in interviews but also inviting me into the Institute for Black Catholic Studies community. Finally,

Fr. George Clements. The Black Power protest movement that fought for (and won) his appointment as pastor was the first story I tried to tell. Fr. Clements met me for multiple interviews, patiently put up with numerous phone calls, and always did so with an encouraging smile and a kind word. Thank you for your life's work, which continues to inspire everyone you encounter. This book is but one of the many stories that can, that must be told of Black Catholics. It is dedicated to them. Thank you all.

My research would have gone nowhere if not for the tireless efforts of several archivists. Many thanks go to Lesley Martin at the Chicago History Museum Research Center; Julie Satzik and Meg Hall at the Archdiocese of Chicago Joseph Cardinal Bernardin Archives and Records Center; Sr. Veronica Bagenstos and Sr. Maxine Lavell at the Celano Archives of the Sisters of St. Francis; Marcia Stein and Peter Gunther at the Robert Meyers Archives, Chicago Province of Society of the Divine Word; Denise Thuston at the Franciscan Province of the Sacred Heart Archives; and Dr. Stephanie Morris at the Sisters of the Blessed Sacrament Archives.

A number of different institutions, organizations, and intellectual communities have sustained my research over the past six years. I am grateful for the financial support of Northwestern University's Graduate School, the Alice Kaplan Institute for the Humanities (Northwestern), the Cushwa Center for the Study of American Catholicism (Notre Dame), the American Catholic Historical Association, and the College of Charleston's School of Humanities and Social Sciences Dean's Fund. The feedback I've received from audience members, panel participants, and workshop attendees helped refine my argument time and time again. Many thanks to Northwestern's Department of Religious Studies, the Lived History of Vatican II conference, Princeton University's American Religious History Workshop, the Institute for Black Catholic Studies (Xavier University of Louisiana), the American Historical Association, and the American Academy of Religion for creating spaces to present my work and receive invaluable insight. Shannen Dee Williams and Fr. Bryan Massingale both aided and encouraged me at the start of my research. No group was more instrumental in the early stages of this project than Northwestern's North American Religions Workshop. They carefully read everything I wrote and always matched criticism with compassion (and a healthy dose of wine). Thank you Amanda Baugh, Hayley Glaholt, Monica Mercado, Chris Cantwell, Kate Dugan, Jennifer Callaghan, Stephanie Brehm, Ariel Schwartz, and all my fellow NAR-Winians. A special shout out goes to Northwestern's Interfaith Initiative, the student group that hosted my very first presentation of this research in what feels like a lifetime ago. I have also been blessed with brilliant and kind colleagues, first at Earlham College and now at the College of Charleston. Earlham's Midnight Manuscripts writers' workshop was clutch. Three consecutive CofC Writers' Retreats (along with the M&Ms they provided) were essential to the completion of my manuscript. And I never would have finished if not for the caffeine and relative quiet provided by Black Tap, the Malvern Buttery, the Brothers K, and Kudu.

I was privileged to have a number of people willing to read numerous iterations of my manuscript as it moved toward completion. Sarah McFarland Taylor was never short of enthusiasm for my work. Martha Biondi connected (and continues to connect) me to the living history of Black Chicago and honed my understanding of the particular way Black Catholics took up Black Power. My external reviewers made my final manuscript immeasurably better. They truly *got* what I was trying to do, sometimes better than I did myself. Thank you M. Shawn Copeland, Judith Weisenfeld, Curtis Evans, and Kristy Nabhan-Warren. Your feedback clarified my argument and pushed me to write with much more precision. Sylvester Johnson has a knack for naming the most poignant points in my argument and encouraging me to be bolder in making them. Thank you for never ceasing to empower me. My first halting step toward what became my main argument occurred over a conference coffee with Wallace Best. Thank you for thinking with me all these years, for helping me find my own authorial voice, and for the warmth of your friendship. And Robert Orsi, what can I say? You spent countless hours combing each page I wrote at every stage of the process. You were generous with your time and incisive with your insights. You model how scholarship and teaching can be an art, and how we can do both without losing sight of the humanity of everyone we're in relationship with. Thank you.

There would, of course, be no book at all without my editor Jennifer Hammer. My thinking is sharper and my writing is clearer because of your guidance. Thank you for your unwavering support every step of the way. Thanks go to Amy Klopfenstein as well for ushering my manuscript through revisions and production—and for answering ceaseless questions!

I am forever indebted to my teachers. Thanks go to Max Jones and Davis Thompson, who unlocked the magic of words for me and first awakened a love of the intellectual life, and to Mark Huddle, whose civil rights to Black Power course and fortieth-anniversary pilgrimage to Selma ignited my passion for African American history. Most especially, thank you to Susan Abraham, who took me apart and built me back up, brick by brick. You exemplify what it means to be a truly transformative teacher. This book is one more example of how each of you change the world, one student at a time.

Writing can be lonely work. Good friends are a necessity, brilliant friends are even better. Several dear friends, scholars in their own right, provided substantial feedback. All sustained me with their abundant laughter and love (and libations). Thank you to Joe and Allison Sterrett-Krause, Jessica Streit and Hamid El Jaouari, Mari Crabtree, Shari Rabin, Betsy and Joel Schlabach, Noah Silverman and Rena Dascal, Jenan Mohajir and Ali Ammoura, Fr. Dan Riley and the Mt. Irenaeus family, Benjamin Gregg, Joey Lepsch and my whole Bonas crew, Matt Saba, Matt Feminella, Michael Sinnott, Sam Candler, Will Caldwell, Phil Keuhn and Stacey Daley, Trevor Ahrendt, Amir and Brian Thomas-Reed, Brian and Tina Clites, and Rachel and Nathan Bennett.

My families make me whole. To Shelly, Gerry, Ben, Mel, Paul, and all the Case Giesses, thank you for surrounding me with love and putting up with me when I don't feel like playing solitaire. Tom Nadar, you are dearly missed and warmly remembered. Joan and Dick Gaeta, my Nana and Papa, I love you and miss you. Thank you for showing us what family is meant to be. To the Gaeta clan, thank you for nourishing me with good life and good food. *Alla famiglia!* To my sisters and brothers (in-law), Christina and Michael, Joanna and Eric, thank you for reminding me I've really had a wonderful life (and teasing me when I need teasing). As for my parents, John and Maria, there are no words that will suffice. You remain my first and best teachers. You gave me the gift of life. You inspire me in all that I do. Thank you, for everything.

Lastly, my loves. Moira, I could live on your laughter alone. Elena, I was bouncing you in your bouncy-chair with one foot when I typed the first words of what would become this book; now you're building whole worlds with your imagination. The unbridled joy (and frequent exhaustion) you both bring me serve as a steadfast reminder of what is truly important. And Mary Ellen Giess. Writing acknowledgements really puts things in perspective. Mary Ellen literally created human life (twice!) in the time it took for me to complete this book. You are the best wife and friend (not to mention editor) I could ever ask for. The depths of your compassion never cease to amaze me; the amount you're able to accomplish always astounds me. Nothing I do is possible without you.

Introduction

"We, the 10 Black bishops of the United States, chosen from among you to serve the People of God, are a significant sign among many other signs that the Black Catholic community in the American Church has now come of age."[1]

The bishops issued their first pastoral letter, "What We Have Seen and Heard," in which this statement appeared, in 1984 on the Feast of St. Peter Claver, a patron saint of African Americans. They cited Pope Paul VI, who, speaking to African bishops at a 1969 symposium in Uganda, had declared "you must now give your gifts of Blackness to the whole Church."[2] The bishops extended that declaration, saying, "[W]e believe that these solemn words of our Holy Father Paul VI were addressed not only to Africans today but also to us, the children of the Africans of yesterday."[3]

The bishops wrote, "There is a richness in our Black experience that we must share with the entire People of God.... These are gifts that are part of an African past. For we have heard with Black ears and we have seen with Black eyes and we have understood with an African heart."[4] They laid claim to a distinctively Black way of experiencing the world and thus to a distinctively Black way of being Catholic. Black Catholics, they asserted, were distinguished from their coreligionists by Black Spirituality, which the bishops identified as "in keeping with our African heritage" and in contrast "with much of the Western tradition."[5] The bishops also named Black Catholics as inheritors of the Black Church. While Black Catholics "insist upon total loyalty to all that is Catholic," they were united with Black Baptists and Methodists and Pentecostals by a bond forged in "common experience and history."[6]

In extolling their views on the rise of Black Catholicism, the most elegant articulation of the gifts of Blackness came in the bishops' discussion of the liturgy. It would be "through the liturgy," they argued, that "Black people will come to realize that the Catholic Church is a homeland for

Black believers just as she is for people of other cultural and ethnic traditions."⁷ The bishops then proclaimed that, for Black Catholics, liturgy "should be authentically Black. It should be truly Catholic."⁸

Authentically Black, truly Catholic. Reflecting on the pastoral letter mere months after its release, the Black Catholic priest and theologian Edward Braxton used these four words to refer, not to the liturgy, but to the experience of being Black and Catholic in America writ large. This powerful turn of phrase became a synecdoche of sorts for Black Catholicism in the decades that followed.⁹ But while the bishops had spoken of it in timeless terms, the idea that Black Catholicism should be "authentically Black" was a relatively recent one. It would have been foreign to Black Catholics not thirty years earlier.

Take Mary Dolores Gadpaille, for example. Born in 1905, Gadpaille (née Mae Arlene Johnson) became Catholic in 1949 on the Feast of the Seven Dolors, the holy day dedicated to the "seven sufferings" of the Blessed Virgin Mary. Mae Arlene took the name Mary Dolores at baptism, which could be translated as "Mary, Mother of Sorrows." She was one among tens of thousands of African Americans who became Catholic in the middle decades of the twentieth century.

Gadpaille's Catholicism was quite different from what the ten Black bishops described. Upon conversion Gadpaille altered her day-to-day routine to include "Daily Holy Mass, Daily Communion, the Rosary, the Way of the Cross, weekly confession, constant direction of a priest, and the practice of the spiritual and corporal works of mercy." She wrote in letters about how "beautiful" the Latin liturgy was, how "even though one does not understand it wholly, it has a rhythm, harmony and mystery that lifts one out of this world." This was not the "authentically Black, truly Catholic" Catholicism the bishops had in mind. Instead, for Gadpaille, Catholicism "lifts us up above the color line, above the natural vicissitudes of every day life." Gadpaille thanked priests for "restoring to us [Negroes] by just being Catholic a vanished dignity that all the interracial organizations together have not achieved by conference of [sic] legislation. . . . [I]n the place of second class citizenship that America allots, you have given us a passport to citizenship in Heaven, for this earth is 'no abiding city.'"¹⁰

Only twenty-six years separated Mary Dolores Gadpaille's letters from that of the ten Black bishops. What happened in those interven-

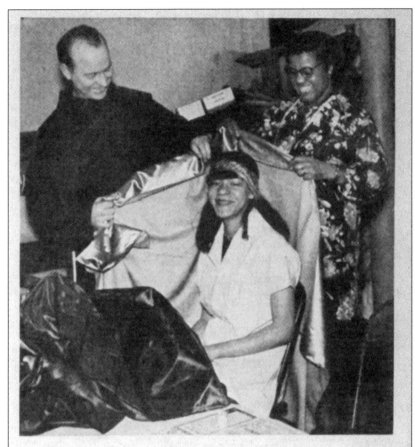

Father Joseph and Mary Dolores Gadpaille adjust the headdress of Thelma Mullin. Mrs. Gadpaille is in charge of all costume making, designing and fitting

Figure I.1. Mary Dolores Gadpaille adjusts costume for performance of the Living Stations of the Cross. Catholic Church Extension Society Records. Courtesy of Loyola University Chicago Archives & Special Collections.

ing decades? How could such a profound transformation in ideas about what being a Black Catholic meant occur in such a short span of time? The answer will take us from conversion amidst the Great Migrations to revolution in the Black Power era.

The middle third of the twentieth century, from the 1930s through the 1970s, was a period of unparalleled growth for Black Catholics in the United States. There were approximately 300,000 Black Catholics in 1940. By 1975 there were almost 1 million, a 208 percent increase, and the Black Catholic center of gravity had shifted from the coastal South to the industrial North.[11] Most remarkable about this fact is that the Catholic world African Americans entered in the first half of the twentieth century did not exist by century's end. Gadpaille and the bishops together witnessed the rise of a *Black* Catholicism, a Catholicism remade in the image of Black Spirituality and the Black Church.

* * *

Today most people are surprised to discover that there are 3 million African American Catholics, or that there are more Black Catholics than members of the African Methodist Episcopal Church.[12] The sheer presence of Black Catholics unsettles some of the most deeply held assumptions about religion in the United States: that Catholics are white and that Black people are Protestant. Those assumptions seem to settle, though, if Black Catholics are situated in the context of the Black Church. People might be stunned to learn that there are Black Catholics but, once informed, they are not so surprised to hear gospel choirs or extemporaneous shouts of "Amen!" in the middle of a Mass. It is, of course, true that most Catholics in the twentieth-century United States were the children and grandchildren of European immigrants, and that the majority of African Americans who are religious are Protestant. And it is true that many Black Catholic churches (many, but by no means all) today share aesthetics and worship styles with other Black Christian communities. But these generalities mask more complicated lives. When African Americans became Catholic in large numbers in the first half of the twentieth century, they joined a Church that juxtaposed itself quite explicitly with evangelical Protestantism. The rise of an "authentically Black" Catholicism was neither inevitable nor uncontroversial. The ten Black bishops who published their letter in 1984 were, literally and figuratively, the result of a revolution that was started on the streets of cities like Chicago by Black laypeople, sisters, and priests in the 1960s. And that revolution began as a struggle between Black Catholics themselves over what it would mean to be both Black and Catholic.

To appreciate the magnitude of this revolution we must understand what came before it. Until the turn of the twentieth century, most Catholics lived in the urban North and most African Americans lived in the rural South. The Great Migrations, which witnessed a mass movement of Black people from the rural South to the urban North and West, initiated the first large-scale encounters between African Americans and Catholics of European descent, especially as Black migrants met white Catholic missionaries in the industrial North and Midwest. When Black families enrolled in Catholic schools parents and children alike were introduced to the rituals, prayers, and habits that defined Catholic culture at the time. They learned new ways of imagining, experiencing, and moving in the world around them. Tens of thousands became Catholic in the process. When they did so, their newfound religious life presented itself in sharp contrast to that in the Black evangelical churches surrounding them. The Great Migrations changed religious life and culture across the country as Black and southern ways of being Christian were remade amidst the "exigencies of the city." Black converts to Catholicism stood apart from this increasingly normative Black evangelical culture. In the place of gospel music and altar calls, Black Catholics celebrated the beauty of Latin and what they took to be the "quiet dignity" of the Catholic Mass that had the power to lift them "up above the color line," as Mary Dolores Gadpaille put it.

The very "quiet" and "dignified" rituals that so many Black families embraced in the first half of the twentieth century came under increasing scrutiny in the 1960s and 1970s, however, as a growing group of Black Catholics sparked a revolution in Black Catholic identity and practice. Black Catholic activists drew inspiration from both Black Power, which championed political and cultural self-determination as the keys to Black liberation, and from the Second Vatican Council, which opened the doors to sweeping changes not just in Catholic worship but also in the ways in which Catholics engaged the modern world. Activists attempted to transform what it meant to be both Black and Catholic. Some even allied themselves with the Black Panther Party, an organization founded in 1966 to provide self-defense against police brutality, and adopted the rhetoric and tactics of the Black Power era.

But the Black Catholicism they fought to bring to life faced opposition from fellow Black Catholics. Bitter debates broke out about how Black people *should* be Catholic and whether Catholics *could* be "authentically Black." Activists worked to introduce and educate their coreligionists about a particular way of being Black and Catholic. Ironically, the very people who criticized Catholic missionaries for convincing Black people to convert to a "white religion" became missionaries themselves, inculcating new ways of being religious. In tracing this revolution from the growing numbers of Black Catholics earlier in the twentieth century to the rise of Black Catholicism beginning in the 1960s, this book explores the inseparability of race and religion. Rather than presume the unanimity of Black identity, the ubiquity of Black activism, or the uniformity of Black religion, it brings to light the lived complexities of debates about what it means to be Black and religious.

The choice to focus on the rise of Black Catholicism in Chicago was not arbitrary. Chicago became one of the most significant Black Catholic communities in the country in this period. The Midwestern metropolis served as the destination for hundreds of thousands of Black migrants from the South. It came to symbolize the Great Migrations writ large. But before Chicago became "the Black Metropolis," it was a Catholic Metropolis. Its landscape was defined as much by parish spires as by smokestacks and skyscrapers. Chicago serves as a microcosm of what happened in cities throughout the United States as Black migrants met Catholic missionaries on the streets of New York, Cleveland, St. Louis, Toledo, Milwaukee, and Detroit. At the turn of the twentieth century Chicago's Black Catholic population, such as it was, numbered in the hundreds and met in the basement of a single church. By 1975 they had surpassed Baltimore and New Orleans in size. Chicago's eighty thousand Black Catholics made the city the second largest Black Catholic population in the country. And importantly, they were at the forefront of the Black Power revolution sweeping through Black Catholic communities in the late sixties, a revolution that left U.S. Catholicism changed in its wake.

* * *

Two clarifications are crucial before we move on. First, this book does not suggest that Black Catholics are solely the product of twentieth-century conversions. It should be stated at the start that there have been Catholics of African descent in the Americas for as long as there have been Catholics in the Americas. The ten Black bishops put it plainly in 1984: "Blacks—whether Spanish-speaking, French-speaking or

English-speaking—built the churches, tilled Church lands, and labored with those who labored in spreading the Gospel."[13] Cyprian Davis, the pioneering historian of Black Catholics in the United States, identifies a Moroccan slave with a Christian name, Esteban or Estevanico (Stephen), among the four survivors of Alvar Nuñez Cabeza de Vaca's ill-fated odyssey across the southern coast of North America in 1536.[14] Historian John K. Thornton argues that it was Kongolese Catholic slaves who rose up against their masters in the South Carolina colony in 1739. They launched what we now know as the Stono Rebellion, the largest slave uprising in the British colonies before the Revolutionary War, on the feast day honoring the nativity of the Virgin Mary. As Linda Heywood and John Thornton have shown, "a year before Columbus set sail for America, an African king was baptized and converted his kingdom into a Catholic nation that lasted nearly 370 years."[15] It is possible that the Kongolese rebels planned to fight their way south to Gracia Real de Santa Teresa de Mose in Spanish Florida. Better known simply as Fort Mose, religious studies scholar Sylvester Johnson describes it as "an African military-religious settlement" just north of St. Augustine, one that "was built by Africans in 1738, was assigned a Catholic priest, and was governed by the African (Mandinga) military commander Francisco Menéndez." The settlement's numbers swelled with escaped slaves, freed and armed by the Spanish crown upon conversion to Catholicism.[16]

Black Catholics in the United States are not the anomaly many imagine them to be. Not all Catholics who crossed the Atlantic were white. Nor were Africans and African Americans somehow naturally inclined to be Christian in evangelical and Protestant ways. It is helpful to remember that, from a hemispheric perspective, Black Christianity in the Americas has been and continues to be majority Catholic, just as Catholicism in the Americas has been and continues to be majority non-white. The populations of Brazil, Haiti, Mexico, and other Latin American nations testify to this fact.

The second clarification is even more important than the first. This book does not argue that twentieth-century converts were not really Black, that they somehow "became white" when they became Catholic. Their contemporaries sometimes did make this claim, ridiculing the Catholic Church as a "white man's religion." Some Black Catholics even adopted this rhetoric themselves in the Black Power era, none more famously than Father Lawrence Lucas in his memoir-manifesto *Black Priest/White Church: Catholics and Racism* (1970). But becoming Catholic did not magically protect Black people from the daily degradations of racism in America. Mary Dolores Gadpaille may have hoped that her Church could lift her up above the color line, but this aspiration did not blind her to what white Catholics were capable of. She recalled in that same letter how, when she first visited a Chicago parish in 1950, "fingers were pointed at me. I was called a 'nigger', and the drug store on the corner would not serve me."[17] Black Catholics bore the brunt of racism in their own Church, as more and more scholars are beginning to show.[18] To quote Malcolm X, "we're not brutalized because we're Baptist, we're not brutalized because we're Methodist, we're not brutalized because we're Muslim, we're not brutalized because we're Catholic, we're brutalized because we are Black people in America."[19] The Church did not remove Gadpaille's Blackness; it restored "a vanished dignity" her country continually tried to rob from her.

Conversion did not hermetically seal Black Catholics off from other African Americans either. (Though, as we will see, becoming Catholic did have its costs.) Such a separation would have been impossible considering the racial landscape of American cities. Chicago was then (and remains now) a segregated city. Historian Beryl Satter has shown that Chicago served as the model of a modern segregated city, one replicated nationwide.[20] White Chicagoans enforced boundaries between Black and white neighborhoods with real estate covenants, neighborhood associations, police surveillance, home bombings, and street warfare.[21] Even the accidental crossing of a racial line could set off a race riot, as it did when a Black boy floated into the white section of a South Side beach in 1919.[22] Segregation did have its unintended consequences, though. The creativity of Black Chicagoans and migrants who took ownership of Black segregated spaces birthed Bronzeville (the famed Chicago neighborhood) and the Black Metropolis (Chicago's city within a city).[23] Black Catholics shared in the experience of being Black in Chicago, in modern America.

This book *does* argue, however, that what it has meant to be both Black and Catholic in the lands that became the United States has changed significantly through the centuries. One could make the case that no period witnessed more rapid change than the middle decades of the twentieth century. This specific period witnessed both the exponential rise of Black Catholics as a population and the rise of a new and enduring understanding of Black Catholicism. Mary Dolores Gadpaille and most of the thousands of African Americans who became Catholic before Black Power did not understand themselves to be Catholic in a distinctively Black way. They did not identify themselves with "the Black Church," nor did they trace their lineage to a "Black Spirituality" sprung from the African continent. They may have celebrated "colored saints," the term used by Father Augustus Tolton, the man known nationwide in the late nineteenth century as the first Black priest in the United States, to refer to St. Augustine, St. Benedict, and St. Monica. But they did so not to signal that they were different from their white coreligionists, but as a sign that they too belonged to the universal Church. From Tolton's perspective, this made the Catholic Church the only "true liberator of the race."[24] It is not that Gadpaille was not *actually* Black while the ten bishops were. Instead, what it meant to be Black and Catholic shifted in crucial ways in the decades between them. Converts became Catholic on the verge of a revolution.

We must be wary of flattening the complexity and diversity of Black Catholic lives in our attempt to restore them to the histories from which they have been so systematically erased. Cyprian Davis is right that the Americas have been home to Catholics from the African continent since the sixteenth century and that the Church could claim African saints well before any Atlantic crossings. But something is lost, historically speaking, when we refer to all those unnamed millions singularly as "black Catholics." Something is certainly gained. Davis used the term "black Catholic" in part for simplicity's sake. It is much less cumbersome than talking about a sixteenth-century *Moroccan* convert, eighteenth-century *African* slaves, and participants in the late nineteenth-century *Colored* Catholic Congresses. Beyond its usefulness as a neutral descriptor, "black Catholic" also serves an ideological purpose. It connects those varied subjects to a broader tradition and roots them in a shared past. This is what historians do, after all.

But when activists in the 1960s and 1970s took to calling themselves *Black* Catholics (emphasis on the capital B) while quoting Malcolm X and referencing Franz Fanon, they meant something specific and quite different from what had come before them. This book speaks of "African

American Catholics" and "Black Catholics" interchangeably throughout, similarly for simplicity's sake. Yet taken as a whole, it aims to historicize the very Black Catholicism Davis takes for granted. As we will find, Davis himself was an active participant in the movement that forever changed what those two words meant when linked together—indeed, he served on the subcommittee that oversaw the preliminary drafts of the bishop's letter, "What We Have Seen and Heard."

* * *

Any study of Black Catholics, this "minority within a minority" as Albert Raboteau put it, is interdisciplinary by its very nature. This book stands at the intersection of a few different fields: it engages scholarship in religious studies, African American studies, Catholic studies, and history. Black Catholics tend to be hidden in the blind spots of each respective discipline. For example, consider twentieth-century U.S. historiography. Migrations and freedom struggles come to mind with regard to African American history. A particular notion of the Black Church takes hold as well. Black Catholics do not fit neatly into these narratives. They were members of a largely white institution at a time when gospel choirs and the cadence of Black preachers reigned in the American imagination, and largely absent from the frontlines of civil rights struggles at a time when Black churches became synonymous with protest. The "American century" figures prominently in the stories told about Catholics too. Waves of southern and eastern European immigrants altered the country's social and religious makeup. By midcentury Catholics managed to make themselves "American" by means ranging from the establishment of school systems to military service and Cold War cultural production. Here too, Black Catholics do not quite fit. The century marked the entrance of immigrants and their children into "mainstream" white America at the expense of Black people.[25]

Black Catholic lives do not adhere to the carefully patrolled borders of the academy. While disciplinary boundaries are necessary inasmuch as they narrow our field of inquiry, they remain the creation of scholars. As religious studies scholar J. Z. Smith reminds us, "the map is not the territory."[26] We must not mistake our categories for our subjects themselves. Studying Black Catholics brings all-too-often isolated disciplines into conversation with one another. It forces us to cross the lines on those maps. Black Catholics have been left on the margins of inquiry because they are not easily incorporated into our comfortable narratives. But if we move Black Catholics from the margins to the center, new narratives emerge. When we listen to what Black Catholics have to say about their own lives, allowing for all the contradictions and complexities that characterize human life, we find that they complicate the categories that define our fields of study. Just as Women's Studies challenges us not just to add women to existing scholarship but to change the terms of scholarship itself, so too the study of Black Catholics shifts the way we think about Catholics, African Americans, and religion in the United States.

The decision to focus on Black Catholics—rather than white Catholic encounters with Black people, or interactions between Black and white Catholics—leads to different insights. Nowhere is this more evident than with regard to the study of Catholics and race. John McGreevy's *Parish Boundaries: The Catholic Encounter with Race in the Twentieth-Century Urban North* (1996) influenced and inspired a generation of scholarship on Catholics and racial justice, including my own. McGreevy explores how white Catholics experienced Black migrations through the lens of a distinctive Catholic culture and institutional landscape, captured in the titular term "parish boundaries." At the heart of his story are "Catholic liberals," often referred to as "interracialists," who set the terms of engagement on "public discussions of racial issues" by the end of the 1950s.[27] Catholic liberals shared the presuppositions of racial liberalism writ large. They argued that the best way to improve "race relations" and eliminate "discrimination" would be to erase race altogether. There is no white race or Black race but one human race, so the saying goes. Or, as a Catholic liberal would have put it, we are all members of the one Mystical Body of Christ. Interracialists fought hard, in para-parish organizations like the Catholic Interracial Council, against so-called "racial" parishes that separated Black and Irish and Italian and Mexican Catholics from one another. And they fought for the civil rights championed in what Jacquelyn Dowd Hall called the "classical chronology" of the civil rights movement, the period between the *Brown v. Board of Education* decision of 1954 and the Voting Rights Act of 1965.[28]

Since *Parish Boundaries*, most scholarship on Catholics and race has been devoted to interracial encounters and interracialism as an ideology. This is one reason why this book avoids substantive discussion of this topic. There are already a number of great books on the subject.[29] But there are also problems with the interracialist approach—people and events it obscures even as it illuminates others. Foremost among the obscured are Black Catholics. Despite the desires of Catholic liberals, Black Catholics in segregated cities tended to be members of majority-Black parishes and tended not to participate in interracial activism. This should not surprise us. Most people did not actively participate in civil rights activism. Part of what makes activists *activists*, after all, is the fact that they are exceptional in the fullest sense of the word.[30] Most Catholic Chicagoans worshipped with people who shared their own ethnic and cultural heritage. One thinks of Martin Luther King's truism that "the most segregated hour in Christian America is eleven o'clock on Sunday morning."[31] Most scholarship on "the Catholic encounter with race," as McGreevy's subtitle implies, is more concerned with white Catholic encounters with Black people than with Black Catholics themselves. When Black Catholics do appear, they tend to be considered *in relation to* white Catholics. Black Catholic scholars are notable exceptions to this general rule, though their prolific work remains marginal in the history of religion in the United States. I am indebted to their trailblazing—to Jamie Phelps, Bryan Massingale, Maurice Nutt, and M. Shawn Copeland in particular.

This book sets out to consider Black Catholic communities on their own terms. When we do so a few things become clear. White missionaries had a far wider impact on Black Catholic communities than white interracialists. As uncomfortable as it might make us, missionaries who prioritized saving eternal souls over solving pressing social problems were precisely the people who encouraged tens of thousands of African Americans to become Catholic. Highlighting a Catholic liberal elite—the hundreds involved in interracialist efforts—misses the lives of most Black Catholics. It elucidates the intersection of religion and politics for some, but at the expense of the everyday lives of most. This is not to say that this book ignores Catholic relationships across the color line. We will spend considerable time examining the relationships white missionaries and Black Catholics forged with one another during the Great Migrations. This did not make them "interracial" in the sense meant by Catholic liberals, though. Instead, the parishes tended to be populated by Black Catholics and controlled by white Catholics. If they could be described as interracial, they certainly were not interracial*ist*. While white-controlled majority-Black parishes did not keep African Americans from becoming or remaining Catholic, their control would serve as a significant factor that compelled some Black Catholics to embrace Black Power.

Which leads us to a second point. An emphasis on Black Catholic communities allows us to see beyond the limits of the classical civil rights chronology. Timothy Neary and Karen Johnson rightly extend Catholic interracial activism into the decades preceding the *Brown v. Board of Education* decision, situating Catholics on the front end of the "long civil rights era."[32] Yet when we focus attention on interracialists, Catholic freedom struggles inevitably end in the late 1960s. McGreevy notes how Catholic liberals lamented that most "African-American Catholics remained culturally conservative." "To the disappointment of liberals," he continues, "few African-American Catholics—clergy or laity—took leadership positions in the civil rights movement. (One white priest publicly wished for a 'Catholic version of Martin Luther King.')"[33] Black Power ended the endeavors of liberals. It contributed to the "collapse of interracialism."[34] As McGreevy put it, "the hope of the interracialists, that racial and ethnic differences would give way to an overarching religious identity, faded amidst the fear that the Church would become wholly irrelevant to African-American concerns."[35] But if Black Power ended the hopes of Catholic liberals, it ignited the Black Catholic freedom struggles. Black Power galvanized some Black Catholics (even as it unnerved others). It provided a generation of activists with the tools to transform their Church.[36] Although there may not have been any Black Catholic equivalent of Martin Luther King, soon enough there were Black Catholic Malcolm Xs, Stokely Carmichaels, and Angela Davises.

If this book calls upon scholars of Catholics and race to pay attention to Black Power, it calls upon scholars of Black Power in turn to pay attention to religion. Recent years have been transformative for Black freedom struggles historiography. Scholars have challenged the classical narrative of the civil rights movement that centered almost exclusively on a male minister led movement that fought segregation in the Jim Crow South through respectable nonviolent Christian protest between

1955 and 1965. This "civic myth of civil rights," as Nikhil Pal Singh calls it, is the story rehearsed every year in celebration of America's progress toward Martin Luther King's dream of the day when children "will not be judged by the color of their skin, but by the content of their character."[37] We now know that Black activists fought for fair housing and equal employment in the urban North ten years before Rosa Parks sat down in that Montgomery bus.[38] We know that nonviolence always coexisted, albeit in tension, with long-standing Black traditions of armed self-defense.[39] We know that Black women were instrumental organizers without whom there would have been no movement at all.[40] And we know that Black Power represented not the death but the rebirth of Black freedom struggles.[41]

One myth persists, though: that of a secular Black Power movement. Black Catholic history seriously challenges this myth. Scholars rightly criticize the Black Christian exceptionalism of civil rights scholarship that polices the parameters of "proper" protest by comparing all activism to King's Christian nonviolence. Yet we should not overstate the case in our attempt to reinstate Black Power in our histories. There is a way in which "militancy" and "radicalism" come to serve as code words for "secular" and "nonreligious." Scholars and popular audiences alike share the perception that Black freedom struggles moved in a more radical direction once freed from the restraints of religion. It is true that Black Power represented a significant critique of racial liberalism as an ideology, interracialism as an objective, and Christian nonviolence as a tactic. But it is also true that some Black religious communities, especially those in urban settings, embraced this critique. By the end of the 1960s a small but growing number of Black Catholics did so. This book features Black Panthers joining Black Catholics in the struggle for self-determination in the Archdiocese of Chicago, priests performing "Black Unity Masses" that incorporated the language and aesthetics of Black Power protest, and parishes adorning their walls with murals to "Black martyrs" like Malcolm X and Fred Hampton. Black Power transformed Black Catholics and Black Catholics in turn engaged the political and cultural nationalisms that defined the Black Power era. And they were not alone. This book joins the work of Angela Dillard and Kerry Pimblott, insisting that scholars of Black Power pay attention to the ways in which religious communities participated in Black

Power as well as the ways in which Black Power forever changed Black religious life in America.[42]

This book likewise enters into ongoing conceptual conversations about "Black religion" and "the Black Church." The study of African American religion has taken a self-critical turn over the past decade, sharing a disciplinary impulse of religious studies writ large. Much work has been done to demonstrate the constructedness of constitutive terms that define the field. "Black religion" and "the Black Church" have been identified as categories produced by people with particular motives in particular moments, not descriptions of essential or singular things. Scholars have encouraged us to observe the variety of African American religions, to move beyond the Black Church in order to see the churches, temples, mosques, and synagogues (not to mention the nonreligious) that make up the fullness of African American life. This book builds on this literature.[43] In the first half of the twentieth century Black Catholics exemplified an African American religious community outside the evangelical Christian tradition, beyond the Black Church. When this book explores the life of Black Catholic schools or devotions popular in Black Catholic parishes, it illuminates ways of being Black and religious that do not conform to popular expectations of Black church life. Black converts embraced practices that distinguished them from other Black Christian communities.

And yet, if their difference signaled Black religious diversity, Black Catholics also reinforced the normative power of "Black religion" and "the Black Church." There is no Black Church, so scholars have said, only Black churches. But, as they crafted an "authentically Black" way of being Catholic, Black Catholics in the Black Power era embraced what they took to be an essential Black Spirituality and learned how to incorporate the traditions of the Black Church (which they took to be singular) into the liturgy. Activists criticized coreligionists who resisted this transformation of Catholic worship as self-hating and escapist, as Black people brainwashed into thinking that "white was right." Black Catholics thus embodied the dilemma Curtis Evans describes as "the peculiar burden of black religion." Black people have been burdened, he argues, to the extent "that a repudiation of those religious and cultural practices deemed singularly 'Negro' provoked criticism for being a betrayal of blackness. To embrace such ideas, on the other hand, was viewed by others as an affirmation of the 'natural' expression of the primitive and emotional passions of an essential blackness."[44] Black Catholics found themselves in this double bind in the middle decades of the twentieth century. Thousands of converts joined the Catholic Church at a time when to be Black and Catholic meant to reject the ritual life of Black evangelical Christianity. They rejected the notion that there was only one way to be Black and religious. This very rejection, though, opened them up to severe criticism as the rise of Black Catholicism recast their distinct devotional life not as Catholic, but as white.

* * *

This book is organized in two parts. The first three chapters describe the rise of Black Catholic Chicago, the growth of a sizable Black Catholic population in the Black Metropolis from roughly the 1930s through the 1950s. Though the chronologies of these chapters overlap, each should be understood as a sequential step in an argument that stretches over the first half of the book, that the Great Migrations initiated mass conversions of African Americans to Catholicism by inculcating new religious practices that set converts apart from other Black Christians in the city. Chapter 1 contends that the convergence of the Great Migrations with Catholic missionary efforts set the conditions for Black Catholic conversion. It reveals how missionaries reimagined Chicago neighborhoods as "foreign mission territories" full of "heathens" in need of conversion and it examines the fraught relationships white missionaries forged with Black migrants as a result. Chapter 2 takes readers into Catholic schools where families rehearsed new rituals, learned new prayers, and developed new relationships. Parochial schools effected a transformation of the religious sensorium and led many Black women, men, and children to become Catholic. Chapter 3 situates Black Catholic converts in the African American religious landscape of migrations-era Chicago. It centers on a nationally renowned performance of the passion of Christ in order to illustrate how devotionalism set Black Catholics apart from the evangelical Christian communities proliferating around them. Chapter 3 argues that Black Catholics shared in the impulse of Black Muslims, Black Hebrews, and others who fashioned ways of being Black and religious beyond the Black Church.

The second half of the book charts the rise of Black Catholicism in Chicago and across the country, a distinctive understanding of how Black people should be Catholic that emerged in the 1960s and came to fruition in the 1980s. Chapter 4 argues that Black Power fundamentally shaped the Black Catholic experience of the Second Vatican Council and birthed a revolution in Black Catholic life in the process. The story begins with a protest movement in the Archdiocese of Chicago in 1968 and 1969. When the archbishop refused to promote Father George Clements, a popular Black priest, Black Catholics joined forces with Black Panthers and other allies to fight for self-determination. Chapter 5 follows the Black Catholic activists who fought to incorporate African and African American traditions into Catholic life. The chapter expands the scope of the book to explore the Black Catholic Movement on the national level at the same time that it examines how this revolution played out in the idiosyncrasies of a particular Chicago community: Holy Angels parish under the leadership of Father Clements. It argues that in their effort to make the Church "authentically Black," activists were forced to become missionaries, working to convert their Black Catholic coreligionists to *Black* Catholicism. If the first part of this book is about African Americans becoming Catholic, the second witnesses what it meant to become Black Catholics.

* * *

Four converts were among the ten Black bishops who announced the arrival of an "authentically Black" Catholicism in their famous letter, and two of them hailed from Chicago. Decades before they championed Black Catholicism, before they were ordained to the priesthood, James Lyke and Wilton Gregory were sons of the South Side who came of age amidst the rise of Black Catholic Chicago. Lyke grew up in the Wentworth Gardens housing project. His Baptist mother enrolled him in Catholic school and paid his tuition in part by cleaning the church's laundry. He and his mother became Catholic, along with a number of his siblings.[45] Wilton Gregory lived with his mother and grandmother in Englewood when Adrian Dominican sisters invited him to enroll at St. Carthage grammar school. There he decided to become a priest before he even converted to Catholicism. Separated by about a decade, Lyke and Gregory were students in parochial schools filled with African

Americans who were not Catholic. Thousands of Black Chicagoans, the daughters and sons of southern migrants, joined them in their journey into the Catholic Church. This was what Archbishop Gregory later called one of the Catholic Church's "moments of glory," when a handful of priests and sisters looked at the neighborhood changing around them and said "this is the community that's here, let's welcome them."[46] It is to those missionaries and migrants that we now turn.

1

Migrants and Missionaries

"Foreign Missions" on the South Side of Chicago

Mary Howard and her twin sister Martha arrived in Chicago on a summer Sunday in 1939. Their train ticket on the Illinois Central line had been a high school graduation gift from their father, who already lived in Chicago's "Black Belt" on the South Side of the city. The twins arrived from New Orleans, not knowing that they would spend the rest of their lives in the Midwestern metropolis. To this point, Mary and Martha's tale resembled that of countless other African Americans from across the South. Between 1915 and 1970 millions of African Americans "voted with their feet" and left the lynch mobs, debt peonage, and segregated spaces of Jim Crow. For many this journey represented nothing less than an Exodus from the Egyptland of the South. Along with their belongings, migrants carried with them dreams of new futures possible in the urban North. Chicago was among the greatest beneficiaries of these "Great Migrations," which one author has called "one of the largest and most rapid internal movements of people in history."[1] The Black Belt boomed as thousands of Marys and Marthas arrived each day, with Chicago's Black population rising from 44,103 in 1910 to 492,000 by the 1950s.

What happened next, though, set Mary and Martha apart in this "Mecca of the migrant mob."[2] As they stepped off the train and onto the platform Mary turned to her father to remind him, "You know we gotta be Catholic, we gotta go to Mass today." It was a Sunday, and it was a mortal sin to knowingly miss Mass. So before they brought their baggage to their father's apartment, the sisters needed assurance that there was a church close by. Their anxiety proved unwarranted because there stood a large Catholic church in the heart of the burgeoning "Black Metropolis," as the South Side was coming to be known. The gray-stoned Italian-Renaissance structure towered over the intersection of 49th

Street and Grand Boulevard, just north of Washington Park. Twin bell towers connected the façade of Corpus Christi Catholic church to its three-story rectory and school. Built at the turn of the twentieth century as a monument to the wealth of its Irish parishioners, the parish, like the neighborhood surrounding it, had become predominantly Black by 1939. Not three decades prior the boulevard had been home to upwardly mobile Irish and Jewish Chicagoans.[3] Now Corpus Christi sat mere blocks from Black Belt intersections affectionately known as "Negro Heaven" and "the Ivory Coast."[4]

A Franciscan friar, wearing the signature brown habit cinched with the white rope of his order, stood outside the church welcoming parishioners and passers-by alike. "Oh, come in, come in," he called out to Mary and Martha. And so the twins entered Corpus Christi for the first time. This would be their parish home for the rest of their lives. That morning they attended the 10 o'clock High Mass. The service was, of course, performed in Latin but this posed no problem. Mary and Martha had both been educated by the Sisters of the Blessed Sacrament in New Orleans, an order of women dedicated to work among Native Americans and African Americans. There they had been schooled in Latin since elementary school. Now they found themselves worshipping in what was fast becoming the largest and most significant Black Catholic church in the city. When the friars invited the twins to involve themselves in the life of the parish shortly thereafter, they accepted with enthusiasm. Mary and Martha would be mainstays of the community through the end of the century. "Once we got here," Mary reflected decades later, "it was just like coming home."[5]

Mary and Martha arrived amidst the rise of Black Catholic Chicago. "The rise of Black Catholic Chicago" in this book refers to the emergence of Black Catholics as a significant, albeit small, constituency in Catholic Chicago and the establishment of the institutional infrastructure necessary to sustain them. At the turn of the twentieth century the city's Black Catholic community numbered just a few hundred people meeting in the basement of a single parish. By 1975 Chicago was home to 80,000 Black Catholics, the second largest Black Catholic population in the country. More Black Catholics lived in 1970s Chicago than in New Orleans or Baltimore, an astonishing fact considering the centuries-long histories of Black Catholic Louisiana and Maryland.[6] This remarkable growth paralleled religious-demographic shifts nationwide. The U.S. Black Catholic population grew from under 300,000 to over 900,000 members from 1940 to 1975 (a 208 percent increase) and, in that same period, the Black Catholic center of gravity shifted from the coastal South to the industrial North.[7]

How and why did this rise occur? The twins' tale proves instructive for answering this question, though perhaps not how we might expect. The vast majority of migrants did not share Mary and Martha's Catholic faith. What is more, most members of Corpus Christi had not been Catholic upon arrival. Instead, what is enlightening is the interaction between the twins and the friars on that South Side street. It might have amazed Mary and Martha to discover that this vibrant parish had closed temporarily not a decade earlier. Once a prominent Irish parish, Corpus Christi's pews emptied in the 1910s and 1920s as more and more African Americans moved to the neighborhood and more and more white Catholics left. The parish the twins entered in 1939 was not peopled primarily by Black Catholics from the historic centers of Black Catholic America, like their native New Orleans, though there were some. Rather, Black converts sustained Corpus Christi, converts who had migrated from Arkansas, Georgia, Kentucky, Alabama, and elsewhere. Priests had baptized nearly two hundred Black children and adults just three months before Mary and Martha's first visit.[8] Corpus Christi was not unique in this regard. On the contrary, it bore a resemblance to most of the parishes that survived the demographic shifts brought by the Great Migrations. (There were many more that did not.) It was a parish born of relationships between Black migrants and Catholic missionaries.

The convergence of southern Black migrants and white Catholic missionaries made the rise of Black Catholic Chicago possible. Beginning with the First World War and accelerating with the Second, African Americans migrated from the rural South to the urban North and West in ever increasing numbers. These Great Migrations have been well documented. Less well known is the fact that they coincided with burgeoning missionary efforts among white Catholic priests, sisters, and laypeople across the country. Missionaries hoped to make the United States Catholic by winning converts to what Catholics considered the "One True Faith." As the Great Migrations remade the American religious landscape, many missionaries came to the conclusion that their

Church's survival in cities depended on African American converts. In Chicago, as in cities across the country, Catholic missionaries reimagined Black neighborhoods as "foreign mission fields" populated by "heathens" in need of "true religion." For most Black migrants, their first encounters with Catholics would be shaped by the desires and anxieties of these missionaries. This Catholic missionary commitment to Black migrants proved quite successful. The meeting of missionaries and migrants led to thousands of Black Catholic converts. Yet it also forged a fraught relationship between missionaries of the "One True Faith" and the "heathens" they served, as missionaries imagined Black Protestant migrants. This asymmetry of power between the converters and the converted sat uneasily at the heart of Black Catholic history in the early twentieth century and would spark a revolution in the 1960s and 1970s.

The Great Migrations Remake the Catholic Metropolis

It is impossible to understand Black Catholics in the twentieth century without first accounting for the impact of the Great Migrations. Indeed, it is hard to overestimate the significance the Great Migrations had on American history and culture in the twentieth century. Nearly 8 million African Americans left the South in the twentieth century. Mary and Martha were two among 391,641 Black migrants who left the South in the 1930s alone—and that was a down decade.[9] At the start of the century, African Americans were a predominantly rural and southern people, as they had been for their entire history in what became the United States. All that changed in the decades that followed. Less than 740,000 African Americans lived outside the South in 1900, only 8 percent of the national Black population. By 1970, 47 percent of African Americans in the United States lived outside the South, more than 10.6 million.[10]

The convergence of a number of factors caused these migrations. Northern and Western industrial economies expanded rapidly during the First and Second World Wars at the same time that the agricultural economy of the South collapsed. White and Black southerners alike traveled north and west as a result, in search of better economic opportunities. But African American migrations also represented bold political statements. The solidification of white supremacy through legal segregation and paralegal mob violence in the Jim Crow South motivated the departure of African Americans, many of whom experienced the Great Migrations as an Exodus comparable to the biblical flight of Israelites out of Egypt. This mass movement was not spontaneous or leaderless. Family members explored potential cities prior to the arrival of their kin; ministers arranged for the transportation of entire church communities; newspapers and labor scouts encouraged migration by spreading tales of opportunity in the North. Together these factors contributed to an unprecedented movement of people, even if Black migrants would quickly discover that there was a major discrepancy between their imagining of Chicago as the "Promised Land" and the reality of an increasingly segregated city often hostile to Black migrants.[11]

Chicago loomed large in the Great Migrations for a variety of reasons. Historian James Grossman points out that while jobs were available in most northern cities, "the decision to go to Chicago, rather than to New York, Detroit, or one of many smaller northern communities" stemmed from a variety of factors that changed over time. The first family members to arrive typically chose Chicago "because of its position at the head of the Illinois Central [Railroad system] and its particularly high visibility in the Black South."[12] Chicago's renown was due in large part to the fact that the city was home to the *Chicago Defender*, a Black-owned newspaper that actively and forcefully promoted migration by means of its extensive communication network in Black communities throughout the South. The *Defender* advertised job opportunities, illustrated the allure of the "Black Metropolis," and narrated the stark differences between North and South. As a result Chicago came to signify the Great Migrations in a special way.

The rise of Black Catholic Chicago was not just an effect of demographic shifts, however. In order to understand why Catholicism became a live option for Black migrants, we must first identify the ways the Great Migrations transformed African American religious culture across the country. And this story starts before the migrations even began, in the years following Reconstruction's collapse. Historian John Giggie has demonstrated how, between 1875 and 1915, reform and revival movements swept Black Christian communities in the Mississippi Delta.[13] The decades immediately prior to the Great Migrations witnessed tremendous contestation over what it meant to be Black and Christian. A group of young Black Baptists "hoped to refine Black religion in the

Delta" and equip coreligionists with the resources requisite for success and respect. Curtailing public religious ecstasy was key to their quest for respectability. "The Progressives," as they called themselves, "desperately wanted members to resist breaking into spontaneous bouts of shrieking, crying, dancing, hand-clapping, and foot stomping during services."[14] Progressives attempted to reign in what they took to be the emotional excesses of Black religiosity. They hoped to challenge white racist assumptions of the primitivism of African American religiosity at the same time that they aspired to better their social and religious standing in their own Black Baptist communities. In other words, they were invested in what historian Evelyn Brooks Higginbotham termed the "politics of respectability"—a politics evident years later among Black Catholic converts in Chicago.[15]

Progressives had their share of critics, though. The most compelling among them were the swelling ranks of Black Holiness and Pentecostal Christians.[16] Holiness-Pentecostalism represented a dynamic religious revival that emphasized the necessity of a "second baptism," known as sanctification, whereby any Christian could be sanctified by the Holy Spirit and cleansed of sin forever. A sanctified Christian received gifts from the Spirit as the apostles once had, including the power to heal illness, to speak in tongues, prophesy, or to exorcise demons. Among the most enduring legacies of the Holiness-Pentecostal movement on Black religious life was its style of worship. In stark juxtaposition to the Progressives, Holiness-Pentecostal Christian worship remained "open to improvisation and spontaneity as men, women, and children reacted to being seized and shaken by the Holy Spirit."[17] The Holiness-Pentecostal movement was uninterested in conforming to the purported "respectability" of modern life, dedicating itself instead to a radical new version of the Christian witness.[18]

This contestation and transformation of African American religious culture did not remain in the South.[19] The religious innovations of the post-Reconstruction South traveled north along the railways with migrants. When Black southern religious culture—Holiness-Pentecostalism in particular—met the exigencies of city life, new urban religious practices emerged in Black Protestant churches in early twentieth-century cities. Wallace Best termed this the "new sacred order in the city."[20] In short, migrants brought with them religious practices rooted in the Black South. Distinctive features of southern Black Christianity, from the religious ecstasy of "the shout" to the distinctive cadence of Black preachers, could now be heard from the streets and in the storefronts of Chicago on any given Sunday.[21] By midcentury Black migrants had made the South Side of Chicago famous for the plurality and creativity of its religious communities. Over five hundred churches, temples, storefronts, mosques, and synagogues filled the narrow strip of Black Belt Chicago by 1940. Soon Baptist, Methodist, Holiness, Pentecostal, Jewish, Muslim, and Spiritualist as well as Catholic communities competed for the souls of Black Chicago.[22]

African American religious communities were not the only ones impacted by the Great Migrations. The migrations fundamentally altered the course of Catholicism in the urban North. When migrants arrived in Chicago, they entered a veritable Catholic Metropolis, a city shaped by a comprehensive Catholic infrastructure. As historian John McGreevy illustrates in his classic book *Parish Boundaries*, Catholics used parishes "to map out—both physically and culturally—space within all of the northern cities," so much so that parish names became interchangeable with the names of neighborhoods.[23] Parishes were substantial architectural and institutional achievements, with each "parish plant" typically including a church, a rectory, a parochial school, a convent, and sometimes even gymnasiums and auditoriums. McGreevy argues that urban parish boundaries must be taken into account in order to understand the encounter between Black migrants and white Catholics. "When African-Americans first began moving north in large numbers," McGreevy notes, "their encounters with the 'white' world were filtered through a distinctly Catholic focus on parish and place."[24]

Lost in most histories of the Great Migrations is the fact that Black migrants arrived in neighborhoods defined by this extensive Catholic built environment. White Catholics might make an appearance in the historiography as antagonists, though they are usually identified as ethnic rather than religious actors—the Irish or the Polish, for example. We might catch sight of them as they take "flight" to the suburbs or fight the efforts of Black families to make new homes, but the gargantuan structures they left behind are rarely mentioned. The fact that historians have long viewed religion as an epiphenomenal rather than essential category, as race and ethnicity are presumed to be, certainly plays a part in this collective lacuna. Migration histories arbitrarily isolate white Catholics and African Americans despite the fact that together they made and remade Chicago neighborhoods, though historians of American Catholics such as John McGreevy, Colleen McDannell, and Timothy Neary serve as notable exceptions.[25] The Black Belt was home to no fewer than six Catholic churches, buildings whose belfries towered over the modest storefronts below.[26] As historian Timothy Neary notes, by the 1930s Chicago's "three black Catholic churches roughly marked the boundaries of Black Metropolis. At 49th Street and South Parkway, Corpus Christi Church stood only a few blocks from the center of Black Metropolis, while St. Elizabeth and St. Anselm fell within its respective northern and southern boundaries."[27]

The architectural and institutional stability of parishes contributed to Catholic success in American cities through the first decades of the twentieth century. Ironically, that stability was soon the cause of a crisis. An extensive urban parish depended on the support of thousands of parishioners. If those parishioners left abruptly, the parish would not be able to sustain itself spiritually or materially. And in contrast to Protestant congregations, Catholic parishioners could not take their parish with them, so to speak. When African American migrants settled in large numbers in the first half of the twentieth century, Catholic parishes soon faced a crisis. What would white Catholics do as the demographics of their neighborhood changed—as white Catholic neighborhoods became increasingly Black and non-Catholic? Many white Catholics resisted, by various means, what they took to be an "invasion" of their turf. The Chicago race riot in 1919 was the most infamous example of violent struggles between white and Black Chicagoans over city space.[28] Less dramatic but much more frequent examples of white Catholic resistance to Black migration included protective covenants and parish organizations that fought to prohibit Black families from buying homes in the neighborhood. When, against all odds, Black families succeeded in doing so, mobs and bombs met them there.[29]

More common than violence, though, was white Catholic abandonment of parishes. White Catholics went to great lengths to remain in the neighborhoods where they had been raised, in the churches where their children had been baptized, in the homes in which they had invested decades of earnings.[30] But despite some reluctance, many white Catholics did eventually move southward and westward as Chicago's Black Belt expanded. By the 1930s and 1940s several South and West Side neighborhoods that had once supported multiple parishes now faced the challenge of meeting monthly costs. The number of parishes impacted by this changing reality increased over the next few decades.

An Archdiocesan report from 1960 gives a clear sense of the impact of the Great Migrations on Chicago's parishes in the first half of the twentieth century. Prior to the migrations that started in earnest in 1915, the city had been home to 44,103 African Americans. Only one parish was "affected" by the Black Chicago population—this meant, in the Catholic ecclesiastical lexicon, that only one parish was located in a predominantly Black neighborhood. The Black population had increased to 102,458 by 1920 and now affected three parishes. By 1930 the number of affected parishes had increased to five. Ten parishes were affected by 1940, thirty-eight by 1950, and seventy-six parishes by 1960.[31]

This demographic shift threatened the survival of Catholic parishes themselves. Since most African Americans were not Catholic, pastors preached to increasingly empty pews and parish buildings fell into disrepair without the financial support of departing parishioners. This transition could occur in a few years or less. When Cardinal George Mundelein, the archbishop of Chicago, decided to allow African Americans to attend St. Anselm's school in Bronzeville in 1932, the enrollment shifted from majority white to majority Black in just one year.[32] Faced with declining white communities, most pastors hoped to prolong the inevitable by reducing costs and halting social services. Others actively supported white Catholic resistance to Black migration. But there were a few who took a different approach. Starting in the late 1930s a small group of priests in Chicago decided that the only viable solution to the crisis facing Catholic parishes amidst the Great Migrations was to repopulate depleted churches with Black converts. They sought to transform parish plants into missionary centers and in so doing, set in motion the making of modern Black Catholic Chicago.[33]

The Movement to Make America Catholic

The impulse to convert African Americans to Catholicism was not merely a by-product of the Great Migrations. Rather, the migrations coincided with widespread fervor among Catholics for converting "heathens," both at home and abroad. The roots of this impulse in the United States date back at least to the late nineteenth century, when a number of prominent prelates and scholars dreamed of making America Catholic.[34] John Gilmary Shea, an influential late-nineteenth-century Catholic historian, published histories extolling the Catholic origins of the American nation and its founding principles. Meanwhile Bishop John Noll challenged anti-Catholicism by insisting that Catholics were not just American, but the ideal Americans with whom the nation's future prosperity rested.[35] In the early twentieth century, these aspirations were responsible for launching organizations dedicated to converting the United States and the world to the Catholic Church. By the 1940s this rising fervor had produced ambitious lay-led organizations such as the Convert Makers of America (CMOA). This group grew out of the broader Catholic Action movement that encouraged laypeople, usually in collaboration with a priest, to use Church teachings as impetuses for action in the world beyond one's home or parish in the hope of transforming the non-Catholic world.[36] The CMOA sought to convert the country through pamphlet racks, information centers, and personal invitation. They enrolled hundreds of "convert making teams" that installed three hundred and fifty-seven pamphlet racks, organized twenty-three information centers, and "made an unaccounted number of actual converts."[37] They claimed to have distributed more than two million pamphlets in 1948 alone.[38]

As the Great Migrations transformed the urban centers of Catholic life in America, some clergy within this broader movement began to identify African Americans as a top priority for domestic missionary efforts. The Chicago archdiocesan newspaper the *New World* documented a number of church leaders who publicly endorsed the African American missionary cause in the late 1930s and early 1940s. Cardinal Mundelein praised African Americans for making the "most splendid Catholics" in his 1938 address to the National Eucharistic Congress in New Orleans. Mundelein insisted that "the great Colored population of the Colored race in the United States belongs in the Catholic Church. It will never reach its destiny until it has been gathered."[39] New Orleans archbishop Joseph Rummel was even more outspoken. "The missions fostered by the Catholic Church of the United States in behalf of the

Negro race," he proclaimed, "may well be called America's mission responsibility Number One."[40]

Pope Pius XII contributed to the special significance of African Americans for U.S. missionary efforts in his 1939 encyclical *Sertum Laetitiae*, which celebrated the one hundred and fiftieth anniversary of the establishment of the Church in the United States. Pius broadly praised "missionary enterprises proper to your own nation which devote themselves with zeal and energy to the wider diffusion of the Catholic Faith." He explicitly referenced "the Negro peoples dwelling among you." Pius confessed his "special paternal affection" for African Americans and insisted "in the field of religion and education We know that they need special care and comfort and are very deserving of it."[41] Catholic missionaries could now cite papal precedent when they insisted that the Church dedicate itself to the cause of African American conversion.

Catholic efforts to convert African Americans eventually caught the attention of national Black publications. The *Chicago Defender* documented record numbers of converts as early as 1927 and took notice as Catholics in Harlem and New Jersey launched conversion drives in the 1930s.[42] By the 1940s, the *Defender* was publishing articles with bold titles such as "Believes Race Is Fast Turning to Catholicism" and "Third of Million Negroes in America Are Catholic."[43] *Ebony* echoed this coverage. In the magazine's inaugural issue in 1945 it published an essay by Claude McKay, the famous Harlem Renaissance poet and recent Catholic convert, on "Why I Became a Catholic" alongside a full photographic spread on "Converts of Color."[44] Another article directly linked African Americans to national Catholic missionary objectives, claiming that the "biggest puzzle bothering the Christian world today is: can the Catholic minority of America become a religious majority?" The answer, according to *Ebony*, lay in the "some eight million Negroes in the United States who claim no religious affiliation whatsoever." African Americans would come to be understood as "the keystone to the Church's campaign to win America."[45]

"Foreign Missions" on the South Side of Chicago

This context shaped the first encounters between African American migrants and the Catholic Church in Chicago. It was a context defined by the transformation of the urban religious landscape brought about by the Great Migrations on the one hand, and the increasing commitment of Catholic missionaries to the conversion of African Americans on the other. This meant that Black migrants were introduced to a particular kind of Catholicism, one taught by missionaries who had the salvation of souls foremost on their minds. What is more, though the migrants did not yet know it, Catholic missionaries had identified them as "foreign missions."

What did it mean to be a "foreign mission"? Generally speaking, Catholic missionary efforts can be categorized as one of two types of endeavors: "home missions" organized to reinvigorate the faith among lapsed or lukewarm Catholics, or "foreign missions" aimed at converting those who did not yet "possess the faith."[46] Despite what the name implied, the designations "foreign" and "home" depended less on geography and more on the faith status of local residents. Missionaries served in a "foreign" missionary field if they served a community wherein most were not Catholic. In this case they devoted their energies toward converting "heathens" and teaching them to be "good Catholics." Since the vast majority of Black migrants were not Catholic, the Great Migrations effectively transformed large swaths of once Catholic metropolises into "foreign missions fields" as far as Catholic missionaries were concerned.

Chicago served as the exemplary model for "foreign" missionary work among African Americans. Cardinal Mundelein's initial response to dramatic demographic shifts in parish neighborhoods was to hand neighborhoods with predominantly Black (and non-Catholic) populations over to missionaries. This began in 1917 when Mundelein invited the Society of the Divine Word (SVD) to "look after the spiritual welfare of the Negroes in his Archdiocese" by taking over St. Monica parish located at 36th and Dearborn Street.[47] Many African Americans, both Catholic and non-Catholic, strongly objected to what they saw as nothing less than the segregation of Black Catholics from the rest of Catholic Chicagoans. Notwithstanding these objections, the archbishop refused to meet with Black Catholics to discuss their petition and proceeded with his plan.

From Mundelein's perspective, the SVD were best suited for work amongst "the Negroes" of Chicago because they were already dedicated to missions across the world. Mundelein endorsed this approach for most of his tenure as archbishop, treating African Americans as a missionary territory in the midst of the Catholic Metropolis. His approach carried with it a number of assumptions that would fundamentally shape what it meant to be Black and Catholic in the first half of the twentieth century. These underlying assumptions become clearer when we attend to the history of the Society of the Divine Word itself. Arnold Janssen, a German diocesan priest, founded the society in 1875. Janssen's spiritual legacy combined an evangelistic orientation toward mission with a commitment to what was called "*devotion moderna*, an attempt to inject concreteness, emotion, and personal piety into the lives of ordinary Catholics." In order to spread this *devotion moderna* across the world, Janssen proposed a seminary that might train German priests for service outside Germany. The SVD quickly evolved into a "mission-sending society of priests and brothers." The seminary trained and dispatched missionaries across the German diasporic and colonial world.[48]

"Always in the background" for Divine Word missionaries, according to historian Ernest Brandewie, "was a robust belief in the adage of the great third century bishop, St. Cyprian of Carthage: *extra ecclesiam nulla salus* ('outside the church no salvation')."[49] This perspective divided the world between those who possessed the "One True Faith" and those who could (and should) be made to embrace it, evangelization ideally to be accomplished through the heroism of missionaries. Seminarians were saturated in this "mission spirit and the missionary ideal and spirituality" starting at a young age.[50] They were encouraged to imagine foreign missionary fields as lands full of danger and ripe for self-sacrifice. Boys were introduced to colorful portrayals of the adventurous lives of missionaries who sacrificed themselves on the frontier "for the sake of souls and the cause of Christ."[51]

The Divine Word missionaries assigned to Black Chicago in the early twentieth century brought with them this vision of the world divided between believers and heathens, Catholics and everyone else. By the early twentieth century the SVD had dedicated itself specifically to work in "the still unconverted world . . . or the pagan world in the wider sense." And as Brandewie notes, it was not a coincidence that the "still unconverted world" corresponded quite closely with "the colonized people of Africa, Asia, and Oceania."[52] The Christian partitioning of the world between the faithful and the pagan already had a long history by the time Divine Word missionaries were sent to support priests serving in the foreign mission fields of German colonies in Africa.

It is clear from the writings of missionaries on the South Side of Chicago that terms like "foreign mission" and "heathen" served as racialized categories as much as religious ones. For instance, Cardinal Mundelein was said to have recruited the SVD in particular because they were renowned for working to "spread Christianity among the non-white races of the world." The fact that neither Mundelein nor Divine Word missionaries felt much need to distinguish between "the Negroes" of West Africa and those in the United States is quite telling.[53] Father Joseph Eckert, the most successful SVD priest in Chicago, wrote in 1927 that his time in Bronzeville had been "real, soul-saving and pioneer missionary work." While most missionaries in urban parishes primarily dedicated themselves to the "reclamation of lost sheep," here among African Americans one had to truly "go out and *get* converts."[54] Another priest shared this sentiment in 1932, describing Corpus Christi parish in the heart of Chicago's Black Belt as "a heathen mission more than a catholic congregation."[55]

Here we see a clear example of how, as religious studies scholar Robert Orsi puts it, "religion is racialized and race is religionized." Modern ideas about the essence of "religion" developed alongside scientific taxonomies of race. "European global adventures" spread both around the world. "From early modernity forward," Orsi writes, "men and women in other parts of the world and with skin colors other than white who lived with the gods really present to them on earth were termed 'savage' and 'primitive.'"[56] The word "heathen" captures this enmeshment of race and religion. For missionaries, "heathen" served as a technical term. It carried no ill intent. It simply named, as a matter of fact, the status of a particular people. A "heathen" was someone who lacked the true Faith. Religious studies scholar Sylvester Johnson has shown, however, that the history of this word is inextricably bound to European colonialism and the racialization of enslaved Africans in particular. He notes that, "in the wake of the Trans-Atlantic Slave Trade and the holocaust of slavery . . . the public meaning of 'Negro' and 'Africa' were finely wedded to 'backward,' 'uncivilized,' and 'heathen.'"[57] Armed with this fact and confirmed by the reigning "sciences" of the time, colonial settlers and missionaries alike embarked on those "global adventures" Orsi references. Heathen

Africans lacked civilization and the gospel, both of which they would require for redemption. The word "heathen" carried this history with it, even if (especially if) missionaries did not know it themselves.

The Divine Word missionaries were not alone in their service to "heathens" in the foreign missions on the South Side of Chicago. They were joined early on by the Sisters of the Blessed Sacrament for Indians and Colored People (SBS) who staffed the parish schools and aided in the attempt to convert African Americans. The SBS shared the commitment to missionary work in the unconverted world. Katharine Drexel, born in 1858 and heiress to the considerable fortune of the Philadelphia Drexel family, founded this order of women religious in 1891. Their constitution, drafted by Drexel in 1907, described the special vocation of the SBS: "to apply themselves zealously to the service of Our Lord in the Blessed Sacrament by endeavoring to lead the Indian & Colored Races to the knowledge & love of God, & so make them living temples of Our Lord's Divinity."[58] Drexel continued to financially support Catholic mission efforts among African Americans and Native Americans throughout North America, the Caribbean, and Africa until her death in 1955. Unlike their founder, though, most Blessed Sacrament Sisters hailed from "East Coast working-class Irish homes."[59] As historian Suellen Hoy puts it, Drexel founded "a congregation of white women dedicated to the 'service and sacrifice' of people of color, Catholic or not," and she "rested the success of her grand plan" on these working-class descendants of Irish immigrants.[60] In the first half of the twentieth century the SBS became increasingly important in Black Catholic communities as teachers in parish schools and as missionaries.[61]

Franciscan friars and sisters joined Divine Word missionaries and Blessed Sacrament Sisters in the foreign mission fields on the South Side of Chicago. Cardinal Mundelein invited friars from the Midwestern Sacred Heart Province to take control of Corpus Christi parish as its white parishioners fled by the hundreds in the face of Black migration to the neighborhood. These were the friars who welcomed Mary and Martha upon their arrival to Chicago at the start of this chapter. The friars converted the church into an African American missionary center in 1932 with permission from the archbishop and the friars called on the services of the Sisters of St. Francis from Dubuque, Iowa, the following year.[62] Franciscan sisters hailed from very different environs than their

Blessed Sacrament counterparts. For the most part, these nuns were raised in large German and German American immigrant families in the farmlands of Iowa.[63] Yet there is a sense in which these Franciscan sisters had even more in common with the Divine Word missionaries than the SBS sisters staffing their schools. Beyond their German heritage, Corpus Christi's Franciscan sisters also held an explicit commitment to the unconverted around the world. This particular community of Franciscan missionaries shared a missionary outpost in Chowstsun, China. Hoy argues that "because blacks generally were not Catholics, they resembled in official church eyes the unconverted Chinese or Native Americans more than the Catholic immigrants from Ireland, Poland, Italy, or Mexico."[64] Dubuque Franciscans *volunteered* to minister among African Americans in Chicago or Chinese people in Chowstsun with the express desire of giving the unconverted the "special attention" they required.[65]

What was the nature of the relationship between white missionaries and Black migrants? In order to answer this question, one must be attentive to the desires and anxieties that informed the lives of missionaries. The history of Christian missions, as mentioned above, is inseparable from the history of European colonial expansion. The missionary objective to convert or "Christianize" always involved introducing native communities not only to new religious beliefs and ritual practices but also to new social, sexual, and aesthetic norms. In other words, becoming Catholic involved a transformation of the self and the body, not just an intellectual assent to new ideas. The relationship between converters and converted was always an asymmetrical one as a result, insofar as the missionary directed the process of self-formation and served as a gatekeeper of salvation.[66]

At the same time, it does not suffice to simply dismiss missionaries as cultural imperialists or colonial agents. Recent histories of Christian missions have, in the words of Ryan Dunch, shifted the focus "from missionaries as agents of a hegemonic Western culture to the actual process of intercultural communication."[67] Missionaries had conflicting relationships with native non-Christian populations, yet they also had conflicting relationships with the communities they had left at home. From this vantage point, the missionary-missioned encounter is less one about the imposition of a monolithic religious system on a passive people and more about the creation of new religious worlds through the encounters between missionaries and missioned.

It is important to keep this in mind when examining interactions between Black migrants and Catholic missionaries on Chicago's South Side. When missionary priests and sisters moved into Chicago's Black Belt, they committed themselves to safeguarding the spiritual well-being of the Black women, men, and children in their care. From the perspective of the Society of the Divine Word and the Sisters of the Blessed Sacrament, the Catholic Church was the "One True Church," the only means for salvation. From their point of view, missionaries best served African Americans by introducing them to the Church and convincing them to convert. Every person baptized into the Catholic Church marked a success for the missionaries that extended out to a cosmological level. Each convert represented a soul "won" for God as well as a soul "saved" from suffering forever in hell. This was not an abstract idea. Instead, it defined encounters between missionaries and African Americans.

The testimonies of Sisters of the Blessed Sacrament serving in two Bronzeville parishes, St. Anselm and St. Elizabeth, provide a glimpse of how missionary sisters experienced their relationship with potential converts. One sister told the story of the Biggs family. In February 1944, Mrs. Biggs came to St. Anselm parish and asked the sisters there if she could enroll her son James in the parish school. Her son had suffered tremendously over the past year. James had been ill with pneumonia and then, when he had refused to enlist in a local gang, was severely beaten. The sisters knew there were no vacancies at the school, yet sympathetic to her needs, they brought Mrs. Biggs to the convent chapel and asked her "if she believed in the power of prayer." When she replied yes, the sisters "explained that we believed in Our Lord's Real Presence in the tabernacle under the form of bread." Mrs. Biggs immediately knelt in prayer for her son. According to the author, Mrs. Biggs prayed in such a way that "would have put many a Catholic to shame," though she was not Catholic herself. This gave the sisters the feeling that "somehow that mother's prayer would be answered." Sure enough, though the school was full, the principal and seventh grade teacher decided James could share a table with another student.[68]

James's enrollment in St. Anselm school and the power of his mother's prayer served as the first steps toward the conversion of the entire Biggs family. The author describes how, once enrolled, James was "among the first at daily Mass before school." It was not long before James and his mother both expressed an interest in converting to Catholicism, a decision clearly influenced by the support these sisters had given to their family in a time of need. Mrs. Biggs expressed "deep gratitude to the Sisters for taking [James] in school and [made] the resolution to embrace the Catholic faith as soon as it was possible for her to come for instructions."[69] James was baptized in the fall of 1944. His mother began attending religious instruction classes in January 1945 and was baptized in May, along with her two daughters and her daughter's children. Mrs. Biggs's husband and mother followed suit in 1946.

The last two lines of the Biggs family story capture the significance this anecdote held for St. Anselm's sisters. "How many more souls will come to God through these people we will never know," the sister concluded. "What if we had refused to take James into school in Feb. 1944!!!"[70] These lines illustrate the ways the missionary desire for conversion was never far from the fear of failure. The author celebrated the conversion of the Biggs family and expressed her hope that their conversion would lead even more people to the Catholic Church. But the "what if" statement cautions readers about what might have befallen the Biggs family. If the sisters had not found room in the school for James, an entire family would have been condemned to a life without salvation, not to mention the countless other souls the Biggs family might have won over to the Church.

A conversion story recounted by another Sister of the Blessed Sacrament, this time at St. Elizabeth parish, captures the entanglement of desire and anxiety at work in a missionary's life. Sister Mary Frances Therese presented a cautionary tale. Born Jane Sophia Kallay in Hungary in 1903, her family immigrated to the United States when she was young. She entered the Sisters of the Blessed Sacrament in 1923 and took the name Mary Frances Therese. By the time Sister Frances Therese published "Despite the Sisters" in the official SBS magazine, she had been a missionary for close to twenty years.[71] The story described Sister Frances Therese's five-year-old kindergarten student, Doris, who "manifested a deep interest in the religion period." The story followed Doris as she enthusiastically asked to be baptized again and again, only to be rebuffed by the sister and the pastor. Children were considered spiritual minors and so, even if children yearned for conversion, they required parental permission in order to be baptized. Sister Frances Therese and the pastor both agreed it was best for her to wait till she was older, "as there were no Catholics in the family and she was more or less a newcomer in the school." "If ever I wanted the saving waters of Baptism poured on anyone," Sister Frances Therese lamented, "it was on Doris." When Doris died suddenly of spinal-meningitis, the sister despaired. "My heart sank as if it were lead within me," the sister recalled. Once they heard the news, the sisters called the Catholic hospital chaplain who had been with Doris in her final moments. "Our hearts leaped up as we listened to Father's account. Realizing that Doris was dying he had poured the saving waters of Baptism over the little one." The story concluded with her imagining Doris flying into the arms of God and whispering "Oh! Here I am, in spite of them."[72]

"Despite the Sisters," even more than the story about the Biggs family, conveys the pressure many missionaries felt in their attempts to bring the Catholic faith to Black Chicago. Sister Frances Therese had recounted an incident wherein she had failed as a missionary, something that embarrassed her but also served as a warning. "Most stories that a missionary Sister would tell would, in the ordinary course of events, reflect her efforts to help souls get to Heaven," she opened her cautionary tale. "The story I am about to tell you is one of a little soul who found her way to Heaven—must I blush to say it—despite the Sisters." Here, the missionary commitment to "help souls get to Heaven" rested in uneasy proximity to the potential for failure. "Despite the Sisters" emphasized the stakes of this failure. If not for the chaplain baptizing Doris on her deathbed, this young girl could never have reached heaven. In other words, there were enormous spiritual consequences for missionary work, at least from the perspective of the missionaries themselves. The sisters thus celebrated each successful attempt. The SBS meticulously recorded the number of African Americans who converted each year, as did other missionary orders such as the Sisters of St. Francis.[73] As we have seen here, the sisters also collected detailed accounts of conversions that simultaneously lionized missionary success and warned of the dire consequences of failure.[74] In these recollections, the missionary sisters made clear how their salvation-oriented ministry shaped their encounters with African Americans.

The relationship between white missionaries and potential Black converts thus was ambivalent. Missionaries held positions of real power over African Americans who attended Catholic churches and schools in Chicago neighborhoods, many of whom were not Catholic. Not only did white missionaries control churches and schools, they also offered potential converts an entryway to salvation understood to be unavailable outside the Catholic Church. This placed white missionaries in positions of power over African Americans. For example, when a Black Catholic man beloved by the Sisters of the Blessed Sacrament passed away in 1937, one sister reflected on the death of their "dear Morgan Park Uncle Tom." The man himself remained nameless. This same sister later spoke fondly of "thirteen little 'pickaninnies.'" These Black children had been gathered together by a white woman for a "long talk and happy lesson" about God.[75] Another missionary sister, a Sister of St. Francis from Corpus Christi parish, recounted the day when the church "opened its doors to the colored child." "Darkies came, and came, and kept coming." One third of these schoolchildren were not Catholic, which meant "the Christianizing of these is a major project of both Fathers and Sisters."[76] Each of these examples testify both to the ways white missionaries understood themselves to be the spiritual guardians best equipped to save African Americans and to the ways missionaries were active participants in the white supremacist discourses prevalent at the time. And these examples just scratch the surface. To cite just one other example, historian Shannen Dee Williams writes extensively on Black women religious bearing the brunt of virulent racism from their fellow white Catholic sisters.[77]

Yet it would be wrong to underestimate the significance of the missionaries' commitment to African American salvation. The Catholic Church in the United States for the most part took little interest in ministering to African Americans until the middle years of the twentieth century. For instance, U.S. bishops ruled at the Second Plenary Council in Baltimore in 1866 that the education and evangelization of emancipated slaves was a "local" concern that did not warrant national attention. When authorities in Rome urged the Third Baltimore Council to deal with "the negro problem" in 1884, the bishops again refused.[78] The council did institute an annual offertory collection "for Indians and Negroes," but even this acknowledgment highlighted Black Catholic marginality.⁷⁹ It categorized African Americans and Native Americans as foreign peoples, overseen not by their local bishops but by a joint Commission for Catholic Missions among the Colored People and the Indians. Thus the Society of the Divine Word and the Sisters of the Blessed Sacrament, as well as other missionary orders who served African Americans, like the Josephite Fathers, were exceptional in Catholic history.⁸⁰ Archbishop Wilton D. Gregory emphasized the importance of missionary orders on numerous occasions in an interview with me. Gregory, who was Chicago's auxiliary bishop from 1983 until 1993 and currently serves as the archbishop of Atlanta, converted to Catholicism after enrolling in St. Carthage parish school on the South Side of Chicago in 1958. He celebrated the "moments of glory" in Black Catholic history when a handful of white priests and sisters challenged the racial status quo and welcomed African Americans in churches and schools.⁸¹ In other words, the imbalance of power inherent in missionary relationships remains inseparable from the fact that missionaries were deeply invested in the Black communities in which they served, a commitment that set them apart from the U.S. Church writ large. Sincere desire on the part of missionaries to save Black souls was not mutually exclusive with white paternalism or racism.

"Methods of Convert-Making among the Negroes of Chicago"

No one embodied the ambivalence between missionary zeal and paternalism, nor exemplified the success of Catholic missionaries among Black migrants in the early years of the Great Migrations, better than Father Joseph Eckert. Born in 1884 to a German family in what is now Poland, Eckert was "the most prominent and well-known SVD engaged in the African-American apostolate."⁸² As with any young man who decided to join the Society of the Divine Word, Eckert was deeply attracted to "life as a missionary" at a young age.⁸³ According to Eckert's unpublished autobiography, he had hoped to be "sent to our Negro Mission in Togo, West Africa."⁸⁴ Deemed physically unfit for missionary life in "the tropics," however, Eckert was transferred to the North American seminary in Techny, Illinois, and soon assigned to mission among African Americans in Chicago. "Instead of landing among the Negroes in Africa," Eckert wrote, he found himself "among Negroes on the south side of Chicago."⁸⁵ Here again, we see the ease with which missionaries conflated the dark-skinned peoples of the world. The innumerable differences between West Africans in Togo and African Americans in Bronzeville mattered much less than the fact that they all were "heathens."

Eckert became pastor of St. Monica in 1921. Three years later, due largely to his missionary efforts, this Black Catholic community had outgrown the small church. To meet the needs of the growing Black Catholic population, Cardinal Mundelein merged St. Monica with St. Elizabeth parish and again gave Divine Word missionaries control of the African American apostolate. By 1932 Eckert had been so successful at St. Elizabeth that Mundelein transferred a third parish, St. Anselm, to SVD control. There, Eckert continued his missionary efforts until 1940. Eckert frequently recalled the archbishop's commission: "Father [Eckert], you are about to undertake a difficult task. If you wish to be successful, you will have to spend yourself."⁸⁶ Eckert took this challenge to heart. He directed his energies toward the conversion of African Americans and over the next twenty years the Divine Word priest became nationally renowned for his missionary efforts in Chicago's Black Belt. It is estimated that he was personally responsible for the baptism of approximately four thousand people.⁸⁷

Eckert's most significant contribution to Black Catholic Chicago was his missionary method. The strategies he employed for converting African Americans served as the model for a generation of priests who contributed to a period of unprecedented growth and vibrancy for Black parishes. In an unpublished essay Eckert recalled Cardinal Mundelein's instructions upon assuming the pastorate of St. Anselm parish in south Bronzeville: "Take good care of all the people in the parish, irrespective of race or color, and make as many converts as possible. Go out, as the Gospel told us last Sunday, and bring the good Colored people into the Church. Fill St. Anselm's Church."⁸⁸ Eckert understood his role as a missionary in the foreign field, seeking converts among the heathens, bringing pagans into the light of Christ. He went about outlining a "program which would consist specially in saving souls and making converts," hoping to encourage Black men and women to "feel like real members of the church which does not approve or even tolerate a smack of prejudice."⁸⁹

Figure 1.1. Father Joseph Eckert with convert class at St. Elizabeth (ca. 1927). Courtesy of the Robert M. Myers Archives, Society of the Divine Word.

How did Eckert intend to accomplish his ambitious task? In his article "Methods of Convert-Making among the Negroes of Chicago," Eckert identified the major obstacle to conversion: "[T]he average Negro harbors a deep and often bitter prejudice against the Catholic Church, and therefore keeps decidedly away from both Church and priests."[90] Missionaries must first subvert these prejudices. Eckert identified six methods to that end.[91] The first could be called personal interaction and invitation. He reflected that whenever he met African Americans in the neighborhood, he asked them where they went to church. "Whatever the answer may be, I heartily invite them to come, at least once, to our services. Should I find out, however, that the person has no Church affiliation whatever, then I try to impress upon him the necessity and advisability of practising some religion."[92] Eckert also developed a more comprehensive approach, going door-to-door inviting people to church. Many were hostile. Some refused to "open their doors when I told them that a Catholic priest would like to find out if any Catholic people were living here. Others spit in my face."[93] But if the invitation was accepted, Eckert was confident that the path to conversion had begun. He boldly proclaimed that "once they have entered the Catholic Church and have overcome that indefinable fear associated in their minds with the very word Catholic, they will return again and again."[94] Though personal contact was always preferable, a second method was publicity and advertisement. Eckert used pamphlets, posted signs, and publications to proclaim the presence of the Catholic Church in Bronzeville as well as to invite African Americans to attend.

The third and fourth methods utilized education. Eckert understood the parish school to be the most effective missionary tool. When he opened St. Monica's school in 1921 roughly one hundred and fifty children attended, "mostly non-catholic and not baptized."[95] Eckert was quite forthright about his intentions in allowing non-Catholic African Americans to attend Catholic schools. "Through the children we reach the children's parents," he reflected. Catholic and non-Catholic children alike learned prayers, attended Mass, and memorized the Baltimore Catechism, the standard text on Catholic doctrine in the first half of the twentieth century. In this way children were introduced to the sights, smells, and sounds accompanying Catholic religious life at the time and schooled in the disciplines involved in being a "good Catholic." When they returned home, children inevitably spoke with their parents "about the Catechism and prayers they have learned, and about the wonderful things they saw when last they visited the 'Catholic Church.'" Eckert hoped inquisitive parents might accompany their children to services.[96]

Worship services and devotional practices offered still more convert-making opportunities. Aware of the fact that most Catholic services in the heart of Bronzeville were bound to have non-Catholics present, Eckert made Catholic worship practices instructive. When the parish crowned their statue of "the Blessed Mother" Mary at the end of May, for example, Eckert took "this opportunity to explain the devotion to our Blessed Mother and to invite the non-Catholics to attend our instruction classes and become acquainted with the teachings of the Catholic Church, especially in reference to the Blessed Mother, so much misunderstood by Protestants."[97] Attendant priests at other Catholic services unfamiliar to African Americans were encouraged to explain their various parts. This was the case with "Tre Ore" services when, on Good

Friday, Catholics commemorated the three hours Jesus Christ spent on the cross by listening to homilies on Christ's final seven words, silent meditation, and participation in the "Way of the Cross."[98] Eckert also emphasized homilies and sermons, convinced that "the average Negro loves and actually enjoys hearing a good, eloquent lecturer, and will likewise go far out of his way in order to hear a good sermon."[99] This led Eckert to insert sermons into services even when it was anomalous in the Catholic tradition. He acknowledged "it is not in accordance with the rubrics of the Church to preach at a funeral," for instance, "but we feel that the Church does not want to bind us in such extraordinary cases."[100] Religious practices generally were redirected toward encouraging conversion.

Eckert's final two methods relied in large part on his firm belief in the supernatural power of Catholic ritual and prayer. Eckert's methods were grounded on ideas about the nature of Black religiosity that became increasingly prevalent in the first half of the twentieth century, as evidenced by his statement that African Americans loved a good sermon. Another example of this was the assumption that African Americans were especially attuned to beauty, an assumption shared by white and Black commentators alike. This is what religious studies scholar Curtis Evans calls "romantic racialism." Romantic racialists contributed to the naturalization of "black religion" as an essential category not by denigrating Black religiosity as primitive and savage but by celebrating Blacks' "special aesthetic capacity over and against arid and materialistic whites."[101] Without knowing it, Eckert participated in this romantic racialist discourse as he drew on the rich Catholic theological heritage that emphasized the power of beauty to mediate the presence of God in the world, or what the noted sociologist and priest Andrew Greeley called "the Catholic imagination."[102] Most of the above methods were intended to entice non-Catholics to attend a service. Eckert was confident about what would happen next. Once they entered the church and attended Mass, there would be no escaping the aesthetic beauty of Catholic ritual. "The beauty of our liturgy," he insisted, "is so pronounced that it is bound to make an impression upon the Negro mind, which is especially receptive to all such things."[103] Missionary priests must make sure that the church is clean, orderly, and "beautiful," that the altar is "beautifully decorated," that "everything, from the decorations down to the conduct of the smallest altar boy, is made to breathe forth the very spirit of harmony and devotion." Then it would be impossible for the congregation not to appreciate "the beauty and significance of our liturgy."[104]

It is clear that for Father Eckert the Mass and other Catholic practices were efficacious in and of themselves, a perspective shared by Catholics at the time. The Mass brought the real presence of Jesus Christ into the world through the sacrament of the Eucharist and hence possessed a power, a beauty, a mystery that was self-evident. Consequently, the primary task for missionaries was simply to encourage non-Catholics to enter a Catholic church for a service. The Mass itself would do the rest. The beauty and majesty of the Mass was not haphazard or happenstance, however. Meticulous attention was to be paid to minute devotional details. Elaborate preparation went into producing this atmosphere of supernatural power and efficacious beauty. Eckert writes that the altar boys were choreographed with "military precision." Moreover, the efficacy of the Catholic Mass stood in sharp contrast with Protestant services, in Eckert's Catholic theology. When Eckert referred to "our liturgy," he meant to contrast the Catholic Mass with Black worship services that increasingly incorporated elements of southern Holiness-Pentecostal worship styles proliferating in Chicago at the time. He recognized that "visitors make intuitive comparisons between *our* way of conducting 'church' and that of those who are in charge of Protestant houses of worship." As they leave the Catholic church, the visitors declare "in the Catholic Church there is always dignity and sublimity," at least in Eckert's imagining.[105]

Yet all these methods, even the ritual beauty of the Mass, would "be futile if they were not accompanied and fructified by the grace of God which, in turn, must be implored by constant prayer." Eckert was adamant that "the grace of God has always wrought miracles of conversions where, humanly speaking, there were no prospects whatever."[106] With this in mind, the missionary could not be satisfied with praying for conversions at night in solitude. He dedicated the parish's "novenas in honor of St. Joseph, St. Ann, the Sacred Heart, etc." to the conversion of non-Catholics. He asked parishioners "to offer up Holy Communion for this particularly noble cause." In the end, "the missionary has no better weapon with which to fight God's battles than continual prayer."[107]

Launching a "Vast Conversion Movement among Negroes"

In 1938, just one year before Mary and Martha arrived on the Illinois Central line, Catholic priests organized the Midwest Clergy Conference on Negro Welfare (MCCNW). Founded to aid clergy assigned to the "Negro Apostolate," the MCCNW was essentially an attempt by priests to pool their resources in order to increase their effectiveness in the foreign missionary fields of Black communities. Faced with "the mass migration of the Negroes from the rural communities to the urban communities," as the official history of the conference put it, the MCCNW aimed to improve missionaries' technical proficiency "in order to start a vast conversion movement among the Negroes."[108] Chief among those gathered was Joseph Eckert. Famous for his convert-making success among African Americans, Eckert was elected to lead the organization in 1939.

While their name—the Midwest Clergy Conference on *Negro Welfare*—implied an interest in the material well-being of Black people in this world, the MCCNW was dedicated first and foremost to the fate of Black souls in the next. When these priests strategized for "Negro Welfare," their principal investment was in the eternal welfare of "the Negroes' immortal soul."[109] This distinguished the Midwestern branch from its Northeastern counterpart led by Father John LaFarge, S.J., a noted racial liberal and founder of the Catholic Interracial Councils.[110] The interracialism of John LaFarge and like-minded Catholic liberals has dominated scholarly treatments of Catholics and race. And yet, the convergence of Catholic missionaries and Black migrants was at least as significant. Though little has been written about them relative to their interracialist contemporaries, priests who prioritized securing salvation over struggles against segregation were instrumental in the very existence of Black Catholic communities across the urban North. Righting racial injustice was not entirely irrelevant for them, but efforts "to overcome racial prejudice and to improve the opportunities of the Negroes" were certainly secondary to salvation.[111]

Midwestern priests committed to the welfare of "Negroes' immortal souls" soon spread their convert-making methods throughout the foreign mission fields of the United States. Their work was not without its ironies. MCCNW publications illustrate how white Catholic missionaries dedicated themselves "to the service of the Colored people" and positioned themselves as the paternalist saviors of Black heathens at the same time. Missionaries both dismissed Black religion as overly emotional and actively disputed racist assumptions about African American religiosity.[112] Take the following pamphlet as an example. "A CATHOLIC Church in America, Or, One Priest to Another" was written as a fictional conversation between two priests. The first is a missionary in the "Colored Vineyard" while the second laments his friend's plight. The missionary challenges many misconceptions about the Negro Apostolate throughout their dialogue. According to the second priest, it seems "in the Providence of God it was meant for the Negro to remain in his emotional semi-superstition." Priests should just let Black people be, he concludes, "just as the Mohammedan must be left in Islamism."[113] But his missionary friend assures him that nothing could be further from the truth. "The emotionalism which some [Negro] sects practice is driving the modern Negro out of those churches. He doesn't want that sort of thing. Dozens have told me it is just this absence of emotionalism which led them to investigate about the Catholic Church."[114] In one fell swoop the missionary denigrates Black religious life *and* dispels racial essentialism. He dismisses Black Protestantism at the same time that he rejects the idea that African Americans are somehow naturally inclined to "emotional" and "primitive" religiosity.

Though it may come as a surprise, the MCCNW was ahead of its time on this point. Arthur Huff Fauset published his pioneering study *Black Gods of the Metropolis: Negro Religious Cults of the Urban North* in 1944, two years after this MCCNW pamphlet. In it, Fauset comprehensively challenged the reigning assumption that urban Black folk were "a carefree, happy-go-lucky folk, given to laughing and drinking, who resolve such troubles as they have in profound and seemingly uninterrupted experiences of religious emotionalism."[115] Contrary to this caricature, Fauset not only found that Black religion was not the irrational outlet many assumed at the time, but he demonstrated that "more than 40 per cent of Negroes never attend church at all."[116] In other words, Fauset argued that Black folk were neither prenatally predisposed to emotionalism nor somehow naturally religious. Half a century passed before his insights were considered essential for the study of African American religion.[117] Nevertheless, Catholic missionaries shared his critique at the time, keenly aware that many African Americans were not affiliated with any particular denomination. Missionaries' awareness of the so-called "unchurched" made it all the more imperative to "win souls" to the cause. John T. Gillard made note of it throughout his various publications. Gillard was a Josephite priest and missionary famous for applying sociological methods to the African American missionary effort. He made note of "non–church going Negroes" in his 1929 book on *The Catholic Church and the American Negro*.[118] He encouraged missionaries again in 1941 when he pointed out that, "of the 13,000,000 Negroes in this country only 5,660,618 even profess to belong to any Church."[119]

But if the unchurched millions were good news for missionaries, this did not mean their work would be easy. The MCCNW pamphlet went on to name the obstacles facing priests in the "Colored Vineyard." Protestant churches throughout the urban North were "still staving feverishly to win the masses of Colored people," an effort that included a vigorous campaign to "Stop the Catholic Church." Taking an anonymous "large Northern city" as an example, he quantified the dilemma by providing a "partial list of some of the 'store-front' churches" surrounding one Catholic church in a northern city:

> Prince of Peace Baptist Church.
> Peter's Rock Baptist Church.
> First Church of Deliverance, Spiritual.
> Light House Methodist Baptist Church.
> Number 1 Sunlight of the Sabbath Church.
> Holy Mount Nebo Pentecostal Assembly.
> St. James Shrine of Prayer and School of Divine Metaphysics.
> Come and See Baptist Church.[120]

The missionary perspective on African American religious plurality was clear. Innumerable churches surrounded African Americans in the migration-era city, yet they all offered nothing but "religious quackery." African Americans yearned for "true spiritual solace," yet received none. Each option was more dubious than the next.

Amidst Black religious plurality, Catholic missionaries tasked themselves with introducing African Americans to the only church that could truly save them. Priests and sisters serving in African American "foreign missions" worked hard to distinguish the "One True Church" from numerous pretenders. In the midst of the wide variety of religious traditions African Americans might choose from in migration-era cities, only one had access to the real presence of Jesus Christ. A recent Black convert recalled going to a "so-called communion service" where the Protestant minister, lacking bread and wine, sent someone across the street to buy grape juice and crackers. "The pity of it," the priest exclaimed. "They yearned for that Life [the Flesh and Blood of the Son of Man, the Eucharist]; came to receive it; and received . . . grape juice and crackers! It would be laughable if it were not so tragic."[121] This reflected a Catholic polemic against Protestants common since the sixteenth century, the argument that the Catholic Church had exclusive access to the real presence of the sacred in the world.[122]

As illustrated in their anxious lists of storefront churches, missionaries understood themselves to be in fierce competition for those millions of unchurched souls. Catholic missionaries preached the "One True Church" to the foreign mission fields of South Side Chicago in the midst of the Great Migrations, as the religious options available to Black migrants proliferated. The encounter between migrants and missionaries was fraught with ambivalences and tensions as Catholics sought to save the souls of "heathen" African Americans. What makes this effort remarkable is that thousands of Black women, men, and children did, in fact, convert. Catholic missionaries helped to spark the rise of Black Catholic Chicago, with individual parishes baptizing hundreds of adults and children each year. Yet even if missionaries succeeded in "winning converts" to the faith, African Americans had their own anxieties and desires. Their motives for becoming Catholic could not be contained by what missionaries intended or planned, nor could they even be contained by converts' decisions, as we will soon see. Why did African Americans enter the Catholic Church in record numbers in the 1930s, 1940s, and 1950s? To answer this question, we must turn to Catholic schools and the children of Black migrants.

2

Becoming Catholic

Education, Evangelization, and Conversion

Randolph had heard stories about priests and Catholicism, though he didn't pay them much mind. He was a father who had managed to raise a large family in Chicago's Black Belt. For most of Randolph's life Catholics were more an idea than a reality. He hardly knew any. All that changed one day when his eldest daughter came home and told him she was going to become a Catholic. Randolph blew up at her. He said quite a few things, not many of which he was proud. But it soon became clear that she had already made her decision. No amount of scolding could convince her otherwise and in time Randolph's daughter received the sacraments.

His wife was next. One by one his other children followed. Despite Randolph's best efforts his entire family converted to what they kept insisting was the "One True Church." More than likely he watched their habits of devotion change. Perhaps he witnessed new rituals at the dinner table, each meal beginning with a brief dance of fingers touching head, shoulders, and chest with "in the name of the Father, and of the Son, and of the Holy Ghost." Or he might have stumbled upon assorted paraphernalia around his home, statues and images he once thought idols. The old family Bible was not Catholic so now a new one would have appeared, joined by other additions to the shelves—the *Baltimore Catechism*, biographies of saints, missals, and devotional guides. It is possible his wife took to wearing a scapular, a swatch of rough cloth worn around the neck to serve as a call to prayer and a constant reminder of Christ's suffering. His wife and daughters now worried about the damnation that awaited his Protestant soul, nervous about an eternal separation that appeared inevitable.

Though he had been a member since he was fourteen, his wife now refused to attend his Presbyterian church. As a Catholic, she was prohibited from even setting foot in "false" churches. If he went to church at all any more, Randolph went with her to St. Elizabeth. St. Elizabeth parish was (and still is) considered the "mother" church of Black Catholic Chicago. It inherited this mantle from St. Monica in 1924 when the two churches merged, a consequence of Father Joseph Eckert's missionary success. At first he simply sat and watched, staging small protests by refusing to participate. Eventually his wife had enough of this sulking man and, exasperated, told him to stay home if he was going to continue to be so disinterested.

This proved his breaking point. Sunday mornings with his wife were important to Randolph, so he continued to accompany her to Mass and began following along. He "decided to do as others would do." He stood and sat and knelt and prayed with everyone, though he had to wait behind in the pews every time his wife went forward to eat the communion wafer—or, as she called it, the Body of Christ. The ritual movements, even the words themselves, became second nature. It was not long before Randolph found himself at St. Elizabeth convent every Sunday at eleven o'clock, after morning Mass, for religious instructions. He fell in love with the same "Sign of the Cross" he had once scorned. It reminded him of Christ's death on the cross. Randolph found his new repertoire of prayers beautiful and inspiring, especially his newfound relationship with the Blessed Mother. As he prepared for his own baptism he whispered the words to himself. "Hail Mary full of Grace the Lord is with Thee..."[1]

This story—of strained familial relationships, of changing habits in the home, of deciding "to do as others would do"—is how Randolph answered "Why I Became a Catholic" in a letter written just before his baptism in 1945. He was one of twenty-four Black Chicagoans completing a course of religious instructions at St. Elizabeth that spring. And they were just a few among the tens of thousands of African Americans across the United States who became Catholic in the Great Migrations. Though we have already considered the desires and anxieties that drove missionaries, what led Randolph's family and so many others like them to join the Catholic Church? Why did African Americans become Catholic? At first glance this seems an obvious question to ask. It was certainly among the most common questions people asked me in the midst of my research, though it is worth noting that no Black Catholic ever did. This deceptively straightforward question—Why?—is packed with a whole host of assumptions about what religion is and how African Americans are presumed to be religious. A historical accounting of conversion, in all its lived complexity, is necessary to fully comprehend the golden age of Black Catholic Chicago. To appreciate this history, we must explore the practices, pressures, experiences, and relationships that led many African Americans to conclude that the Catholic Church was, in fact, the "One True Church." This exploration of conversion will in turn allow us to interrogate operative assumptions about "religion."

Black converts contended with a number of competing conceptions of "conversion." There was only one authentic motive to become Catholic as far as missionaries were concerned: acceptance of the teachings of the One True Church. Catholic conversion centered on recognition of and obedience to the Truth that only the Church taught. But considering the pervasiveness of Protestant Christianity in Black communities, African Americans would have been more familiar with conversion narratives that stressed a personal encounter with God. Enslaved converts, for instance, described in intimate physical detail the moment Jesus pulled them back from the pit of Hell and set them on the path to righteousness. "God struck me dead," they said, so that they could be "born again." Conversion was understood, in this formulation, to be an emotionally charged transition from sinfulness to salvation datable to a specific moment and initiated by divine intervention.[2] This conception was rooted in the Protestant Reformation and served as the model for modern scholarship on the subject. While Catholics stressed submission to external authority, the modern concept of conversion emphasized sincerity and an internal transformation. At home as easily in academic institutions as in tent revivals, twentieth-century sociologists took up this modern concept too, though they spoke in socioeconomic rather than salvific terms. Conversion came to be commonly understood as a freely made and intensely personal "choice" made among a variety of options.[3]

Becoming Catholic, then, required not only learning new ways of being religious but also learning a new way of conceptualizing conversion. Catholic education is key to understanding Black conversion in this historical moment as a result. "Education," here and throughout, is used to describe instruction in schools in the narrow sense, as well as a broader inculcation of habits and sensibilities. Becoming Catholic in this particular time and place entailed a transformation of how one experienced the world. For some converts, like Randolph, this transformation took place in church and at home. For even more it happened in and around schools where students and their parents practiced new prayers, rehearsed new rituals, and developed new relationships. The significance of schools in this process was not an accident. Missionaries in Chicago's "foreign missions" explicitly linked evangelization with education and reimagined schools as convert-making machines. But even those with no direct connection to parochial schools became Catholic only insofar as they cultivated new ways of being religious. Before Randolph "believed" what the Catholic Church taught, he "decided to do as others would do." Converts did not "choose" to join the Church so much as they came to know—in their knees and hands and heads and hearts—that this was the only church for them. This knowledge was inculcated through discipline and practice. Conversion was an education, one that came at great cost.

"Convert Makers" and Their Chicago Plan

If we were to ask missionaries at the time why African Americans became Catholic in such large numbers in the first half of the twentieth century, they probably would have pointed to parochial schools. This was certainly the answer I heard anecdotally and read in the existing scholarship.[4] One way to answer the question would be to explain how education became so central to evangelization in Chicago. Father Joseph Eckert's foreign missions on the South Side of Chicago met with success, yet his success had its limits. In 1938, near the end of Eckert's tenure in Chicago, only three parishes were committed to conversion work and none of them were diocesan. Divine Word priests and Sisters of the Blessed Sacrament staffed St. Elizabeth and St. Anselm, while Franciscan friars and sisters led Corpus Christi. So long as the archbishop left Black Catholics segregated from the rest of the archdiocese, under the jurisdiction of missionary orders, there could be no grand plan to convert Black Chicago.

This changed in 1938 when two young white priests, fresh from seminary, requested an assignment in a Black parish. Martin Farrell and Joseph Richards shared at least two things in common. They witnessed the ways migration changed neighborhoods firsthand and they were inspired by Eckert's missionary impulse. Farrell was baptized in Visitation parish, an Irish community considered "one of the largest and most important [parishes] in the Archdiocese" in the 1930s. Just a few decades later it had become an infamous hub of white Catholic resistance to the perceived "Black invasion." Parishioners with the support of the pastor founded the Garfield Boulevard Improvement Association to keep African Americans out of the neighborhood and, by the 1960s, resorted to hate mail, death threats, and vandalism to discourage Black families from settling in the neighborhood.[5] Farrell recalled his childhood parish as "a bastion of white supremacy."[6] Joseph Richards was baptized into the then-Irish St. Elizabeth parish in 1913. By the time he turned fifteen most of the original congregation had left, his neighborhood had become Bronzeville, and Father Eckert was pastor of the now-Black St. Elizabeth. Eckert's charismatic presence proved instrumental for the formation of both Richards and Farrell, the former as a parishioner and the latter as a frequent visitor.[7]

Farrell and Richards attended the Archdiocese of Chicago's St. Mary of the Lake Seminary together from 1932 to 1938. Dubbed "the convert makers" by historian Steven Avella, the two priests hoped to follow in Eckert's footsteps and expand the city's foreign mission territories. This set them apart from their contemporaries, to say the least.[8] Most priests could not fathom African Americans being Catholic. They assumed, in Farrell's words, that "these people were Baptists, Methodists." "Nobody thought of them being Catholic outside of the SVDs and some Franciscans."[9] "It was alien," unheard of for a diocesan priest to work in a Black parish, let alone request one. "The diocesan priest moved out of a parish when it became black."[10] But request it they did and in July 1938 Cardinal George Mundelein reversed his policy of transferring diocesan parishes to missionary orders when the neighborhood became majority Black. He assigned Farrell and Richards to St. Malachy parish on the West Side and the young priests set out to prove their contemporaries wrong.[11]

Much like Corpus Christi and St. Elizabeth on the South Side, St. Malachy was a parish in decline when Farrell and Richards arrived. The parish peaked in the 1920s, but as white parishioners left and Black migrants came to call the neighborhood home, the parish shrank from 1,400 to just 300 members by 1930.[12] Farrell and Richards's task was clear: save the parish by repopulating the pews with converts. They did not so much invent a plan as systematize and expand on Eckert's. The Divine Word missionary had said that the Church reaches parents "through the children."[13] So, in the fall of 1938 Farrell and Richards set about remaking St. Malachy school into a missionary center. First, they opened the school to African Americans, which, almost by default, meant welcoming non-Catholic enrollment. Second, they actively recruited Black students (and their parents) who were not Catholic. The two priests "unabashedly went door to door, personally inviting people to come to the parish and send their children to the school."[14] Teams of priests, sisters, and laypeople became "self-taught demographers," counting the Catholics in the neighborhood and gauging the interest of those who might enroll their children.[15] Third, and most crucially, they welcomed non-Catholic enrollment on the condition that both children and parents agreed to attend religious instruction courses as well as Mass. Parents need not convert to secure their child's enrollment. In fact, Father Farrell later explicitly identified that as an unacceptable motive for conversion. Parents *were* obliged to become students of Catholicism along with their children, however.

While Corpus Christi and St. Elizabeth on the South Side remained the most prominent Black Catholic parishes in the city, it was this West Side parish that allowed the rise of Black Catholic Chicago to continue from the 1930s all the way into the early 1960s. St. Malachy recorded over four hundred and fifty conversions in Farrell and Richards's eight-year tenure.[16] In 1946 Cardinal Samuel Stritch, Chicago's new archbishop, doubled down on their parochial-school conversion plan. He transferred them to two more declining parishes, respectively. Farrell was reassigned to St. James, which sat on the north end of an ever-expanding Black Belt. When he opened enrollment in the school to Black children regardless of their religious affiliation, the church flourished. By 1949, just three years after Farrell's arrival, "more than 700 men and women had been baptized, and St. James Church soon became known as one of the largest mission parishes in the United States."[17] Meanwhile, Stritch reassigned Father Richards to Holy Angels. Once among the most prominent parishes in Chicago's "old Gold Coast" neighborhood, Holy Angels had ex-

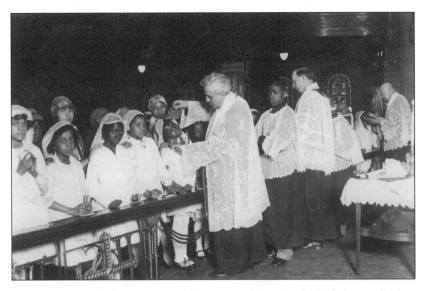

Figure 2.1. Father Joseph Eckert baptizes a convert class at St. Elizabeth (ca. 1927). This photograph bears a striking resemblance to one published in the *Chicago Defender* in 1927, though it is unclear whether they were taken on the same date (see "Catholics Baptize Record Class of Converts," *Chicago Defender* [May 14, 1927]: 4). Courtesy of the Robert M. Myers Archives, Society of the Divine Word.

perienced a precipitous drop in membership to just a few hundred white parishioners in an increasingly Black neighborhood. In Richards's first few years, three hundred and seventy-seven parents—one in every three who completed a religious instruction course—and three hundred and seventy-four children converted.[18] By 1959 over eight thousand Black women and men had attended religious instruction classes and more than three thousand had converted as well as close to five thousand children.[19]

Farrell and Richards's respective reassignments had a cascade effect. They introduced their methods to new priests, priests who brought this plan with them when they were reassigned. The formula was replicated across Chicago. Parishes encouraged Black enrollment, made religious instruction courses mandatory for non-Catholic enrollment, and baptized hundreds of new Catholics. The chronicles kept by Corpus Christi's friars first recorded that non-Catholic parents were expected to accompany their children to Sunday Mass and attend a full course of religious instructions in September 1946, though they were not "obliged to join the Church." Four hundred adults entered religious instructions that fall and nearly three hundred and fifty became Catholic by December the following year.[20] St. Elizabeth baptized over one hundred new members nearly each spring in the 1940s.[21] In the words of historian John McGreevy, the convert makers "created a veritable African-American Catholic empire."[22] In this way, Black Catholic converts saved a number of parishes across the city that might have closed for lack of members.

Their missionary strategy soon gained such renown that it was known across the Midwest simply as "the Chicago Plan."[23] Thanks to the Midwest Clergy Conference on Negro Welfare, priests from Louisville to Milwaukee attended workshops on "*The Chicago System (recruiting non-Catholics for Instructions through the School)*" and "Obligatory Mass Attendance for Non-Catholic Parents."[24] Their circle expanded in 1960 when Father Richards and one of his protégés, Father Patrick Curran, organized "The Catholic Church and the Negro in the Archdiocese of Chicago."[25] This two-day conference for diocesan priests outlined the demographic shifts that had transformed white parishes into predominantly Black non-Catholic neighborhoods over the past four decades and detailed the essential elements of the Chicago Plan. Curran argued that this plan—explicitly linking education with evangelization—represented the only viable solution to the city's shifting religious landscape. If parishes were to survive at all, priests must become missionaries and declare "'total warfare' on the non-Catholic community."[26]

"Why I Became a Catholic"

But Black converts did not think of themselves as captives in some spiritual war game, souls to be "won" by missionaries. Missionaries set some of the conditions for conversion, to be sure. If priests had not opened parochial schools to Black students, for instance, who knows how the history of Black Catholic Chicago would have played out. Once enrolled, though, missionaries could not contain the forces and factors that moved people to join the Church. When we listen to Black women, men, and children themselves, we find that "convert" is not the first word they used to describe themselves. Instead, we find people who wanted to be "good Catholics."

African American Catholics often insist that *faith* makes them Catholic.[27] This might seem redundant, but it is deeply felt and defended for good reason. Black Catholics in the United States have long been deemed suspect by their sheer presence. They are familiar with the presumption, especially on the part of white Catholics, that African American Catholics must be converts. Black religiosity in the United States has been so thoroughly associated in the popular imagination with evangelical Protestantism, and U.S. Catholicism with whiteness, that Black Catholics appear anomalous—this despite the fact that Catholics of African descent have been in the Americas as long as any Catholics have. Black people "born Catholic" in the United States, meaning African Americans born into Catholic families and baptized as infants, often name the generations who preceded them to disabuse people of that presumption.

African American *converts* to Catholicism face a different set of suspicions. Sociologists in the last decades of the twentieth century were fascinated with why African Americans would convert to Catholicism.[28] The most prevalent answer given was for greater social and economic mobility, a hypothesis I heard and read often. African Americans chose to join Catholic churches because they provided high quality educational institutions and promised better futures for their children. This reigning perspective drew on nearly a century of scholarship that stressed social structures and economic interests as determinative factors in religious identity. A related, albeit more polemic, response was that African Americans became Catholic because they wanted to be white.[29] Catholicism, according to this line of argument, represented a restrained and "respectable" mode of religious life amenable to upwardly mobile Black people who aspired to escape their second-class citizenship by emulating whiteness. These explanations, however, preclude from the start that African Americans may have found Catholicism compelling *as Catholicism*. Lost in this literature is the possibility that Black women and men, like Randolph with whom we opened this chapter, may have been moved by the ritual movements of the Mass, that they may have found something in those habits of devotion that felt right. Those I met in the course of my research made this point plain. On my first trip to St. Malachy on Chicago's West Side, as I chatted with the pastor and a parishioner, I expressed my frustration with the implications that plagued these sociological studies. The parishioner, who had converted in the

1940s, chuckled. Why were he and his family Catholic? He shook his head and stated matter-of-factly, "We're Catholic because we kept the faith."[30]

This conversation resonates with what Black Catholic converts have left in the archival record and in memoirs. As historian Cecilia Moore has shown, "how and why many African Americans chose to leave the comforts, supports, and familiarity of the Black churches and their attendant institutions in the second third of the twentieth century in order to become Roman Catholics was the subject of numerous conversion narratives and articles published in *The Catholic World, Jubilee, The Interracial Review, Commonweal, America, The Torch* and other Catholic publications between 1930 and 1960."[31] These sources attest that when converts reflected on why they became Catholic, they did not mention clergy conferences or demographic shifts or evangelization plans, nor did they talk about social or economic opportunities. Instead, they spoke of divine assistance, steadfast faith, and their discovery of "the Truth." This was on display in the December 1936 issue of the *Interracial Review*. In it, an anonymous author attempted to answer the question that "white Catholics, in friendly curiosity, often ask the Negro convert . . . How did you 'happen' to become a Catholic?" The author offers a catalogue of possibilities. Perhaps it was their upbringing under "devout Christian parents," the fortune of "having contact with very good Catholics," or coming "under the influence of a brilliant man of my own race who had just become a convert." By the end it is clear that none of these reasons were sufficient. "How does one 'happen' to become a Catholic?" the author asked again, this time rhetorically. "By the grace of God I am what I am."[32]

The collection of letters written by converts at St. Elizabeth in 1945, of which Randolph's story was just one, also emphasized "faith" as the prime mover for conversion. Randolph was among the twenty-four students in Sister Mary Frances Therese's religious instruction course that year. Readers will recall Sister Frances Therese from the previous chapter where we discussed the cautionary tale of a child convert that she published as "Despite the Sisters." If priests like Joseph Richards and Martin Farrell pitched and promoted the Chicago Plan, teaching sisters such as Sister Frances Therese brought it to life. Catholic schools were staffed primarily by women religious. Sisters had come to outnumber priests in the United States by 1820 and, as historian James O'Toole notes, "by the twentieth century, in many places sisters outnumbered priests by factors of five and six to one."[33] Furthermore, historian Margaret McGuinness has shown how, "with the exception of celebrating Mass or administrating the sacraments, sisters were more actively involved in the everyday lives of Catholics than priests."[34] This was no less the case in Black Chicago. "By the 1950s," according to historian Suellen Hoy, "close to one hundred missionary sisters resided in African American neighborhoods."[35] Parents and students alike interacted with sisters with greater frequency than they did with priests. Women like Sister Frances Therese, then, often introduced African Americans to the Catholic Church. That year she gave her students a special assignment: write a letter to Mother Katharine Drexel, the mother superior and founder of her order, about "Why I became a Catholic."

Each letter presented a different life story. They differed in tone and style, ranging from the marginally legible to the meticulously polished. Taken together, the writers shared a desire to be good Catholics, a desire seemingly born of the certainty that all that the sisters and priests said about the Church was true. "My instructions completed," one letter writer wrote, "I was then convinced that there was no other Religion for me. Its magnificent heart, simplicity and truth entranced me and each day my love for it increases." Others echoed this sentiment, presenting their conversion less as a choice among options than the only alternative available upon consideration of the facts. One writer felt she should "offer myself to the True Church of God, as I now know the Catholic Church to be." Another said that, having surveyed other options, "non [sic] of them seem to teach the doctrine of the true Work of Christ. It was the only Church that had a real understanding." None were more direct than the woman whose letter consisted of a single run-on sentence: "I want to become a Catholic because it is the only church that teaches the truth and the only one that knows the truth and the only one that cares about the truth."[36]

Now, it is not entirely surprising that prospective converts would write that they wished to become Catholic because they believed "it is the only true church of God." After all, they wrote their letters under the instruction of a sister who occupied a position of authority over them in the process of conversion. They addressed their letters to an even more prominent Catholic. We should expect their answers to conform to missionary expectations. Belief in "the One True Church" was the only legitimate motive for conversion at the time as far as the Church was concerned. Ellen Tarry, an African American writer and convert to Catholicism, said as much in her autobiography. When, as a young girl, she asked for a definition of the word "convert," her schoolteacher responded, "those who study the teachings of the Church, accept them, and become Catholics."[37] Father Martin Farrell confirmed this in *The Parish Catechism, Written Especially for Instructing Non-Catholic People in the Basic Teachings of Religion*, published in 1954. "The only sufficient reason for joining the Catholic Church is this. . . . You are convinced that the Catholic Church is the only true church and that you cannot save your soul outside of the Catholic Church." (There were, of course, a whole host of wrong reasons: "I like it. My wife is a Catholic; therefore, I should be. My child is in the Catholic school, and wants to be a Catholic.")[38]

Given the fact that most conversions occurred in and around schools, catechists and theologians were wary about purely instrumental decisions to become Catholic. Present-day observers and historians may harbor similar doubts, if for different reasons. Was conversion in this context a consequence of coercion? Is there reason to be suspicious of converts' sincerity? These questions are understandable and it is necessary to be aware of demands placed on African Americans by the exigencies of their environment—by, for example, the conflicting expectations of both Catholic missionaries and Protestant kin. But the questions also imply a certain understanding of "conversion" and "religion" more broadly, namely, that religious choice is not real or genuine unless it is freely chosen. This dichotomy between the authentic religious choice on the one hand and the instrumental one on the other has been fundamental to the post-Enlightenment understanding of religion. Privileging privately held beliefs over communally enacted rituals, scholars distinguished sincere beliefs that have been "chosen" from inauthentic ones that have been "coerced."[39] Adam Seligman, Robert Weller, Michael Puett, and Bennett Simon diagnose this dichotomy in their recent book *Ritual and Its Consequences*. They note that "ritual has had something of a poor reputation in the contemporary world, relegated to a form of deviance in the structural-functionalism of midcentury American sociology, or extirpated as an empty, external husk, lacking in ultimate spiritual significance, or again, condemned as a form of authoritarian control and dominance."[40] "Real religion," so it is said, cannot be coerced.[41]

The problem with this dichotomy is that it compels a judgment that the historical record, when approached from another angle, does not warrant. An account of conversion that begins with what African American converts say about their own conversions can help us move beyond the limits of this dichotomy. Faced with letters and memoirs like those from Randolph's instruction class it becomes much more difficult to cast conversion as the result of a utilitarian decision to enroll children in a better school, or a choice to improve one's social status. Accounts of conversion that do not seriously consider claims made by converts themselves—namely, the significance they placed on "faith"—miss an essential aspect of the experience itself. This does not mean, it should be said, that we must uncritically take converts' explanations as the final word on the matter. Nor does it mean that scholars should avoid asking questions about the economic factors that impact parental decisions about where to enroll their children in school or the dynamics of social status that shape neighborhoods. No one explanation alone can account for why African Americans converted, not even that of Black Catholics themselves. As we will see, Black converts' lives were structured and shaped in ways they were not fully conscious of. Becoming Catholic involved much more than intellectual assent or individual agency. It involved inculcating different ways of being religious. Converts' words do not close our inquiry; they shift it. If, as my sources insist, faith caused conversion, then what makes faith possible in the first place? This line of inquiry is what theorist and anthropologist Talal Asad had in mind when he posed the question: "What are the conditions in which religious symbols can actually produce religious dispositions? Or, as a nonbeliever would put it: How does (religious) power create (religious) truth?"[42]

Inculcation in the Classroom

Converts were not made, nor did they simply "choose" to believe. Rather, they became someone new as they learned (and were taught) to feel, imagine, and experience the world in new ways. Becoming someone new tended to happen in and around Catholic schools for two reasons. First, Black families' encounters with Catholics more often than not occurred in schools. Most migrants were not Catholic and many harbored suspicions about Catholicism. It was unlikely that Black newcomers would wander into a Catholic church on a Sunday morning in search of community, especially when one considers that most Catholic churches were white spaces hostile to Black people. Catholic schools were a different matter—at least those in predominantly Black neighborhoods and open to Black enrollment. Catholic schools attracted Black parents in large part due to a dearth of alternatives. Public schools became segregated for all intents and purposes as white families abandoned them when faced with the arrival of Black families. South and West Side schools quickly became separate and unequal, underfunded and overcrowded.[43] Too few teachers and too many students, all with inadequate resources, inevitably led to ill discipline and poor performance.

Catholic schools in those same neighborhoods were able to avoid these problems in large part because of the dedication of vowed women religious. On a basic level, teaching sisters kept parochial schools relatively affordable since their salaries were quite low in comparison to lay professionals. Women religious took vows of poverty. But beyond affordability, women religious were instrumental in creating the disciplined educational spaces that became so attractive to many Black parents. Sociologists St. Clair Drake and Horace Cayton, in their classic *Black Metropolis: A Study of Negro Life in a Northern City* (1945), reported "many parents felt that the parochial school offered a more thorough education in a quieter atmosphere and personal attention."[44] Historian Timothy Neary illustrates that, already by the 1940s, "word spread among Bronzeville residents that Catholic schools provided individual attention, discipline, and rigorous academic instruction often missing in public schools."[45] Even when they were not Catholic, parents appreciated the "moral education" that defined Catholic classrooms.[46]

The second reason becoming someone new occurred in and around Catholic schools is that, at the time, the whole of Catholic educational philosophy was devoted to doing exactly that. Parochial schools were not mere alternatives to public education. They were institutions explicitly established by Catholics to counter what they perceived to be the dangerous moral deficiencies of public schools, deficiencies that stemmed from the fact that public schools were, from the Catholic perspective, de facto *Protestant* schools.[47] "Educational objectives, as far as Catholics were concerned, were twofold," according to the preeminent Catholic education scholar Harold A. Buetow. There was an ultimate objective and an immediate objective. The immediate aim was to produce people capable of working for their own well-being and for the common good, the specifics of which changed with historical circumstances. "The ultimate aim," on the other hand, "remained ever the same—knowledge of God in view of man's eternal destiny."[48]

All of Catholic education, from religion to arithmetic, was put in service of this ultimate aim. Rev. Daniel Feeney put it this way in an address at the 1929 meeting of the National Catholic Educational Association: "Catholic Education does not mean secular education plus the recitation of prayers and a knowledge of the Catechism." Rather, religious training informed "the entire curriculum and permeate[d] the whole child every minute of every day."[49] Catholic education was designed to be the formation of "good Catholics." Monsignor George Johnson in a 1944 essay described the "the goals of Christian [by which he meant Catholic] education in American democratic society" as including "physical fitness," "economic literacy," "social virtue," and "cultural development." "Moral perfection, or saintliness," however, was "the crown of all the rest, achieved in and through all the rest, fulfilling the purpose of man's existence, because it purifies him and unites him with his God."[50] "Johnson's influence on the Catholic elementary school curricula in the United States since 1943," according to Buetow, "is incalculable."[51]

The success of the Chicago Plan makes more sense when we take this pedagogy into account. Conversion in Catholic schools is often rendered as a utilitarian choice. Parents want their children to be educated, parochial schools represent the best available option, therefore families enroll and eventually convert. While each individual point may be technically true, this formula misses the extensive self-formation students and their families underwent in the process. Schools are by definition in the business of self-formation. In this, Catholic schools were no different than any other. They sought to mold youth into dedicated democratic citizens just as public schools did. As Robert A. Orsi discusses in *History and Presence*, Catholic educators differed insofar as "they worked within an environment that made no special allowances for children in terms of moral formation, doctrinal instruction, or devotional and sacramental practice."[52] For instance, a model religion curriculum for the Archdiocese of Chicago circa 1930 encouraged instructors, as Orsi put it, "to address the full sensorium of childhood—sound, movement, color, smell, and taste—as befits a [Catholic] religious imaginary in which the supernatural is fully present to the senses." They were also enjoined to "drill children in the highly technical terminology of Catholic doctrine in all its scholastic opacity."[53] In other words, the making of good Americans from the sisters' perspective was equivalent to the making of good Catholics.

What makes this so interesting with regard to *Black* Catholic schools is that these objectives and methods defined the educational experience for non-Catholics as well as Catholics. Jacqueline Jordan Irvine and Michèle Foster capture this in their edited volume *Growing Up African American in Catholic Schools* (1996). Irvine attended a segregated Catholic school in 1950s Alabama and notes how, though "99% of the 250 students" including herself were not Catholic, she "attended mass and catechism classes five days a week in school."[54] Religious formation extended beyond formal religious instruction as well. Teaching sisters taught geography "primarily within the context of religious discussions or proselytizing. For example, [she] learned about Mexico in the context of Our Lady of Guadalupe, Italy through reference to St. Francis of Assisi."[55] Foster shared Irvine's experience despite growing up in an entirely different context. Foster was just one of a few non-Catholic Black students at a French Catholic school in 1950s Massachusetts. Nevertheless, she too notes "all students were expected to participate in the ritual activities of the Catholic Church." "Like every other student," she "memorized catechism, attended mass and other religious ceremonies, sang Gregorian chant, prayed in Latin, English, and French, recited the altar boy's responses to the priests' prayers, watched as my classmates received the sacraments—went to confession, made their first Holy Communions, and were confirmed—and hoped that I would go to limbo instead of hell as the nuns preached for those who were unbaptized would."[56]

The transformation of the ways children understood, imagined, and moved in the world, then, sat at the heart of Catholic education. Students learned a repertoire of devotional prayers and practices that shaped their religious worlds on a daily basis, whether or not they were Catholic. In order to understand why a Black child might wish to become Catholic, even if his or her siblings and parents and friends and neighbors were not, we must examine the impact this kind of formation might have on the students who underwent it. There is no better place to begin to understand the process of becoming Catholic than inside a parochial school classroom.

Formation took place in what might be called "traditionally" religious settings—in chapel for Mass, at a shrine for devotion, in catechism class. Sisters of the Blessed Sacrament teaching at St. Elizabeth and St. Anselm left evidence in their annals of what this looked like. The Marian Year of 1954 serves as a notable example. Inaugurated by Pope Pius XII on the Feast of the Immaculate Conception in December 1953, the pope's hope was to increase faith worldwide by dedicating devotion to the Blessed Mother. Observances ranged from families gathering to pray the rosary in their homes to public spectacles that filled sports arenas. A number of scholars have illustrated how Catholic anticommunism, born of the perceived threat "godless communism" posed to Catholics worldwide, contributed to a preponderance of Marian apparitions and the proliferation of Marian devotion in the 1950s.[57] But other themes likely overlaid this Cold War one for African American students in Chicago Catholic schools.

The Sisters of the Blessed Sacrament teaching at St. Elizabeth's grammar school and high school in 1954 worked hard to inculcate the right relationship between students and the Virgin Mary. Students at St. Elizabeth periodically made a pilgrimage to Marian shrines around the city. The sisters erected shrines to greet students as they entered school and enlisted students' aid in the construction of classroom shrines. Each student helped to decorate the shrines with her or his own prayers, pictures, and poetry. They said a rosary and recited the official Marian Year prayer each day in class. If this were not enough, the sisters sent them home with a large portrait of the Blessed Virgin and scapulars for their families to wear, along with instructions on proper devotion to the Blessed Mother.

A student who was not Catholic—for simplicity's sake, let's call our hypothetical student "Joan"—would have been well prepared once it was her turn to take home the class's Mary statue. For one whole week the statue would be under Joan's protection, as she remained under the Blessed Mother's. Now, like her peers before her, Joan would have been expected to invite her family and their neighbors to join her in saying the rosary. She would have brought booklets home to help. But for her, the prayers had long become second nature.

Joan may not have been Catholic, but perhaps she wanted to be. She yearned to join Our Lady's Sodality, the group especially devoted to the Virgin Mary who got to stand in front of the whole class, veiled in white, to crown her Queen come May. She tired of watching friends process to the communion rail when their class went to Mass, each of them receiving the real body and blood of Jesus Christ while she could only imagine from the pews. Joan may well have wanted to be special like her Catholic classmates, to be received into what her classmates, teachers, and the parish priest told her was the only True Church. But to become Catholic she would need her parents' permission. After all, how could she be a good Catholic if her parents refused to bring her to Sunday Mass or, worse still, if they undermined the sisters at home? So, when *she* recited the Marian Year prayer—when she called on the Blessed Mother to "convert the wicked," when she prayed that "all men [might] feel the attraction of Christian goodness"—she thought of her Protestant aunts and uncles who mocked Catholics as "Mary worshippers." She prayed that their hard hearts might be softened. And she dedicated a rosary to her parents, that her whole family might become Catholic together.[58]

"Joan" may be hypothetical, but her story was quite common. Her story was one I encountered in archives and in books, not to mention in anecdotes in formal interviews and informal conversations. The desire to become Catholic stirred in schools. Children learned how to be Catholic even if their families were only nominally Christian. And they learned how to be Catholic before they expressed any desire to become Catholic themselves. They memorized prayers, studied doctrine, and developed new habits. Peculiar ways of moving limbs and esoteric turns of phrase became instinctual. And these were the sorts of things teaching sisters *intended* to inculcate. A whole host of other forces moved beyond the sisters' direct control and no less shaped the students. If all children were required to attend Mass, but only some (that is, Catholics) could fully participate, it was almost inevitable that envy and resentment would ensue. If the foremost authority figures in students' lives outside

Figure 2.2. First Holy Communion Procession, Corpus Christi Catholic Church. Courtesy of the Celano Archives of the Sisters of St. Francis, Dubuque, Iowa.

their families—priests and sisters—taught that the unbaptized were destined for limbo, referred to their siblings as "pagan babies," or told them they "would all burn in hell if we did not convert," as Irvine recalled her teachers telling her class, it would not be surprising if children began to believe them.[59]

But, as alluded to above, religious formation was not limited to these "traditional" settings. Reading, writing, and arithmetic were put to use in the making of "good Catholics." Orsi notes, for example, how sisters cultivated a sensibility toward the supernatural through handwriting exercises. "Catholic teaching sisters spent an enormous amount of time and effort during the school day instructing children to write correctly, legibly, and *perfectly in cursive*." The immediate aim, to borrow Buetow's phrase from above, was to teach students how to write in cursive. This was inseparable, though, from the ultimate objective: fostering right relationship with God. To this end, penmanship lessons taught "self-control, concentration, and precision" as students practiced writing the names of saints and the words of prayers again and again and again. In this way, a handwriting lesson could be "an end unto itself" and "a devotional practice" simultaneously.[60]

This would have been routine for students at Black Catholic schools as well. It is evident in a book of poetry composed by seventh grade students at Corpus Christi School under the guidance of Sister Mary Roman in 1963. Sister Roman introduced students to basic poetic conventions (rhyme, meter, etc.) in class. Then she asked them to take a hand at it themselves. The resulting booklet reveals how porous boundaries could be between a poetry lesson and devotional writing. One student's poem read "Lent is the time of the year, / When we should all just want to cheer. / To think that we have all this time, / To make up for our awful crimes. / To tell God that we love him so. / And hope that He will always know." Another wrote the guilt-ridden "He Walks Alone."

> Where was I when He took the Cross?
>   Upon His bruised and beaten shoulder?
> Where was I when it weighed Him down
>   And fell upon Him like a boulder?
> Where was I when they nailed Him up
>   Without a care or worry?

>   Where was I? All drapped [*sic*] in sin
>   Unworthy of His glory.

Christ's crucifixion and death resonated as a theme throughout the religious poems, perhaps indicating the liturgical season when they were written. An especially colorful account was simply entitled "Sufferings." "When you get a needle prick, / You cry and say it hurts, it sticks. / But did you know that Christ our Lord, / Was jabbed in the side with a rusty sword? / We can't really cry about our pricks, / Christ didn't cry about the thorns / When the cruel soldiers of the city / Treated Christ without Love or Pity."[61]

Together these poems illuminate the inculcation of Catholicism by children, in this case in an English class. Not every student chose such somber subject matter. Nor was each poem explicitly religious. (One poet rhymed about frying bacon, another about a "little green man" from Mars.) What is more, it is impossible to know definitively which student poets were Catholic. One boy wrote "Jesus died for us you see, / On the hill of Calvary. / Soldiers beat Him mocked and scorned / But Jesus did not scream or mourn." This poem alone cannot tell us whether he was born Catholic, hoped to convert one day, or attended no church at all. Nevertheless the poems do give a glimpse of the kind of Catholicism cultivated among students. The poems that deal in religious themes shared an emphasis on the suffering of Jesus and the sinfulness of the poet, underwritten with equal parts of guilt and gratitude. In this they conformed to portrayals of Christ's passion popular in the first half of the twentieth century. (They very likely were informed by a passion play Corpus Christi parishioners performed each Lent.) The vivid imagery and personal nature of the poems confirm that, as Orsi argues, "children's religious formation was to be based not solely, or even primarily, on their intellects, but especially on the stimulation of their emotions, desires, and imaginations." Devotional poems written by seventh graders exemplified the work of teaching sisters who had spent years exciting imaginations and disciplining bodies so that their "youngsters would enter the company of supernatural figures really present to them in the sacraments and in their everyday lives."[62]

Sister Roman's presence throughout the self-bound book, as teacher and editor, gives an even clearer sense of sisters' expectations. Half the poems in this collection would be described as "secular," but Sister Roman made sure to frame those between two pages of devotional poetry at the beginning and another two at the end—pages she augmented with illustrations of crosses and the IHS insignia (a Greek acronym for JESUS later adopted as a Jesuit emblem). Sister Roman also included a composition of her own that serves as an apt analogy for the religious formation instilled by teaching sisters. "My Treasure Chest" imagines students as gemstones—"garnet, ruby, and pearl"—gifted by God to teach. "In each eye there trod / That precious diamond soul / Reflects the will of God." These boys and girls needed to be properly shaped. They may be jewels, but jewels viewed "through the rough." This is where teaching sisters stepped in. Souls might reflect the will of God, but without proper guidance they remained unprepared for the trials and temptations of the world.

> Through discovery, attention
>   File the edges, cast the lime,
> For these gem sets before me
>   Polish well each day of time.

Her hope was that "When comes that grand finale / And they sparkle through the test, I will signal to the Almighty / That's my Little Treasure Chest!" The stakes of religious formation, then, were high for sisters and students, even in an English class.

These lessons made lasting impressions on students. No amount of religious formation in and of itself "made" converts out of children; not all nominally Christian students became Catholic by graduation. Few of Jacqueline Jordan Irvine's classmates converted, for instance, despite the fact (or perhaps because) they were told they would burn in hell otherwise. Nonetheless, sources record children adopting Catholic practices *before* they became Catholic. Ellen Tarry wrote about her profound experiences with the Eucharist as a non-Catholic child attending Catholic school. Tarry described how the priest's Eucharistic blessing during Mass moved her deeply, despite knowing nothing of the doctrine of transubstantiation. "Each morning a miracle took place in front of my eyes," she wrote in her autobiography, "and Jesus was present upon the altar before which I knelt."[63] Sisters prepared children like Tarry to experience the real physical presence of Jesus Christ in the bread and wine of the Eucharist. The realness of Jesus's body and blood was impressed upon them at a young age as they were trained to comport themselves in special ways in the spaces surrounding it. Children made other Catholic practices their own too. Chicago papers publicized the story of a non-Catholic fifth-grade boy who baptized his dying father before a priest could arrive. The boy was confident he had followed the correct ritual procedure since he baptized just as Sister Mary Verda demonstrated in class.[64] These stories illustrate the ways formation "worked," regardless of whether or not conversion was the end result.

Educating the Entire Family

Religious formation shaped the parents of pupils as well. Schools served as gateways into the Catholic Church for Black children. Children by necessity brought their parents with them, by necessity not only because the transformation of children inevitably impacted the parents but also because parents had to make promises to enroll their children in Catholic school in the first place. Sister Mary Clarice Sobczyk captured what this looked like from the parents' perspective in her dissertation, a study of African Americans in five Chicago parishes between 1946 and 1949. Sister Sobczyk taught elementary school at Holy Angels parish as she completed her Ph.D. in sociology at DePaul University. These happened to be the same years Father Joseph Richards implemented the Chicago Plan at the parish. She describes how, in order for non-Catholic parents to enroll their children, mother and father together had to be interviewed by parish priests. This interview impressed upon the parents the moral weight of this decision and the conditions upon which their child's enrollment rested. "Both parents must promise to come twice a week for a course of instruction in Christian doctrine," the priests informed parents, "and to attend Holy Mass on Sunday and holy days [of obligation] with their child or children."[65]

These conditions were part and parcel of the missionary plans that linked education with evangelization. But another premise operated behind this one, namely, that Catholic schools were designed to educate entire families, not just children.[66] This came through in the conversations priests and sisters had with non-Catholic parents prior to their child's enrollment. Sister Sobczyk paraphrased this conversation:

> Nancy is your child and you are asking us to help rear Nancy in the right way. If Nancy is accepted the priests and nuns will do their part. . . . Nancy will be taught the Catholic religion and it is the duty of the parents to know what is being taught. For Nancy may at home talk about the religious doctrine which she had heard in school. She may need your help. What will you do? If you ignore her, refuse to talk about religious matters, mock or contradict what she had learned in school, you are going counter to the training which the Sisters are giving.[67]

Parents became deeply involved in Catholic education regardless of whether or not they were Catholic. Their child's enrollment depended on their extensive involvement.

Enrollment for children meant months of classes and Masses for parents, classes and Masses that served as religious formation for entire families. Twice a week parents attended religious instruction classes for an hour and a half, which accumulated to some fifty-one hours of catechism over the course of the semester. This posed quite a challenge to parents already working hard to support their families, so priests and sisters offered three different class times to accommodate various schedules.[68] Once there, formation trained them to move and think as "good Catholics" and reinforced the fundamental principle that there is no salvation outside the Catholic Church.

A typical course of instructions, such as those Sister Sobczyk described in her study, roughly followed the order of Father Martin Farrell's *Parish Catechism, Written Especially for Instructing Non-Catholic People in the Basic Teachings of Religion* (1954). Farrell modeled his *Catechism* on the Baltimore Catechism that served as the standard since the Third Council of Baltimore (1885). What distinguished his was that Farrell tailored it for the express purpose of instructing non-Catholics, which for him meant non-Catholic Black Chicagoans. Early classes covered basic religious truths, such as the existence of God and the necessity of prayer. Later classes progressed through the practicalities of Catholic life such as the sacraments and commandments.

Many of the "truths to believe," as Farrell termed them, would have been familiar to most Christians. Priests and sisters devoted most of their time to topics that would have been controversial among non-Catholics. One of the most difficult was the Catholic Church's exclusive claim to truth and salvation. Sobczyk notes how parents raised few objections until the lectures on the exclusivity of the Catholic Church. Most were shocked "when it comes to the fact that Christ established the Catholic Church, that they must accept the authority of the Church as the only Church, and that every one is obliged to join her and accept her authority or otherwise nothing will be gained."[69]

Whether or not they agreed, parents participated in the same religious formation as their children. The primary teaching method employed by teachers at the time was a pedagogy of practiced repetition called "drilling." Just as athletes re-form their bodies for physical endurance through exercises and drills, so too priests and sisters sought to re-form non-Catholic bodies and minds through repetition and habituation. Over the course of a year parents memorized and repeated short answers to a succession of Catholic doctrinal questions, such as:

206. How many churches did Jesus Christ establish?
    Jesus Christ founded only *ONE* church.
        There are over 259 kinds of Christian churches in America today.
        Only one of them is the true church of Christ.
207. Which church is the true church of Christ?
    The church recorded in the Bible is the true church of Christ.
208. Which church is the church recorded in the Bible?
    The only church that could possibly be the church that Christ founded
    is a church that is 1900 years old, namely, the Roman Catholic Church.[70]

Drilling extended beyond theological principles. Much like a religious instruction course, Farrell's *Parish Catechism* also inculcated religious obligations through drilling. In writing, seeking to impress upon potential converts the moral gravity of their decisions, bolded and capitalized typeface seemed to shout at readers again and again: "**ATTEND MASS EVERY SUNDAY AND HOLY DAY OF OBLIGATION. GIVE UP YOUR SERIOUS SINS.**"[71] Drilling, whether read in a catechism or repeated aloud in a classroom, operated in the hope that persistent repetition would bring to life the reality it taught.

These moral disciplines intensified once a student, parent, or child decided they wished to become Catholic. If a priest deemed them fit for baptism—priests would assess motivations for conversion—prospective converts then entered another set of classes. These stressed the everyday impact of the doctrines they had been drilled on for months. Converts trained in proper conduct in Church, practicing "genuflecting, kneeling and saying some prayers." They learned the necessity of fasting before church and arriving on time.[72] They were taught to move their bodies in particular ways—to touch their foreheads, shoulders, and heart with holy water upon entering the church, to genuflect toward the tabernacle when taking their seats, to kneel without touching the seat of the pew, to receive the Eucharist on their tongues without chewing, to pray silently on their knees until the priest returned to his seat. And if classes were not enough, parish publications reminded the newly converted each week. Parish bulletins admonished "speeders" who sped out of Mass after communion, for example, along with "end men" who guarded the last seats in the pew, and "the late-late show" who always arrived late for Mass. A regular column "WHAT EVERY GOOD CATHOLIC KNOWS" served as a corrective for unacceptable habits.[73] They learned to move their bodies in distinctively Catholic ways.

It is no surprise then that, having been so instructed, those who did convert insisted that the Catholic Church was the One True Church. Religious formation awakened this in them. Faith in the exclusivity of Catholic truth claims came through clearly in the letters written by converts, who described the Church variously as "the head of all churches," the "only true Church of God," the only church that teaches "the truth," and the only church with "real understanding" of the "doctrine of the true Work of Christ."[74] Parish bulletins bore this out as well. One parishioner at one of Chicago's convert-making parishes, for instance, published a poem titled "Our Church" that insisted that "Others may preach and may lecture / And say whatever they please," but "We have the seven sacraments," "We have our Lord ever present," "Our Church is Catholic, Apostolic, Infallible, Holy and One," and "We have the Truth Eternal."[75] Even *Ebony* magazine captured this in a 1946 feature story on "Converts of Color." There they noted that becoming Catholic required converts to "renounce former religion, attend class for an average of three months, [and] learn the 'catechism.'" Months of class and Mass culminated in their absolution from past heresy, baptism, and the profession of a vow to adhere to the "Catholic Faith, outside of which nobody can be saved."[76]

The Contingency and Cost of Relationships

But neither a history of the Chicago Plan nor an exploration of life in Catholic schools—neither convert makers' strategies nor students' inculcation of new ways of being—can completely capture the unpredictability at the heart of becoming Catholic. African Americans became Catholic in the ever-changing circumstances of their lives. They became someone new in webs of relationship not just between missionaries and the converted but also between parents and children, between committed partners, even between human and nonhuman beings. These unanticipated encounters generated something not entirely in the control of any one person, a point inevitably missed when conversion is reduced to either choice or coercion, when it is given a functionalist explanation. Any attempt to understand why so many African Americans became Catholic in this period, to understand the conditions that make faith possible, must acknowledge the contingencies and relationships that define everyday life.

Returning to Sister Frances Therese's instruction class of 1945, our twenty-four letter writers repeatedly called attention to the relationships that initiated and facilitated their entrance into the Catholic Church. Some attended instruction because their fiancés were Catholic. For a Catholic to marry a non-Catholic at the time required special dispensation from the bishop. Permission would only be granted on the condition that both spouses would raise their children Catholic. And, since Protestants were considered heretics, their souls would be eternally separated at death. Romantic relationships thus provided powerful motivation (and applied tremendous pressure) to become Catholic—even if "My wife is a Catholic; therefore, I should be" was not considered a legitimate motive for conversion. Falling in love with a Catholic was not incidental to becoming one. This is what led one letter writer to go to Mass and religious instructions in the first place. She attended at the insistence of her boyfriend, who made clear his disappointment when she failed to do so. Another letter writer noted that she went to religious instructions once she was engaged to a Catholic, matter-of-factly stating, "we want to be married in church."[77]

Romance was not the only, or even the most frequent, relationship cited. Intimate connections people had with supernatural beings were integral to conversion. Some letter writers recalled supernatural presences convincing them to join the Catholic Church. One woman joined a group that prayed the "Novena to our Sorrowful Mother" and began to attend Mass before she became Catholic. When a doctor informed her that she needed an operation—a prospect that "terrorized" her—she began to pray to St. Bernadette. Perhaps she had met Bernadette through the popular, critically acclaimed film *The Song of Bernadette* (1943). Or maybe friends told her stories of her spiritual power.[78] One thing was certain for this despondent woman, though. After thirty days of prayer her doctor said she did not need surgery. If her relationship with the Blessed Mother and St. Bernadette were not enough to convince her, a young Catholic man soon requested her hand in marriage. Now she knew she had to convert.[79]

Another woman, raised Baptist, was also visited by a Catholic saint in a time of need. Feeling like something was missing in her life, she "prayed so hard" for guidance that a "very high Saint came to me in a vision," carried her to the Catholic Church, and told her to find help there. "From that day," she recalled, "I decided to become Catholic." She later identified this figure as St. Jude, the patron saint of hopeless causes whose national shrine was based on the South Side of Chicago.[80] Stories like these illustrate the wide resonance of Catholic saints in the early twentieth century when public devotion was at its height.[81] In this case, relationships between non-Catholics and Catholic saints could initiate the process of becoming Catholic.

Other relationships were not with beings so much as with rituals, which, after all, involve the body in relationship with other bodies and a host of physical objects. Letter writers bore witness to the ways participation in Catholic practices might lead to becoming Catholic, not the other way around. Many spoke of the special efficacy of Catholic prayer in their lives. One woman described sitting for hours and reading a Catholic missal, with God at her side, when she found herself in trouble. It was common for converts to mention Mass attendance as integral to their eventual conversion. One woman credited her conversion to a close friend who brought her to Mass. She attended Mass with her several times and "fell in love with its Doctrines." Her belief that this was "the only true Church of 'God'" flowed from this experience of Catholic worship.[82] Yet another convert pointed to his first Mass as the turning point in his life. When he accepted the invitation of a sister, he "liked it so much" that he went back and began religious instructions.[83]

Belief followed practice for Black converts to Catholicism. People did not choose to convert and then, after having intellectually assented to certain doctrinal propositions, start doing Catholic things. Quite the contrary, converts were well versed in Catholic prayers and well practiced in Catholic devotional habits *before* they made their professions of faith, regardless of whether we are talking about grammar school students or their parents. Black Catholic conversion in this way inverts common presumptions about how religion works. Converts became Catholic because it *felt* right. This was not metaphorical. Nor was it simply internal affect, somehow divorced from the external environs surrounding and shaping converts. It was something felt in converts' bodies—smelled in the incense that lingered around altars, tasted in the Eucharist that clung to the roof of one's mouth, and ached in one's knees in prayer while beads passed through folded fingers. One letter writer put it this way: "I would feel different when I would enter the doors."[84] And as we have seen, this religious formation cultivated this feeling. Catholic education created the conditions under which becoming Catholic could "feel right."

This feeling did not come without cost, however. Conversion held serious social consequences. When converts joined the "One True Church," they tacitly agreed never to attend "non-Catholic Churches even for social affairs." As Father Farrell put it at the time, "they must realize without hostility that they have the truth, and those outside the Catholic Church have not."[85] Cecilia Moore notes that "for Black converts to Catholicism—especially before the Second Vatican Council (1962–1965) signaled the willingness of the Roman Catholic Church to engage more directly and collegially with Protestants—the process of conversion and the commencement of a Catholic life meant cutting important religious, social, cultural, and familial ties."[86] Since most African Americans were not Catholic, conversion threatened to sever significant familial and social ties. Moore describes how this church teaching "put off limits most of the traditions of the Black church like attending homecomings, women's days and men's days, New Year's Eve Night Watch services, Easter Sunday Sunrise services, and even weddings of friends because to attend meant entering a Protestant church and worshipping in a Protestant context."[87] Attending family reunions hosted by a Baptist church or a funeral for a Presbyterian parent now put the souls of the newly converted in grave danger. Socializing with Protestants carried grave consequences.

The Catholic Church at the time taught that Protestants were condemned to eternal damnation as heretics. It is not difficult to imagine the confrontational position in which this notion might place a convert in relation to his or her kin. Confrontations could continue after death. Priests sometimes fought with non-Catholic families over the burial of deceased converts, as Catholics were supposed to be buried in a consecrated Catholic cemetery. For instance, in 1958 a parish priest at Corpus Christi refused to give a deceased parishioner a Catholic burial because the family refused to bury the person in a Catholic cemetery.[88] This particular dilemma led a convert and Corpus Christi parishioner, Mary Dolores Gadpaille, to publish an entire book on the subject. Entitled *That You May Die Easy* (1959), Gadpaille hoped to preemptively thwart the kinds of conflicts that could arise at the time of death in "mixed homes, [comprised of] Catholics and non-Catholics alike."[89] Conversion thus had the power not only to separate African Americans from past religious communities, but even to alienate converts from family and friends for eternity.

Catholic teachings on marriage and sexuality presented further challenges still. Fully one third of the classes on Catholic sacraments were devoted to "holy matrimony," a telling fact when one considers that marriage was only one of seven sacraments. Instructors not only offered a history of marriage and the practical steps required for the sacrament, but also listed the "sins against matrimony" and "faults harming marriage." Father Farrell's catechism mirrored this overemphasis on Catholic teachings on marriage. Farrell devoted fourteen pages to the sacrament of holy matrimony, in contrast to just three on baptism and six on the Eucharist.[90] Potential sins were extensive and included divorce, birth control, abortion, and "unlawful separation of husband and wife."[91] To quote just one example from Farrell's *Catechism*,

> Separated or divorced people are not permitted to keep company. A separated or divorced person is still married, therefore, commits serious sin by keeping company with another.[92]

Most Christian churches at the time allowed for divorce, so it is possible that a significant number of parents attending instructions may have been separated, divorced, or remarried. Abiding by these teaching might radically alter long-standing, deeply felt relationships

These teachings on marriage and sexual relationships would have been especially difficult for women and men in the migration era. Some likely left spouses in the South when they moved to Chicago and others may have shared homes with unmarried partners. If they followed Father Farrell's *Parish Catechism*, priests and sisters would have informed these mothers and fathers that Protestant churches were to blame for the widespread collapse of marriage, that common law marriage brought people "down to an animal level of living," that divorce put your soul in mortal danger of damnation, and that divorced Catholics were absolutely forbidden from "keeping company" with members of the opposite sex.[93] The dangers were greater still outside marriage and Farrell reminded potential converts that "Any use of the sexual passion and instinct outside of marriage is a mortal sin."[94] Catholic conversion might alter, or even end, intimate relationships or spark fierce debate between partners hoping to convert each other. Catholic teachings on marriage and sexuality served as a breaking point for many would-be converts, who either refused to or could not become Catholic due to these regulations. Lectures on "the true meaning of marriage" even made it into parish bulletins on occasion.[95]

Becoming Catholic

Attempts to answer why African Americans became Catholic with a straightforward or causal explanation miss the contingencies and costs of human relationships. Attentiveness to them, on the other hand, demonstrates just how mysterious the process of becoming someone new could be. Yes, convert makers and their evangelization plans set some of the terms by which African Americans first encountered the Catholic Church. Yes, Black parents enrolled their children in Catholic schools for the opportunities they afforded. But these plans and opportunities cannot contain the unexpected circumstances that might bring someone to seek baptism. A chance encounter on the street might yield an invitation to attend Mass; a friendly introduction at a party could lead to lifelong romance with a Catholic. These relationships were essential, not incidental, elements of religious transformation. And costs, often unanticipated, came with the territory. This has the added effect of illustrating just how compelling converts found Catholic life. Changing, not to mention severing significant relationships weighs on you. When Randolph's wife took it upon herself to convert her husband, no amount of faith on her part could forestall a fight or prevent pregnant silences at the dinner table. When a Catholic schoolboy brought home his class statue of the Blessed Mother, his earnestness would not lessen the sting of cousins' snickering. Yet tens of thousands of African Americans became Catholic all the same. It is worth pausing to appreciate what this tells us about the power of religious formation.

The role power plays in processes of self-formation is precisely what Talal Asad has in mind in his discussions of how one becomes Christian. Asad has spent much of his career attempting to shift the study of religion away from its obsession with agency, interiority, and symbols. "It is not mere symbols that implant true Christian dispositions," he notes in *Genealogies of Religion*, "but power—ranging all the way from laws (imperial and ecclesiastical) and other sanctions (hellfire, death, salvation, good repute, peace) to the disciplinary activities of social institutions (family, school, city, church) and of human bodies (fasting, prayer, obedience, penance)."[96] Here, power is not an antonym for agency and it is not necessarily negative. Power, Asad points out in an essay entitled "Comments on Conversion," can be "both productive and repressive . . . at once torment and ability."[97] This productive power is what we have observed among African American converts to Catholicism. Rather than the result of a rational choice among religious options or an instrumental decision for socioeconomic advancement, Black migrants became Catholic at the nexus of motivations and pressures, hopes and fears, and unexpected daily occurrences. They were educated and formed, body and soul, by forces of which they were often unaware. These were the conditions that made faith in the One True Church possible in the first place. This did not render their conversion insincere or inauthentic. It was the result of their being human.

Are converts sincere or do they make an instrumental decision? Is conversion a choice or is it coerced? Examining conversion at the intersection of religious formation, relationships, and the contingencies of everyday living can lead us beyond the dichotomies that have defined much of the study of religion. Approaches that emphasize choice, that imagine converts as free agents weighing options and choosing a church in some sort of spiritual cost-benefit analysis, miss the ways that becoming someone new involves forces that cannot be contained by any one person or institution—that exist beyond the control of either the converted or their would-be convert maker. It is not just that conversion is a process rather than a decision, though this is certainly true. Rather, the whole is greater than the sum of its parts.

Women and men and children became Catholic when all these things—the evangelization of missionaries, the religious formation of parochial schools, the sensations of Catholic devotional life, the crisscrossing of lives intersecting with each other, and yes, the choices people made—came together. Months, sometimes even years, of classes and Masses culminated in baptism. It was common for Black parishes in the 1940s and 1950s to practice group baptisms. Though the Easter Vigil Mass was the traditional day for the entrance into the Church, most churches were forced to designate extra days in the summer and winter in order to accommodate the sheer number of converts each year. Baptismal records identify converts ranging from six years old to sixty. Priests often baptized entire families together on the same day.[98] On their given day candidates arrived at the church joined by their sponsor, someone either chosen or assigned to serve as their guide in their new lives as Catholics. Lining up at the communion rail, sometimes in the aisles of the church, attendant priests baptized converts with three splashes of water.

What did it mean, now, to be Black and Catholic in the Black Metropolis? What did it mean to be a member of the "One True Church" in the midst of Black religious plurality?[99] As we will see, becoming Catholic amid the existential intricacies of race had complicated consequences. One last story from Sister Frances Therese's letter writers illustrates this. Freddy, a young man hoping to be baptized, emphasized the comportment of Catholic bodies when he answered "Why I want to be a Catholic." He reflected that the way Catholics "carry themselves makes any one notice them in a respectable way." Freddy especially admired the way sisters and priests "carry themselves." His attentiveness to embodiment, the ways Catholics moved their bodies in the world, led him to the conclusion that "the Catholic church is the one and only true church." Now Freddy looked forward to what he knew would be the happiest moment of his life, his baptism, and swore that he was "going to try very hard to be a good Catholic."[100]

Becoming Catholic involved a comprehensive transformation of religious life. Freddy's story hints at the ways in which transformation cannot be understood apart from the politics of race internal to Black communities. African Americans did not become Catholic in a vacuum. When converts embodied new ways of being religious they inadvertently, and sometimes intentionally, distanced themselves from other Black Christians. The "quietness" of Catholic worship that converts celebrated contrasted with other modes of African American religiosity, especially the evangelical worship styles spreading through Chicago's storefronts by the hundreds. When converts spoke of the "dignity" of the Mass, they hinted at the ways their comportment distinguished Black Catholics from most other Black Christians in Chicago, or at least how they hoped it might distinguish them.[101] Whether or not they were cognizant of it at the time, when we situate Black Catholics alongside the Black Pentecostals and Baptists as well as the Black Hebrews and Muslims who also called the Black Metropolis home, it becomes clear that for them, to be Catholic changed what it meant to be Black.

3

The Living Stations of the Cross

Black Catholic Difference in the Black Metropolis

The scent of incense still hung in the air of the sanctuary in the heart of Bronzeville following morning services at Corpus Christi Catholic church. The pews were full again, but now white and Black pilgrims from across the city joined Black parishioners. Silence settled on the congregation as the lights dimmed. A brown-robed friar, flanked by altar boys bearing a cross and candles, made his way to the wall where the first of fourteen wooden carvings was mounted. These fourteen "stations" marked the *via crucis*, the "way of the cross" Christ made from condemnation to crucifixion nearly two millennia ago. The devotion popularly known as "the stations of the cross" was designed to transport pilgrims to Jesus's side through prayerful movement so that they might better identify with his suffering and death.

Another friar, who had unobtrusively taken his place in the pulpit, broke the silence. "The First Station. Jesus is Condemned to Death. We adore Thee, O Christ, and we bless Thee." Together the congregation dropped one knee to the kneeler at their feet as they responded—Catholics by force of habit, others perhaps as instructed by their programs—"Because by Thy Holy Cross, Thou hast redeemed the world." Up to this point the devotion was familiar enough to most. Catholics were accustomed to "making" the way of the cross each Lent as they prepared for Easter with forty days of fasting. But then something extraordinary happened. The stations came to life.

Devotees were accustomed to gazing at a carving, or perhaps a painting or mosaic, on the wall as a priest led them in reflection. But now nearly forty Black women, children, and men entered the sanctuary from either side of the altar. Behind the bronze gates of an inlaid communion rail, standing five steps above the sanctuary floor, Black actors took their places in front of the altar. Clothed in silk they appeared to those present to have stepped out of the Bible itself. Pontius Pilate was present, accompanied by spear-and-shield-bearing Roman guards. Priests and Pharisees surrounded them, as did a crowd. Not a word was spoken; even the children were hushed and still once they assumed their staged positions. Last to enter was Christ himself. There he stood, ready to embrace his fate. His robe was white and his skin was brown. Christ was a young Black man.

Close to forty people were arranged in front of the altar. Mary Howard, whom readers will recall from the opening of chapter 1, was among them. She was tasked with embodying Procula, Pilate's sister-in-law. Mary was practiced in the art of pantomime. These parishioners had trained together for weeks, but she had performed for years by now. Tradition holds that Procula was the one who urged Pilate to eliminate this rabble-rouser. It pained Mary to reenact this scene. Decades later she still recalled how sad she felt, speaking as if she had been present at the foot of the cross itself. Mary felt complicit. She was a performer, posed so that pilgrims might gain an even deeper sense of the significance of the Son of God's crucifixion. "But at the same time," she said, "you're living it . . . you just felt like it was happening." She found herself at a loss for words. "It is so . . . You just . . . You're sorry you're in it, but you live it." She paused and then repeated, "you just witnessed yourself as being there when they crucified Jesus, [be]cause you just living it, you understand?"[1]

This *living* of the stations was especially intense when pilgrims and performers together reached the twelfth station, "Jesus Dies on the Cross." The already-dim lights faded into darkness. One spotlight remained, illuminating the cross an eerie green. Before the altar now stood a Black man on a cross. His arms held taut with fists balled against the wood. His skin was exposed, naked to the waist. The disciple John stood to his left, face hidden in hands. His mother Mary wept at his right hand, face downturned and hands clasped in prayer. Mary Magdalene lay collapsed on his nailed feet. The congregation knelt for an extended period of time as they listened to detailed descriptions of Jesus's torture and death. When knees ached and backs felt numb, the pilgrims were encouraged to relate their fleeting discomfort to the incomparable suffering of Christ. While they listened to the priest's meditations, the Black Christ held firm his pose. Black Catholics brought a bleeding and broken Christ to life on the South Side of Chicago.[2]

Figure 3.1. Corpus Christi's Living Stations of the Cross make the cover of *Extension: The National Catholic Monthly* (March 1953). Catholic Church Extension Society Records. Courtesy of Loyola University Chicago Archives & Special Collections.

"The Living Stations of the Cross," as they came to be called, drew interracial and interreligious crowds almost as soon as they first were staged in 1937 and parishioners performed them annually for thirty years. Located at the intersection of 49th Street and Grand Boulevard, Corpus Christi was a dominant architectural feature in the Black Metropolis. Its parish boundaries included the intersection known as "Negro Heaven" and the church stood not far from the iconic Regal Theatre and Savoy Ballroom where people thronged to see the likes of Louis Armstrong and Lena Horne.[3] This was the "largest colored Catholic church in America," pioneering sociologists Horace Cayton and St. Clair Drake noted in their famed study of the city within a city, home to over four thousand Black Catholics.[4]

The Living Stations was but one of many practices that characterized Black Catholic ritual life in the Black Metropolis. By focusing on a prominent ritual performance at a prominent parish, we can situate Black Catholic life in the midst of the religious transformations underway in the Black Metropolis in the first half of the twentieth century. Conversion entailed a transformation of one's body and senses as much as a change in beliefs. African Americans became Catholic to the extent that they embraced new ways of being religious. And by the end of the 1950s, just two decades after Father Martin Farrell and Father Joseph Richards had launched their "Chicago Plan" in a West Side parish, Black Catholic Chicago had grown to fifty thousand members. Parishes once near closure, now repopulated by converts, bore witness to the vibrancy of Black Catholic devotion. These parishes thrived in ways both spectacular and quotidian, both sharing in and contributing to Bronzeville's cultural flourishing in the first half of the twentieth century.

At the same time, Black Catholic ritual life differed dramatically from widespread expectations of Black religiosity. The Living Stations and other more mundane habits of devotion set Black Catholics apart from the evangelical Christian congregations proliferating around them. In this they were not alone. Black Catholics shared in the same impulse as Black Hebrews, Moorish Americans, and Black Muslims. Much like these migration-era religio-racial movements, Black Catholics adopted religious practices and bodily disciplines that distinguished them from what many were coming to consider normative Black religious life. The Holiness-Pentecostal movement arrived in Chicago with southern migrants. People could be seen and heard "catching the Holy Ghost" in storefront churches across the city and increasingly, even in established institutions. Gospel music became the soundtrack for this "new sacred order of the city," as historian Wallace Best termed it.[5] And at the same time, this new sacred order was beginning to be seen as emblematic of Black religion itself. This was the context in which Corpus Christi parishioners performed the Living Stations and this is why Black Catholic devotionalism could stand as a sign of difference. Predicated on disciplined control of bodily movement and structured silent prayer, Catholicism represented a compelling alterative to Black evangelical Christianity.

The Stations Come Alive on the South Side of Chicago

Father David Fochtmann, a Franciscan friar at Corpus Christi, organized the parish's first "pantomimed" stations of the cross in 1937. The friar was inspired, it seems, by a parishioner who attended the internationally renowned passion play in Oberammergau, Germany.[6] Fochtmann designed the pantomime in collaboration with about forty Corpus Christi parishioners. A local carpenter constructed the necessary crosses and stands for the stage. Women from the parish formed a sewing circle and made costumes. They hoped to capture what the cast and directors "imagined the dress at the time of Christ might have been" and drew inspiration from images on the large stained glass windows in the church.[7] The pantomimed stations were initially intended to serve the spiritual needs of Corpus Christi. Every Friday in Lent that year African American costumed cast members silently reenacted the suffering and death of Jesus for their fellow parishioners.

Over the next few years friars like Fochtmann came and went. But the cast made sure that the Living Stations of the Cross became an annual tradition. Many of the original cast members continued to act in the pantomime for years. They managed to sustain their enthusiasm and maintain their continuous production until 1968. As a result of this steadfastness, the parish became renowned in Chicago for "their faithfullness [sic] and their devotion to the Living Stations."[8] But what exactly was it that the cast devoted themselves to? A closer examination of this devotion's history and its performance in the Black Metropolis will provide a framework to better understand the nature of Black Catholic ritual life in the first half of the twentieth century.

Corpus Christi's Living Stations were rooted in the long devotional history of the stations of the cross. The *via crucis* or "way of the cross" was originally a pilgrimage path through Jerusalem that retraced Jesus's footsteps from condemnation to crucifixion. Artistic representations and reproductions of the *via crucis*, known as "stations," became prevalent throughout Christendom in the thirteenth and fourteenth centuries as pilgrimage to the Holy Land became dangerous, a consequence of the Crusades. By the early eighteenth century, Pope Clement XII had authorized the erection of "stations of the cross" in churches throughout the world. By the twentieth century, stations of the cross had become ubiquitous in Catholic churches and making the way of the cross was commonplace.

The stations told the story of the *via crucis* through numerically sequenced images (paintings, bas reliefs, and sometimes statues). The images' story begins with Pilate condemning Jesus to death. Collectively, they narrate the road from Jerusalem to Calvary, as Jesus carries his cross (the second station), falls three times (the third, seventh, and ninth stations), and encounters other figures along the journey—his mother; Veronica, who wiped the sweat and blood from Jesus's face; Simon of Cyrene, who helped Jesus carry the cross; and the weeping women of Jerusalem (the fourth, fifth, sixth, and eighth stations). The stations end with Jesus's crucifixion and death, with Jesus stripped of his garments (tenth), nailed to the cross (eleventh), dying on the cross (twelfth), and finally his removal and burial (thirteenth and fourteenth).

This devotion operated on at least three levels. It transported participants through space and time to the passion of Christ, it encouraged a personal identification with the suffering and death of Christ, and it attempted to make Christ's passion real through prayer. Personal meditations directly connected the passion with the lives of participants and participants prayed that they might truly live the passion.[9] It accomplished these three objectives through a devotional kinesthetics. The entire congregation "made" or "prayed" the stations, prayers that included genuflection, the sign of the cross, standing, and kneeling. For most of the service the congregation remained silent, responding in unison at specific moments. The passion of Christ thus became real through movement and disciplined stillness, silence and scripted spoken prayers, by the involvement of the body as well as the mind in the prayer.[10]

Corpus Christi's Living Stations took the act of spiritual transportation one step further. They enlivened the passion with the vivid performance of its pantomimes, allowing pilgrims to watch the stations unfold before their eyes. The *Chicago American* reported, "attired in the robes of Biblical times, the actors perform the scenes . . . with stark realism."[11] Elaborate costumes and props evoked biblical imagery familiar at the time, so that the Roman soldiers and Jewish priests appeared "authentic." The congregation saw Jesus stand before the throne of Pilate, surrounded by crowds of silken-robed priests and shield-bearing soldiers. When Jesus was crucified, everyone watched a young Black man nailed to a cross just yards from where they sat.

The Corpus Christi friars and parishioners involved in the Living Stations hoped that the pilgrims praying in the pews would imaginatively engage the scene, and that pilgrims would relate their own lives to the passion of Christ so as to better follow in Christ's footsteps. A friar aided this personal experience of the passion by reading meditations at different points throughout the service. A sense of what these meditations might have sounded like may be gleaned from Catholic devotional literature of the time, in the absence of any record from Corpus Christi. When Jesus was condemned to die on a cross, congregants reflected on the crosses they bore each and every day. They were emboldened by the endurance of Jesus, as he lifted his frail body up three times under the weight of the cross. Mothers and fathers in the congregation were called to bear pain and persecution as Blessed Mother Mary did when she met her son, with sober strength. Congregants watched as Simon the Cyrene, the African conscript, helped Christ lift the cross and they were encouraged to share and bear Christ's cross as Simon did. When they saw Veronica tenderly wipe the blood and sweat from Christ's face, they thought of ways to serve others as Veronica once served Christ. The congregation was ashamed for Christ as he was stripped of his garments, laid half-naked along the altar steps for all in the church to see, and reflected on the earthly attachments they could strip themselves of in their own lives. They shuddered each time actors struck hammer to wood as the blows to Jesus's body echoed throughout the church, timed rhythmically with the readings. Congregants meanwhile meditated on the depth of God's love for them and the power of Christ's sacrifice.[12]

The depth of feeling Corpus Christi's parishioners invested in their performance enlivened the devotion. Both photographic and journalistic accounts of the Living Stations capture how emotional these silent pantomimes could be: without uttering a word they conveyed the anger in the faces of those shouting for Christ's crucifixion, the anguish of the weeping women of Jerusalem, the ferocity of the soldiers as they hammered nails into wood. But it should be stressed that one of the reasons the Living Stations drew such emotional responses from those present was because the pantomiming parishioners communicated wordlessly, with frozen faces and still bodies. Cast members modeled extreme discipline of movement and sound for those gathered in prayer in the pews who were also called on to speak and move at prescribed moments. In this way, the Black Catholic reenactment of Jesus's passion and death fit neatly into Catholic devotional culture popular in the first half of the twentieth century. "Making the way of the cross" occupied a central place in the Catholic imagination insofar as it represented and reinforced a particular understanding of the human person as sinful and in need of discipline.

Corpus Christi parishioners were reminded of this fact every Lent. A 1945 article in Corpus Christi's lengthy parish bulletin titled "Why Do Violence to Ourselves?" exemplified the Catholic fixation on sinfulness and self-discipline. Though self-control is "demanded in every department of life," from athletics to business, the "deeper reason why we must practice mortification" is that humanity is a "fallen race" who "sinned and rebelled" against God. Humans have an "inordinate desire for evil in any form, be it to anger, to drink, to pride, to sensuality." As a result, "if we are to lead rational lives and not become growling, snarling beasts that no one can live with, we must practice self denial." Christ left them "the Cross and the splinters" to aid Catholics in the trials of self-mortification and denial.[13] The cross was in this way intended to be an agent in one's daily life, one of the primary means through which Catholics experienced physical discomfort and pain each day during Lent and ideally throughout their lives. When Catholics suffered they were encouraged to imagine themselves carrying their own crosses. The stations of the cross belonged to what Robert Orsi has identified as the American Catholic "devotional ethos of suffering and pain," whereby physical distress of all kinds were understood as "an individual's main opportunity for spiritual growth."[14]

It is clear that the Corpus Christi community staged the Living Stations with this longer devotional history and ethos in mind.[15] Franciscan friars and Black parishioners hoped to spiritually transport the congregation to Calvary so that pilgrims might reinterpret their lives through the torture and crucifixion of Christ. This is evident in the way the stations were advertised. The Living Stations were not intended to be a theatrical presentation or, as the parish bulletin phrased it, a "mere unfeeling stage play." The Franciscan friars and Black parishioners staged a "religious drama of a high type," a "genuine devotion" meant to increase "devotion toward our Savior's passion."[16]

Corpus Christi enlivened the stations in order to evoke an experience of Christ's passion for the congregation, to transport them to another time and place. Another *Parish Gleanings* article offered the rationale behind this ambitious aim. All Christians pledged themselves to "follow the way of the Cross, to learn to be meek and humble of heart, to suffer for Him who died for us." But in order to properly follow the way of the cross, "you must know it" and "you must LIVE it." How can Christians know and live the way of the cross two millennia after the death of Christ? The Living Stations answers this question. The author insisted that "to live, we must experience; to live the way of the Cross, we must experience its weight." What better way to experience the weight of the cross than by witnessing the passion in the flesh? Corpus Christi parishioners made it possible to "see and hear the story of your Savior's Passion and death."[17] More concretely than paintings or bas-reliefs, the Living Stations brought Christ's condemnation and crucifixion to life. Performers of the Living Stations aspired to imprint the way of the cross in the memories and imaginations of all present and thereby better facilitate the embodiment of Christ's suffering and death in daily life.

The Living Stations serve as a helpful model for understanding Black Catholic ritual life in the period prior to the Second Vatican Council and Black Power, which, as we will see, together revolutionized Black Catholic life beginning in the late 1960s. This performance was but a dramatic example of daily devotions that marked what it meant to be Catholic at the time. The stations of the cross had their roots in medieval Europe, remade in American cities such as Chicago by European immigrants in the nineteenth and twentieth centuries. The devotion consisted of repetitive motions and wrought prayers that intervened in shared silence at scripted moments. Through this ritualized movement and speech, participants embodied a particular conception of the human person, one that was sinful and in need of self-discipline or, as the parish bulletin might have put it, spirits that needed to be chastened through "violence to ourselves." These features of the Living Stations—its European roots, its structured silence and movement, its emphasis on human fallenness and self-control—could be observed in much more mundane religious activities as well. Every Catholic Mass, for instance, reenacted the sacrifice of Christ's body and blood for the sins of humanity. Each time parishioners prayed the sorrowful mysteries of the rosary, prescribed words led them through Christ's passion one bead after another. Every year when parishioners processed the Eucharist around the neighborhood in a golden monstrance, whether or not they knew it they carried on the tradition Irish Catholics had instituted on the South Side of Chicago before them and that could be dated back to a twelfth-century saint. These represented defining features of Black Catholic ritual life in the Black Metropolis.

"The New Sacred Order" in the Black Metropolis

This passion was not performed in a vacuum, however. Black Catholics brought the stations to life in the midst of a Black cultural renaissance. Black Chicago witnessed a flourishing of cultural production from the 1930s through the 1950s, a flourishing that drew on and extended the Harlem Renaissance of the 1920s. Black Chicago authors Richard Wright, Arna Bontemps, Margaret Walker, and Gwendolyn Brooks expanded on the Black aesthetic movement that combined artistic achievement and political activism to give voice to a "New Negro" identity. Musicians Louis Armstrong and Thomas A. Dorsey as well as artists William Edouard Scott and Archibald John Motley, Jr. contributed to this Black Chicago Renaissance as well.[18] (It is worth noting, if only as an aside, that both Scott and Motley were Catholic.) Historian Adam Green has demonstrated the ways in which this renaissance even included cultural producers outside the traditional "arts."[19] According to Green, Bronzeville's cultural leaders and institutions contributed to the emergence of "New Negro" identities that "encouraged [the] imagination of a Black national community, and made new notions of collective interest—and politics—plausible."[20]

Corpus Christi exemplified the success of Catholic missionaries in the first half of the twentieth century. It was a convert community par excellence.[21] And by the 1940s Corpus Christi understood itself as one of the central institutions in the burgeoning Black Metropolis. The pastor insisted as much in the inaugural issue of Corpus Christi's bulletin. Parishioners, he argued, should work to convince "our local merchants and men of profession of the fact that Corpus Christi Parish is the largest organization of the South Side." Parishioners collectively had "a buying power that will bring greater success in their business and professional ventures once their message is sold to the public through our parish paper."[22] If the advertisements that filled the bulletins over the next decade serve as any indication, Bronzeville businesses agreed. All the signature entertainment venues of the Black Metropolis advertised in the bulletin, inviting parishioners to attend theaters and clubs located mere blocks away.

But Corpus Christi stood apart from its surrounding environs even as it shared in the collective success of the Black Metropolis. Its ritual life differed from what Black religion was increasingly presumed to look, sound, and feel like. This is because at the heart of this Black renaissance was a transformation of African American religious life, a transformation that had an enduring impact on how people would understand Black religion for decades to come. The Great Migrations brought southern Black Christians into urban industrial cities in the North. When Black southern religious culture met the exigencies of city life, new ways of being religious were born. This new sacred order in the city not only changed African American religious life, but also contributed to the emergence of a specific conceptualization of "Black religion" itself.

As we have seen, when African Americans left the South for the urban North they brought with them a distinctive religious culture deeply influenced by the Holiness-Pentecostal movement sweeping the South. Wallace Best draws on W. E. B. Du Bois to characterize this culture.[23] Du Bois defined the "religion of the Negro slave" and more broadly,

Black southern religious culture, according to three key characteristics: "the Preacher, the Music, and the Frenzy." Preachers represented the central religious authority of Black southern communities and by the early twentieth century had developed a distinctive sermonic style with its own rhythm and cadence. Southern Black Christians shared a soulful style of singing that, according to Du Bois, was born in America but "sprung from the forests of Africa." Finally, southern Black religion was most famous for its "frenzy," something that might appear "grotesque or funny" to the uninitiated but was truly "awful" (meaning full of awe, astounding) for those who witnessed it. This was "the Frenzy or 'Shouting,' when the Spirit of the Lord passed by, and, seizing the devotee, made him mad with supernatural joy . . . [which could vary] in expression from silent rapt countenance or the low murmur and moan to the mad abandon of physical fervor—the stamping, shrieking, and shouting, the rushing to and fro and wild waving of arms, the weeping and laughing, the vision and trance."[24]

The arrival of Black southerners by the hundreds of thousands thus brought a new religious culture to the Black Metropolis. The sheer number of migrants led to intense competition as communities vied for congregants. African Americans now had an array of religious options. If new arrivals found the worship styles too restrained in Black Chicago's established churches—the preaching uninspired or the music unmoving—they could leave and found their own community. Abandoned storefronts provided migrants with readily available and affordable spaces within which a wide range of innovative practices and theological eclecticism might be possible. By the time the Living Stations of the Cross first graced Chicago newspapers in 1938, the Black Metropolis was already home to two hundred and twenty-three of these so-called "storefront churches." Best describes storefront churches as "an original institutional creation among urban Blacks in the twentieth century." These original creations were essential elements for the establishment of the new sacred order of the city.[25] And while W. E. B. Du Bois coined "the Preacher, the Music, and the Frenzy" to describe southern Black Christians at the turn of the century, he used those exact same words to describe storefront churches in the urban North nearly sixty years later. In his introductory essay to social documentarian Milton Rogovin's storefront church photograph series (circa 1958–1961),

Du Bois wrote that the images "of Negro church-goers in Buffalo" took him back to what he had written in *The Souls of Black Folk* fifty-eight years earlier. An extended excerpt from Du Bois's original essay on the preacher, the music, and the frenzy annotates Rogovin's photos of mid-twentieth-century Black Baptist and Holiness churches. Du Bois concludes by noting that "it is astonishing and yet easily understandable that this description of the religion of the slaves still fits the practice of present conditions among the poor, black workers recently come to cities like Buffalo."[26]

This proliferation of options, especially storefront alternatives to established Black churches, fundamentally changed the religious landscape of Chicago. The Black Belt's established churches at the turn of the twentieth century had "placed great emphasis on preaching that was 'orderly' and worship that was 'decorous.'"[27] Now they were forced to either adapt or diminish. As African Americans experimented with new practices in storefront spaces, more and more traditional Protestant churches hoped to attract and retain members by adopting the cadence of southern preaching, the rhythm of southern musical styles, and more freedom of movement in worship. In this way the influence of the southern Holiness-Pentecostal movement spread through many of Chicago's Black churches.

More and more churches allowed for direct interactions between the minister and the congregation, with the testimony of the preacher frequently supported by the community present in the pews. Many Black Chicagoans began to feel the physical power of the Holy Spirit possessing their bodies in the act of worship, an experience that could lead to dancing, shouting, weeping, and even shaking strong enough that fellow congregants might hold each other upright.[28] Members of Olivet Baptist learned to encourage their speakers with shouts of "preach!" and "amen!"[29] The saved "fell out in the Spirit" at Elder Lucy Smith's All Nations Pentecostal church.[30] Crowds thronged to hear the Hammond organ propel Rev. Clarence Cobbs's famous gospel choirs at First Church of the Deliverance Spiritualist.[31]

Black Catholics stood apart from this new sacred order in a number of significant ways, though we should be careful not to overstate those distinctions. Though there were no Catholic storefront churches, Corpus Christi could be compared to another type of migration-era church:

"the institutional church." Faced with the assorted crises set in motion by the unprecedented movement of people that was the Great Migrations, Black churches that could afford to do so provided migrants with a whole host of social services. Like its peer institutions, Corpus Christi housed a credit union, served as a recreation center, hosted a variety of different social clubs, and helped to connect parishioners to potential employers. Nor were Black Catholic parishes alone in their cultivation of high-church—what some called "high-class" or "respectable"—ritual. St. Edmund's Episcopal Church sat just over ten blocks south of Corpus Christi. Its history paralleled that of Black Catholic Chicago in interesting ways, a church abandoned by its white parishioners and repopulated by new Black members. Religious studies scholar Colleen McDannell notes that, like Corpus Christi, St. Edmund's too boasted "highly choreographed ritual" that emphasized "memorized movements and texts."[32]

These comparisons notwithstanding, Black Catholics embodied ways of being religious that distinguished them from both the southern evangelical Christian practices growing in popularity in migration-era cities as well as what was fast becoming the normative conception of "the Black Church." To be clear, the two—practices in Black churches and the concept of "the Black Church"—are not equivalent. As a number of scholars have shown, there is no singular "Black Church." Even excluding Catholics for the moment, there are a variety of Black Protestant churches, churches whose shared experience as Black in America did not negate histories of doctrinal debate and divisions over worship styles. An African Methodist Episcopal church is not a Black Baptist church. Denominational differences matter.[33] That said, in the first half of the twentieth century academics, filmmakers, musicians, and churchgoers popularized a particular idea of what Black religion *is*. This idea took hold both for those who celebrated "Black religion" as an authentic spirituality otherwise absent in the modern white West as well as for those who rejected it as primitive and irrational emotionalism. "Black religion," in the singular, shared a resemblance with the southern evangelical Christianity brought north in the Great Migrations. Thus, while Du Bois's "preacher, music, and frenzy" cannot stand in for African American religious life writ large, scholars and lay audiences alike increasingly took it to be equivalent to "Black religion" itself. Within this context, Catholicism was one of many religious possibilities for African Americans. Black Catholics stood in contrast not to a single "Black Church," but to the assorted practices that came to stand in for "Black religion."

Thousands of Black converts swelled the ranks of the One True Church in these decades. Black Catholic ritual life differed in important ways from both the new sacred order changing African American religious life in the Black Metropolis and the normative notion of what Black religion was supposed to be. The Living Stations exemplified this difference. The Living Stations drew inspiration from medieval practices reinvigorated by the devotional culture of European immigrants and their children in the United States. They were predicated on a particular theological conception of the sinful self and encouraged all present to embrace suffering as Jesus had in his passion. And the Living Stations accomplished all this through a ritual performance that emphasized silence and stillness.[34] Though identification with the suffering Christ would certainly be familiar to many Black Christians at the time, the history and habits of this devotion set Black Catholics in sharp relief amidst the new sacred order of the city.

The Living Stations and Black "Authenticity"

The Living Stations were very popular across Chicago almost as soon as they were first performed. Just one year after their inaugural run the Living Stations drew thousands of people to the Bronzeville parish. The cast continued to embody the stations each Friday, but now added Sunday performances as well for hundreds of Chicagoan and suburban pilgrims who packed the pews. Interracial and interreligious crowds sometimes stepped into a Catholic church for the first time to witness them. Prominent patrons of the arts joined with Chicago Catholic leaders to sponsor pilgrimages to the church.[35]

White journalists at the time appeared to be at a loss to explain why pilgrims lined up by the hundreds to view Black Catholic parishioners reenact the passion of Christ. Perhaps they should not have been so surprised. A number of stage performances of Black religiosity gained national renown in the 1930s. Willa Saunders Jones, a Black Baptist migrant to Chicago, wrote and produced a passion play in 1926 that continued to run for the better part of sixty years.[36] Marc Connelly's Pulitzer-Prize-winning play *The Green Pastures* (1930) was by far the most famous production. This wildly successful Broadway production (adapted for theatrical release in 1936) transposed biblical stories to contemporary Black Louisiana and reveled in what Connelly took to be the childlike simplicity of a southern Black religiosity "unburdened by the differences of more educated theologians."[37] But another production bore the closest resemblance to Corpus Christi's Living Stations. Members of Atlanta's Big Bethel AME Church first performed the pantomimed morality play *Heaven Bound* in 1930. (They continue to perform it to this day, eighty-five years later.) The play was so successful that it was reproduced around the country. While *The Green Pastures* employed southern Black dialect and played on Black stereotypes, theater scholar Winona Fletcher describes *Heaven Bound* as "nearly hygienic in its avoidance of stereotypes." The play relies heavily on pantomime, which Fletcher speculates was "a deliberate choice in the 1930s to avoid the dilemma of saying what constituted real 'Negro life and art.'"[38]

One thing is clear in hindsight: public performances of Black religiosity, including the Living Stations, were popular because they were perceived to be "authentic." What precisely did "authenticity" mean in this context? For Corpus Christi's Living Stations it meant that those who attended experienced them as "real." The Living Stations were experienced as "authentic" in part because the costumes helped to successfully transport participants to another time.[39] Beyond attire, the intensity of the emotions portrayed and evoked by the pantomimes contributed to this authenticity. Tears were to be expected.[40] The idea that the Living Stations accurately depicted the crucifixion of Christ and facilitated an authentic experience of the passion recurred in journalistic treatments over the next two decades. As the *New York Amsterdam News* put it in 1951, the Living Stations of the Cross looked "like a picture from the days of Christ, depicted to the minutest detail."[41]

But even more than tailoring and tears, pilgrims seemed to experience the Living Stations as especially "authentic" because *Black* women, men, and children performed them. Of course, this Black devotional performance signified different things for white pilgrims than it did for Black pilgrims. White journalistic coverage indicated that "Blackness" played a role in the success of the stations. One article described the Living Stations as a "Unique Lenten Program," despite the fact that it described another pantomimed stations of the cross on the same page.[42] The Living Stations were not unique in terms of their subject matter. Theatrical and filmic portrayals of Christ's passion thrived at the time in Chicago and across the country.[43] Instead, Corpus Christi's stations of the cross were unusual because Black people performed them. The *New World*'s Ryan expressed this fact when she wrote about "an unusual drama [that] will be enacted during Lent, at Corpus Christi . . . when living Stations of the Cross will be presented by a Negro cast." Ryan felt the need to repeat herself. "This cast, all Negro parishioners, includes men, women, and children, mostly recent converts."[44]

Thousands of white pilgrims traveled to Corpus Christi in the late 1930s and 1940s to witness a Black reenactment of suffering and death. For white pilgrims, Black pantomimes seemed to imbue the stations of the cross with a special intensity. The *New World* reflected in 1942 that when "colored parishioners portray in pantomime the Way of the Cross," they demonstrated "a devotion deep within the souls of the parishioners, a love they are anxious to convey to others."[45] A contemporaneous article attributed the principal difference between Corpus Christi's stations and another contemporary live performance to how much "more vividly" they were enacted.[46]

In this sense, the Living Stations exemplified the ways urban working-class bodies have frequently been imbued with special spiritual power throughout American religious history. White voyeurs sought out "authentic" experiences in working-class communities, simultaneously anxious about the rapid transformation of urban space and nostalgic for the presumed simplicity of a premodern, preindustrial age. Orsi has written about this "recurrent impulse in American urban history." Drawing on Victor Turner's conception of the "powers of the weak," Orsi characterizes this impulse as "the extraordinary capacities of feeling and being, of spiritual vitality and erotic potency, that those with social power first attribute to the most marginalized populations in their midst and then wrest from them for their own purposes and pleasure."[47] Davarian Baldwin identified this practice specifically in the context of the Great Migrations and the New Negro movement in Chicago. What he termed "sacred slumming" manifested in "an obsessive white focus on gospel music's emotional musicality and 'Holy Ghost' dancing [that] confirmed a romantic belief in the invigorating powers inherently found in Black bacchanalian decadence."⁴⁸ White interpretations of the Living Stations of the Cross resonated with this tradition of "sacred slumming" in some ways, even as it also deviated from it in others.

Here again the Living Stations bear comparison with Big Bethel's *Heaven Bound*. Fletcher describes how white and Black audience members reacted differently to the morality play. *Heaven Bound* intentionally avoided the caricatures of Black religion that marked *The Green Pastures*. This intention notwithstanding, most white viewers of the early productions looked for and found "the exotic, the primitive, and the naïve" in the Black pantomimes. Fletcher, for instance, quotes one white reviewer who described the play as "sprung from the soul of a primitive people" and another who praised its "child-like, easy-going" nature.⁴⁹ There was a notable difference between the audiences of *Heaven Bound* and the Living Stations, however. *Heaven Bound* was a stage-play in a Black Protestant church and allowed for "the presence of communal audience action" common in Black churches. Fletcher describes "spontaneous participation" on the part of audience members, ranging from people surging into the aisles for better views of the action to shouts of "Amen" and "Bless de Lawd."⁵⁰ The Living Stations, on the other hand, required those present to participate in the disciplines of Catholic devotionalism. Those in the audience were expected to be silent and still for long stretches, punctuated by prescribed movement and scripted prayers. Both *Heaven Bound* and the Living Stations invited emotional responses, but they cultivated different kinds of catharsis. If *Heaven Bound* garnered applause, laughter, and dancing, the Living Stations called for tears and quiet reflection.

One of the first and most extensive articles on the devotional performance, Father Aidan Potter's 1938 review for the *Franciscan Herald*, captures both the similarities and the differences between this Black Catholic performance and other productions of Black religiosity at the time. Potter thought the Living Stations brought the passion of Christ to life with a "childlike simplicity and straightforwardness" comparable to medieval miracle plays and St. Francis himself. He credited the success of this "colored cast" to their amateur status. "They are just ordinary men and women, and children, of the parish," he insisted. The audience witnessed not "trained acting, but the actual living of their parts." "With a simple artlessness," these Black Catholics forgot "calculated ef-

The intense drama of the pantomime is reflected on the faces of the congregation who become a part of each scene enacted by the players. 800 to 1,000 people from all over Chicago attend the devotion each week

Figure 3.2. Black children (front right) watch white pilgrims as they view the Living Stations (1953). "The Living Stations of the Cross," *Extension: A National Catholic Monthly* (March 1953), Catholic Church Extension Society Records. Courtesy of Loyola University Chicago Archives & Special Collections.

fects" and expressed "unfeigned emotions."[51] Potter praised the Black teenager playing Christ in particular, who pantomimed "so sincerely and unaffectedly . . . a better portrayal could scarcely be desired."[52]

This commentary belied an important distinction between the performance of African American religiosity in the Living Stations and the sacred slumming Baldwin describes, or even the reactions white audiences had to *Heaven Bound*. Those slumming in Black churches typically came in search of emotionalism, imagining Black religious bodies as gateways to a spiritual primitivism that could transport them to premodern religiosity.[53] But when crowds gathered in Corpus Christi to make the way of the cross, they did not come to witness overly emotional primitives. Instead, commentators were met with the meticulous bodily discipline of these performers. Aidan Potter noted that the actors were "drilled" by the director, Father Fochtmann, whose "excellent direction of the cast drew favorable comment."[54] Rev. Evans marveled at "colored players" so "finely trained in the medieval art."⁵⁵ The *Chicago Tribune* made mention elsewhere of how "colored actors" had been trained by a priest to pantomime according to "medieval patterns."⁵⁶ Black journalists, unaccustomed to Black Catholic devotional practice, also took note of these disciplines. The *Chicago Defender* remarked how "the requirements of pantomime demand more skill than normal acting because each gesture and movement must tell what the spoken word would ordinarily convey."⁵⁷

Rather than emotionalism or primitivism, Black bodies disciplined by Catholic devotional practice drew white pilgrims to the Living Stations. Here we can see the ways the Living Stations' enduring popularity was predicated in part on Black Catholic difference. Throughout the stations pilgrims watched and wept and prayed as Black men, women, and children kept still and silent for minutes at a time. A friar narrator filled some of this silence with personal meditations that made the scene created by these Black performers a medium for understanding one's own struggle with sin and relationship with Jesus in daily life. In other words, the bodily disciplines involved in the African American reenactment of the persecution and violent death of a criminal made it possible for pilgrims to relive the Christ's passion and reinterpret their own lives.

The Black Gods of the Metropolis and the Cultivation of Religious Difference

It is clear that Corpus Christi's Living Stations defied white expectations of Black religiosity. However, religious difference was not simply perceived by white spectators. Black Catholics cultivated it themselves. They fashioned for themselves a way of being Black and religious that contrasted with the new sacred order of the city in significant ways. And Black Catholics were not alone in this. Black Catholics were part of wider efforts to forge new "religio-racial identities," as religious studies scholar Judith Weisenfeld puts it, through distinctive practices in the midst of the Great Migrations.

If the new sacred order of the city represented one way the Great Migrations transformed African American religion, another was the emergence of charismatic Black innovators who launched new religious movements—innovators whom Arthur Huff Fauset famously named "the Black Gods of the Metropolis." These movements accomplished a number of things. For one, as religious studies scholar Sylvester Johnson argues, they

> promoted theologies and practices of ethnic heritage that redeemed converts from social death, a condition marking them as people without peoplehood, relegated as nonmembers of the American nation. The result was a new religious order that asserted Blacks were a people with peoplehood, with history and heritage that transcended the space and time of the American experience of slavery and racism.[58]

The Commandment Keepers Ethiopian Hebrew Congregation of the Living God, the Moorish Science Temple of America, and the Nation of Islam all declared that African Americans must accept their true ethnic and religious heritage if they were to have any hope of confronting the violence of American racism. The Commandment Keepers, popularly known as the Black Hebrews, claimed descent from the Falasha Jews of Ethiopia. The Moorish Science Temple (MST) insisted that African Americans were actually Moorish Americans and members received new names and identification cards to prove it. The Nation of Islam (NOI) argued likewise that African Americans were an Asiatic people, members of the original Black human race. For these groups, entrance into a religious community was inseparable from the assertion of a new identity that sought to transcend white supremacist conceptions of Black rootlessness and primitivism. Weisenfeld coined the term "religio-racial movements" to characterize the groups that shared this impulse to fashion new identities during the Great Migrations. Across theological and political differences, they rejected the negative implications of "Negro racial identity" in the American racial hierarchy and instead endowed Blackness "with meaning derived from histories other than those of enslavement and oppression."[59]

At the heart of these movements was an explicit rejection of Christianity as inescapably a white religion. As Johnson notes, each was premised on the claim "that Christianization and slavery were essentially processes of cultural destruction."[60] This marked a significant shift in African American religion writ large. Black charismatic leaders argued that Christianity was inherently foreign to African Americans insofar as it was a "white religion" integral to the enslavement of Africans. Noble Drew Ali, the founder of the Moorish Science Temple, identified Christianity as the religion of European "pale skins." The head of the NOI, the Honorable Elijah Muhammad, railed against Christianity as the religion of "blonde-haired, blue-eyed devils" inimical to Islam, the true religion of Black people. According to this logic, Christianity was essentially incompatible with Black identity.

Considering the fact that the overwhelming majority of religious African Americans were Christian, denunciations of Black evangelical Christianity came as the logical extension of their critique of Christianity as a white religion. The Nation of Islam's most famous minister, Malcolm X, was renowned for his criticism of "the Black Church" as otherworldly, interested in "the pie in the sky after you die" at the expense of the plight of Black people here and now. Malcolm frequently railed against Black preachers for their "yelling and spitting out foam all over the pulpit" and was renowned for "fishing" for converts among Black Christians as they exited Sunday services.[61]

But even more important for our purposes are the critiques these movements leveled at Black Christian practices in particular, practices prevalent in the new sacred order of the city. Arthur Huff Fauset captures this critique in *Black Gods of the Metropolis*, published in 1944. His discussion of Prophet F. S. Cherry's Church of God, a community of Black Jews in migration-era Philadelphia, makes frequent note of the disdain Black Jews had for speaking in tongues and other aspects common in Holiness-Pentecostal worship. "The business of speaking in tongues is a joke," a Mrs. I. testified. "All the whooping and yelling, dancing, falling out and the like is indecent."[62] Similarly, Fauset opens his chapter on the Moorish Science Temple with the testimony of H. R., who expresses his disgust at his mother falling out in a church. "He hated all that foolishness."[63] Sylvester Johnson takes note of a similar tendency with Rabbi Wentworth Matthew, the founder of the Commandment Keepers. Matthew insisted that Black people reject the "niggerations" of Black churches in favor of their true religion, Judaism. He derided Christianity "by demeaning the Christian worship of African American migrants from the South whose cultural proclivities toward rhythmic dance and spirit possession were drastically transforming the religious landscape of the urban North."[64]

Religio-racial movements were well known for their adoption of distinctive religious practices and bodily disciplines. As Judith Weisenfeld puts it, "adopting new modes of dress helped to produce and maintain a member's sense of self in light of a commitment to a particular set of beliefs about the nature of religion and race."[65] These movements distinguished themselves from those they called "so-called Negroes," for example, by dressing distinctively—Moorish American men wore red fezzes and Black Muslim women donned veils, to name just two examples. These "self-making performances," to borrow Weisenfeld's phrase, extended to diets as well. The Black Hebrews observed traditional Jewish dietary laws, for instance, and Black Muslims adhered to certain Islamic notions of halal as well, foreswearing pork, alcohol, and tobacco.[66] Taking into account their critique of the new sacred order, it is important to note that these practices and disciplines were designed to, among other things, differentiate Black Hebrews and Jews, Black Muslims and Moors not only (or even primarily) from white Christians but also from Black Christians, especially those migrating from the South. Restricting pork consumption was not just a way to keep kosher or halal. It also rejected a key ingredient in Black southern "soul food"—the Nation of Islam also forbade the consumption of collards, okra, and cornbread.[67] "Clothing the body or eating in ways that disrupted expectations about how people of African descent should express themselves religiously," Weisenfeld concludes, "undoubtedly made a political statement about race, embodiment, and citizenship in this period."[68]

This cultivation of religious difference came to the fore in worship itself. In describing the worship of Black Jews and Moorish Americans in *Black Gods*, Fauset notes again and again how worship was explicitly contrasted with popular evangelical practices. "Speaking in tongues, a common criterion of holiness worship, is looked upon with disfavor," Fauset notes of the Black Jews.[69] Their critique was not simply rhetorical. In the case of the Black Jews, Prophet Cherry structured the singing of the congregation by beating a drum methodically. Members repeated brief prayers in unison. Prophet Cherry himself ordered worship, conducting the congregation in recitation and unison that did not allow for the "excess of emotion" members loathed in Holiness churches.[70] The contrast between the new sacred order and the Black gods of the metropolis rings clear in Fauset's description of ritual in the MST as well. A typical service began with the congregation "chanting a hymn softly." In case the implied contrast was not evident, Fauset restated the point: "Unlike the singing in many Negro services, the chants of the Moors are very soft."[71] Later on he emphasizes again that "all services are extraordinarily quiet, belying the generally accepted beliefs regarding the Negro and his religious worship." The congregation exudes a "tomb-like stillness," "exclamations from the congregation are few and almost inaudible," and "there is a complete absence of that emotionalism that is considered characteristic of Negro services."[72]

Of course, religio-racial movements were not always as successful at achieving this distance from Black Christians as they imagined themselves to be. In reference to the same Fauset passage about Moorish Science Temple worship quoted above, Weisenfeld notes that "at the same time that the worship culture within MST temple space differentiated Moors in dramatic ways from their neighbors, the incorporation of Christian hymns, spirituals, and gospel music connected them to black Christian communities."[73] Elsewhere she points out that the influence of Rabbi Wentworth Matthew's "Christian background was apparent in the [Commandment Keeper] congregation's worship space and practices in the group's early years, as a visitor noted in 1929, describing a sanctuary decorated with stained glass featuring a cross and crown and placards reading 'Wait for the Power That Fell Pentecost' and 'People Prepare to Meet Thy God. Jesus Saves.'"[74] MST and Black Hebrew congregations repurposed Christian hymns and used instruments common in Holiness and Pentecostal storefronts at the time. We should be wary, then, of overstating the difference cultivated by religio-racial movements. Nevertheless, the desire to differentiate oneself from Black Christians tells us something about how members of religio-racial movements crafted their new identities regardless of whether or not they were consistent or entirely successful in their attempts.

Black Catholics are not usually compared with Black Muslims or Black Hebrews—and they certainly would not have done so themselves. Nevertheless, our examination of the Living Stations illustrates the ways in which Black Catholics cultivated religious difference from the new sacred order around them. African Americans who converted to and practiced Catholicism in the first half of the twentieth century shared in the formation of new religio-racial identities. Black Catholics did not assert a new national heritage but, as we have seen, they did separate themselves from former social worlds when they entered the One True Church. Black Catholics did not articulate an alternative ethnic history, but they did actively embrace a new devotional tradition rooted in the medieval European past. Black Catholics adopted what they took to be the "quiet dignity" of the Mass as an alternative to those practices "deemed singularly Negro" in the words of Curtis Evans, practices associated with "slave religion" and the Black Church.[75] In other words, Black Catholics can be compared with Black Hebrews, Black Jews, Black Muslims, and Moors insofar as the "self-making performances" and bodily practices characteristic of the Catholic Church in this period set Black Catholics apart from Black evangelical Christians.

If the Living Stations of the Cross represented a dramatic performance of religious difference, other devotions did so as well. Take Black Catholic devotion to the real presence of Jesus Christ in the Eucharist, for instance. As a Corpus Christi parish bulletin reflected, the Eucharistic presence of Christ "makes it possible for us to receive a blessing from Jesus as direct as that which the children whom He was want to bless, received; as direct as that which the Apostles themselves received."[76] The authenticity (and subsequent superiority) of the Catholic Church was often attributed directly to this Eucharistic presence. Corpus Christi, a parish named for the "body of Christ," proclaimed this real presence each year on the Feast of Corpus Christi when parishioners processed their Eucharistic Christ around the neighborhood in a golden monstrance. These processions concluded with benediction, when the priest raised the monstrance for a blessing. As the bulletin reminded readers, it was not the priest who blessed those present, "but Jesus Himself. There is nothing like it outside of Heaven."[77] A less public proclamation of Eucharistic difference was the Forty Hours Devotion. Parishioners collectively made prayerful vigil with the Eucharistic Jesus for forty straight hours. On these special days, all were asked to genuflect with both knees when entering and exiting church. Everyone was also assigned a special designated hour to worship Jesus, "exposed on His Sacramental Throne above the Tabernacle," so as to assure that "Our Lord is never left without adorers."[78]

Devotions served simultaneous purposes, often unbeknownst to Black Catholics themselves. The fact that Corpus Christi had enough volunteers to keep vigil with the Eucharist for the Forty Hours Devotion,

Figure 3.3. Feast of Corpus Christi procession, Corpus Christi (undated). Courtesy of the Franciscan Province of the Sacred Heart Archives.

or that photographs record scores of parishioners processing behind the monstrance as it made its way around the block, gives us insight into Black Catholic ritual life in the first half of the twentieth century. Many Black Catholics enthusiastically took part in a Catholic devotional tradition that had, until recently, been the domain of European immigrants and their children in cities like Chicago. Corpus Christi processions and Forty Hour Devotions would have ceased to exist in many South and West Side Chicago neighborhoods if not for the commitment of Black Catholic converts. At the same time, insofar as these devotions occurred in what were now predominantly Black and Protestant neighborhoods, they also set Black Catholics apart. When Black Catholics processed the Eucharist through the streets of Bronzeville they pronounced their difference to neighboring churches even if, for Black Catholic participants, the procession was less about their neighbors and more about their devotion to the real presence of Jesus Christ.

At other times Black Catholic difference was more overt. Black Chicago historian Timuel Black interviewed a Black Baptist minister who illustrated this point. Rev. A. P. Jackson recounted the violence he faced when he built his Bronzeville church in the vicinity of Corpus Christi. According to him, when Black Catholics discovered that some "foot-stomping, hand-clapping Baptists were coming over, they said, 'Oh my God, now the neighborhood will go to the dogs, and we can't let this happen!' So, when we started building the church, they used to break our windows, and twice they even tried to set the church on fire." When he caught the perpetrators, he asked the Black youth why they were vandalizing his church. Their response was "this ain't no church. Not a real one." When Jackson challenged them, they pointed across the street to their parish. "Our priest told us. That's a real church over there!"[79] Historian Timothy Neary recorded a similar story in an interview with James Williams, who "remembered 'Holy Rollers' meeting in tents along South State Street in the summertime, shaking tambourines and shouting. 'I figured the only people doing that sort of thing were the ignorant blacks, who didn't know any better,' he said."[80] Father George Clements, a Black priest and former Corpus Christi parishioner, also recalled confrontations with Black Protestants from his childhood. Non-Catholic children in the neighborhood teased him and other kids from Corpus Christi as "Cat-lickers," resentful of what they took to be Catholic arrogance.[81] The accusation of a superior attitude bore some truth, he noted. Priests and nuns urged African American Catholics to think of themselves as better than their non-Catholic neighbors.

Lifted "Up above the Color Line"

Corpus Christi's Black Catholic pantomimes reached the height of their fame in the 1950s. In March 1953, the Living Stations featured on the cover of *Extension* magazine (a national Catholic monthly modeled on *Life*). A full photographic spread illustrated for readers "this soul-stirring realization of the sufferings of the Saviour."[82] Perhaps as a result of this national coverage the Living Stations soon captured the attention of Bishop Fulton Sheen, the Catholic television celebrity famous for his highly rated show *Life Is Worth Living*. Corpus Christi welcomed Sheen for Holy Week in 1954. There the bishop witnessed the Living Stations in person and led the parish's Tre Ore service on Good Friday, which commemorates the final hours of Jesus's life. That same year, Corpus Christi's pantomimes put on the Living Stations in the Chicago Coliseum, where they were filmed and broadcast on local television. Corpus Christi was now known as "the Shrine of the Pantomime," at least for the duration of each annual Lenten season.

While the pantomimes drew the eyes of celebrities in 1953 and 1954, Mary Dolores Gadpaille worked away quietly behind the scenes. Readers will remember Mary Dolores as the Black Catholic convert from the Introduction who was baptized on the Feast of the Seven Dolors in 1949. Gadpaille was in charge of designing, making, and fitting all the costumes—costumes that, *Extension* agreed, gave the production an added sense of "authenticity." Though she remained out of the spotlight, she was an especially enthusiastic and vocal member of the parish. In her time at Corpus Christi, Gadpaille wrote numerous letters to Father Pius Barth. Barth was the Provincial of the Franciscan Province of the Sacred Heart in the late 1950s, meaning he was roughly the equivalent of a bishop in the Franciscan order. Taken together her collected writings, meager though they may be, convey just how deeply Catholic disciplines and practices could shape the daily lives of Black Catholics.

When Gadpaille introduced herself in writing to Father Barth she summarized her spiritual journey thus: "I am a Franciscan Tertiary [meaning she was a member of the Third Order of St. Francis, a fraternity of laywomen and men who sought to model themselves on the life of Francis of Assisi], converted and baptized in Boston, Mass. by a Passionist; started my spiritual growth under a Jesuit; developed and grew to fruit and flower under a Franciscan. I started looking for God at five years. I never abatted [sic] that search until I found Him at the age of fourty [sic] three." She had promised God that "if I ever found Him, I would stay at His feet as did Mary." When she did find God in the Catholic Church, she understood "staying at his feet" to mean performing the ritual obligations and habits of devotion central to Catholic life at the time. This meant "Daily Holy Mass, Daily Communion, the Rosary, the Way of the Cross, weekly confession, constant direction of a priest, and the practice of the spiritual and corporal works of mercy."[83] Since she had pledged to attend Mass every day for the rest of her life (barring illness) the Mass assumed a special power in her life. In another letter Gadpaille thanked Barth for "offering up the Holy Mass" at Corpus Christi and described the experience as "beautiful." She loved that she could follow his Latin chanting and "even though one does not understand [the Latin] wholly, it has a rythm [sic], harmony and mystery that lifts one out of this world."[84]

Gadpaille's letters offer an important reminder in the midst of our discussion of Black Catholics in the Black Metropolis. To borrow language from our discussion of conversion in the preceding chapter, African Americans who became Catholic inculcated and embraced new ways of feeling, imagining, and experiencing the world around them. It is true that Black Catholics participated in Catholic devotionalism at the height of its distinctiveness in American history and culture. It is also true that this set them apart from other Black Christians in Chicago at the time. It would be a mistake, however, to conclude that Catholicism served solely as a negative identity; that Black converts embraced Catholicism more for what it was *not*, namely, evangelical Protestantism, than for what it was. As we have seen, year after year hundreds of Black women and men and children came to know that the Catholic Church was the "One True Church"—a knowledge they felt in their bodies as they rehearsed rituals and practiced prayers. Gadpaille's writings happen to capture, quite poetically it must be said, the power Catholic devotional culture held for growing numbers of Black Chicagoans. Catholicism never served only, or even primarily, as a marker of difference for Black Catholics themselves. Nevertheless, surrounded by the religious transformations underway in Black Chicago during the Great Migrations, their Catholicism set Black Catholics apart from their environs whether or not they were aware of it.

Mary Dolores Gadpaille was an exceptional figure—the majority of Corpus Christi parishioners did not attend Mass daily and certainly did not write letters to the Franciscan Provincial. Nevertheless, her description of the Mass resonates with the reflections of other converts. It was common for converts to comment on the capacity the Mass had to allow them to transcend the trappings of the temporal world, even if only momentarily. A letter composed in Sister Mary Francese Therese's 1945 religious instruction course perfectly encapsulated this experience of Catholic worship. The convert's letter consisted of three short sentences:

> Why I wanted to be a Catholic. First I believe it is the only true church of God. And I like the quite-est [sic] of the service even tho I didn't understand it and again I would feel different when I would enter the doors.[85]

Here we see how, for this convert as for others like him, belief that the Catholic Church "is the only true church of God" cannot be separated from the special feeling facilitated by a perceived quietness in Catholic worship. Black Catholics at the time frequently used the words "quiet" and "dignity" to name what they took to be this unique quality of the Catholic Mass.

The compelling power of Catholic quiet was a common refrain among Black Catholics. But what makes something "quiet" in the first place? Quietness is, after all, comparative by definition. Considering what we have already discussed regarding the new sacred order of the city and its religio-racial movement critics, the celebration of Catholic quiet dignity should be understood in juxtaposition to the perceived "noisy" emotionalism of Black evangelical churches. The connections Black Catholics made between quiet worship, the dignity of discipline, and the authenticity of the "One True Church" differentiated them from other Black Christians. Black Catholic characterizations of the Catholic Mass as quiet contrasted with the shouting and clapping common in Baptist churches. Catholic comportment was considered "dignified" and "respectable" at least in part in distinction with the ways Pentecostals shouted, laughed, danced, wept, and "fell out in the Spirit." In other words, whether or not it was intentional, an embrace of the Catholic Mass over the altar call or Eucharistic Benediction over speaking in tongues embodied Black religious difference in the Black Metropolis.

Black Catholic cultivation of quiet bore strong parallels to the Moorish Science Temple, as we have already seen. But Black Catholics espoused a universalism over and against the particularity of race as advocated by most religio-racial movements (Father Divine's Peace Mission movement would be one notable exception). Commandment Keepers, the Moorish Science Temple, and the Nation of Islam all embraced the particularity of Black identity in order to transcend race and racism in the United States. They accomplished this by adopting alternate ethnoreligious histories and heritages. Though white supremacy had marked them as "Negroes"—as a people without peoplehood or history—Black Hebrews, Moorish Americans, and Black Muslims argued that African Americans were in fact the descendants of ancient and original peoples (Hebrews, Moors, Asiatics), original peoples who were Black. When Black converts entered the One True Church, on the other hand, they became members of a transnational, multiracial, and multiethnic religious community. The silent prayers, scripted responses, and structured bodily movements they adopted oriented Black Catholics toward the sacred in ways that connected them not only to Catholics throughout the United States, such as Bishop Fulton Sheen and the thousands of Catholic pilgrims who attended the Living Stations, but also to Catholics in Oberammergau, Germany, and elsewhere throughout the world. Catholic devotional practices and bodily disciplines, then, distanced Black Catholics from the Black evangelical churches proliferating around them on the South Side of Chicago not through the embrace of a distinctive ethnic identity but rather through an attempt to transcend race altogether. The Living Stations of the Cross exemplified this universalism inasmuch as it attempted to revive medieval European pilgrimage practices and connect Corpus Christi's Black parishioners to Catholics across time and space.

This universalism was neither an abstract nor an unimportant aspect of Black Catholic life. Here it is helpful to return to the letters of Mary Dolores Gadpaille once more. In one letter to Father Pius Barth, she identified her arrival at Corpus Christi as "the first time I had ever come upon a group of people in whose philosophy, religion and actions there was no color line." At Corpus Christi she finally felt that Black people "were one with the human race and children of God."[86] Gadpaille thanked the Franciscan friars for "the Spirit that makes you treat a people not like 'Negroes' so called, not like second class citizens, not like inferiors but as children fo [sic] the living God." As we read in the Introduction, Gadpaille lauded the Franciscans for lifting Black Catholics "up above the color line, up above the natural vicissitudes of every day life and pours into our souls, dignified by it, such a love of God and His Church that we can not only love and serve God ... but our enemies as well." Gadpaille argued that "by just being Catholic" these Franciscans had restored in Black Catholics "a vanished dignity that all the interracial organizations together have not achieved by conference of legislation." "In the place of second class citizenship that America allots," Gadpaille concluded, "you have given us a passport to citizenship in Heaven, for this earth is 'no abiding city.'"[87]

Gadpaille was not alone in her interpretation. Black Catholics had long invoked the universality of the Catholic Church as a solution to "the race problem" in America. Claude McKay, the Harlem Renaissance writer born in Jamaica, was baptized Catholic in Chicago in 1944. In a 1946 *Ebony* magazine essay titled "Why I Became a Catholic," McKay took great pride in the fact that he now belonged "to the authentic church of Christ—the Holy Roman Catholic Church." He only wished "the Negro people" knew more about it. If they did they would discover, as he had, that "there never was any race or color prejudice in the Roman Catholic Church from its beginning up until the Reformation." Though the Church "may have made mistakes," McKay felt "proud of belonging to that vast universal body of Christians" nonetheless.[88] Historian Nancy M. Davis records an exasperated Black Catholic named Pierre Carmouche writing, in 1915, "As American citizens and as Catholics too, you and we are not 'Negroes?' How can it be? How can a person be a Negro? Catholic?" Carmouche wrote in protest of the archbishop of Detroit's attempt to effectively segregate Black Catholics. He rebelled against the very notion that Catholicism could contain separate races, quoting his pastor as saying "I don't see how I can consider my parishioners as Catholic 'Negroes' or 'Negro Catholics.' . . . All I know is that they are Catholics."[89] Father Augustus Tolton, the man known nationwide as the first Black priest in the United States, called "the Catholic Church the true liberator of the race." He toured the country in the 1890s, fund-raising for his fledgling Chicago parish with sermons about "the church which knows no point of the compass," the "broad and liberal . . . church for our people."[90] The list could go on. Gadpaille, McKay, Carmouche, and Tolton all understood themselves to be members of a *universal* Church. If most religio-racial movements rejected the second-class status of the "so-called Negro" by embracing a distinctive ethnic heritage—Hebrew or Moorish or Asiatic—Black Catholics like Gadpaille shared in the rejection but differed in the solution. Black Catholics adopted silence, structure, and discipline that they felt lifted them "up above the color line."[91]

The Living Stations End on the Eve of a Revolution

Corpus Christi parishioners last performed the Living Stations in 1968. Their popularity had begun to wane. Yet the fact that 1968 marked the end of this devotion held symbolic significance beyond this one parish. The Living Stations were modeled on centuries-old Catholic habits of devotion. The power of this Black Catholic performance was predicated on their cultivation of silence and stillness, contrasting the practices prevailing in most Black Christian communities at the time. This silence and stillness was seen by many Black Catholics as a way to embrace Catholic universality and reject the particularity of race. Universalism that transcended ethnic and racial boundaries was certainly a doctrinal ideal for the Catholic Church at the time, one that missionaries foregrounded in their efforts to convert African Americans. When Black converts adopted new devotional habits and bodily disciplines, they effectively incorporated this universalism in their religious lives.

Black Catholics were never naïve about the fact that white Catholics in the United States fell well short of this ideal, however. In 1968 a small but vocal group of Black Catholics took inspiration from the political and cultural nationalism of Black Power and launched a vociferous challenge to purported Catholic universalism. One aspect of this challenge was a struggle to secure the institutional power necessary for Black Catholics to determine the destiny of their own communities. Another aspect, though, was a sharp critique of Black Catholic practices with roots in European devotionalism. Practices like the Living Stations were not "universal," they decried. They were white. If Black Catholics were to remain both Black and Catholic, they would need to control their own parishes and be able to incorporate "authentic Black" practices into their religious lives. These Black Catholic activists sparked a revolution of identity and practice that would end devotional performances like the Living Stations and forever change what it meant to be Black and Catholic in the United States.

4

Black Catholics and Black Power

Concerned Black Catholics and the Struggle for Self-Determination

"When did you first think of yourself as Black and Catholic?" I asked Father George H. Clements.[1] "I can pinpoint the exact moment that the change took place," he replied. "April the 4th, 1968, a bullet whizzed through the head of Martin Luther King and it was then that I went into the bathroom at the rectory, looked in the mirror, and the face staring back at me was a clergy prostitute." Clements recalled the commitment he made to himself that day: "From now on, I'm gonna be a *Black* man."

This moment, which Clements described as a conversion experience, brought to light a painful recognition: he had prioritized advancement up the "proverbial clergy ladder" over the needs of the Black community. He laughed, ruefully remembering how he "was no threat to anybody," how he "went through the whole buffoonery of pretending that whatever they were saying made sense, especially when it comes to Black people . . . I definitely wanted to become a monsignor and I wanted to eventually become an auxiliary bishop."[2] This is what he meant when he called himself a "clergy prostitute." Clements had experienced an awakening to Black racial consciousness, an experience soon shared by Black Catholics across the country.

By December 1968 Father Clements was embroiled in controversy, one that proved to be just the first of a controversial career.[3] Chicago's archbishop, Cardinal John P. Cody, refused to promote Father George Clements to the pastorate of his South Side parish despite the backing of parishioners and clergy alike. Supporters took to the streets in protest and forged a coalition that included Concerned Black Catholics, white Catholic allies, and members of the local Black Panther Party, among others. What began as a local church controversy quickly gained national notoriety and as it did, its ramifications extended well beyond one Black priest in one parish. At stake was nothing short of Black Catholic self-determination.[4]

While we have thus far been charting the rise of Black Catholic Chicago since the 1930s, the turning point of the late 1960s begins what I call the rise of *Black Catholicism* in Chicago. By the 1960s Chicago had already become one of the most important Black Catholic communities in the country. Thousands of African Americans became Catholic over the better part of a half-century as migrants met missionaries in schools on the South and West Sides. Chicago's Black Catholic population would soon eclipse New Orleans and Baltimore, the historic capitals of Black Catholic America. The Black Metropolis laid claim to the largest Black Catholic church in the country, Corpus Christi, which, as we have seen, was famous nationwide for the Living Stations of the Cross. What changed in the late 1960s was not *that* there were Black Catholics but *how* they were Black and Catholic. Converts in the first half of the twentieth century joined the "One True Church," making that choice amidst an ever-increasing plurality of Black churches and temples. They embraced devotionalism brought by European immigrants and celebrated the "quiet dignity" that defined their worship. In a matter of years, though, the rituals once taken to be signs of a universal faith would be criticized as "white." A growing number of Black Catholic activists began to argue that they were not Catholics who happened to be Black but Black people who deserved and demanded a distinctively *Black* Catholicism.[5]

The story of Father Clements and the St. Dorothy Church controversy from December 1968 to June 1969 illuminates the origins of this revolution in Black Catholic life across the country. Black Power fundamentally shaped the ways in which Black Catholics experienced the changes ushered in by the Second Vatican Council. The Council (Vatican II for short) met from 1962 until 1965 and propelled profound transformations in Catholic life. In the years that followed, Black activists initiated a broad shift in the philosophical principles, political tactics, and cultural aesthetics of Black freedom struggles. A growing group of Black Catholic activists, Father Clements prominent among them, took up Black Power and confronted the U.S. Catholic Church as a "white racist institution." They called for Black control of Catholic institutions in Black communities as well as for the integration of what they understood to be "authentic Black" practices into worship. These demands met with stiff resistance, however. Foremost among the critics of these activists were many Black Catholics themselves. The debates sparked by the convergence of Black Power and Vatican II changed the course of Black Catholic history.

What Does Vatican II Have to Do with Black Power?

Pope John XXIII surprised the world in 1959 when he announced his plan to convene an ecumenical council of the Catholic Church—there had only been two councils in the four preceding centuries, the Council of Trent (1545–1563) and the First Vatican Council (1869–70). The Second Vatican Council opened in October 1962 after three preparatory years and gathered more than two thousand bishops each fall until the Council closed in December 1965. Bishops discussed a range of topics in these four ten-week sessions, addressing issues as diverse as the role of laypeople in the Church, the proliferation of nuclear weapons, the use of vernacular languages in the liturgy of the Mass, and the role Jews played in the death of Christ.

It was not entirely clear at the outset why the pope had convened the Council in the first place, though one word quickly became the most prevalent way the Council was described by both clergy and media alike. "*Aggiornamento*" was the Italian word John XXIII regularly used to characterize his intentions for the Council before his death in 1963. Defined variously as "bringing the church up to date," "adaptation," and "modernization," many Catholics understood *aggiornamento* to indicate the spirit of change and openness to the modern world they hoped the Second Vatican Council might inaugurate.[6] Not all bishops at the Council agreed with this assessment, however. Council sessions witnessed vigorous debates between two factions of bishops. A small group of cardinals firmly established in the administration of the Vatican, known as the Curia, wanted Vatican II to reaffirm precedents set by previous ecumenical councils and actively resisted attempts to institute major changes in Catholic theology, ecclesiology, or practice. Other European bishops considered more theologically liberal took Vatican II to be an opportunity to adapt the Church to the changing circumstances of the modern world. Over the course of four Council sessions the influence of the liberal faction increased and by 1965 the bishops had produced sixteen documents that introduced the most significant changes in the Catholic Church since the Protestant Reformation.

Scholars continue to debate the extent to which the Second Vatican Council represented a break with prevailing ways of being Catholic or whether it marked a culmination of shifting attitudes and practices.[7] Regardless of which perspective one takes, the ways Catholics interpreted and implemented the Council and its documents shaped in extraordinary ways what it meant to be Catholic in the years that followed. Vatican II instituted certain changes in the Church in the 1960s and 1970s. Catholic laypeople, priests, and women religious also drew their own conclusions from these documents, which occasionally brought them into conflict with other Catholics. Those who celebrated the Council insisted that the event had ushered in a "spirit" of reform and renewal that extended beyond the formal proceedings of the event itself. Vatican II could take on a life of its own in the hands of Catholics willing to interpret *aggiornamento* broadly. Any attempt to understand the reception and impact of Vatican II on Catholics themselves thus must address the ways it coincided with changing local circumstances.[8]

For Black Catholics in the United States, local circumstances were increasingly defined by Black Power. The Council had closed and changes in Catholic life were already underway in 1966 when the newly elected chairman of the Student Nonviolent Coordinating Committee and future "Honorary Prime Minister" of the Black Panther Party, Stokely Carmichael, first called for "Black Power!" in Greenwood, Mississippi. These two words signaled a broad tactical and ideological shift in Black freedom struggles, even if ideas later associated with Black Power—Black nationalism, community control, and self-defense—were not new.[9] Black Power is best understood not as a singular movement but instead as a constellation of ideas and practices embodied differently by various activists and intellectuals.[10] Black Power was no more monolithic than the "civil rights movement." Across debates and divides, Black Power activists generally were committed to a critique of postwar liberalism as well as an embrace of Black self-determination and self-definition. Self-determination, as I use it here and throughout, is quite simply the power (political, economic, social) to control the resources of one's own community and thereby determine its destiny. But what constitutes a community? This is where self-definition comes in. Ideas about what it meant to be "Black" always intersected with and informed arguments for community control. How one defined self-determination, and whether self-determination bore radical or conservative consequences, largely rested on how one defined the parameters of "the Black community." Black Power thus included ideas not only about the proper distribution of power (politics) but also about identity and self-representation (culture), what could be called "Black consciousness."[11]

Black Chicago witnessed the full force of this transition from civil rights to Black Power. Martin Luther King, Jr. came to Chicago in 1966 to confront racist real estate practices and urban poverty in an attempt to extend the Southern Christian Leadership Conference's efforts into the urban North. King's coalition was called the Chicago Freedom Movement (CFM) and unfortunately, is most famous for dramatizing the insufficiency of southern civil rights strategies when met with the subtleties of systemic racism and the intransigence of white resistance to urban and suburban integration. The CFM's failures bolstered local activists who already had misgivings about the effectiveness of nonviolent direct action in cities outside the South. Organizations committed to self-determination rose in popularity as a result.

When Black Catholics in Chicago engaged the *aggiornamento* of Vatican II, they did so in a city already influenced by Black Power and its impetus toward self-determination and self-definition. As we will see, the ways Black Catholics understood and engaged the Council became indecipherable apart from debates about Black Power. In 1968 Black Catholic activists began to interpret Vatican II as an opportunity to incorporate Black Power in Catholic life. They soon set the terms of the discussions that developed among Black Catholics generally. With the Council intimately tied to Black Power, how best to be Catholic in the wake of Vatican II was bound up with ideas about what it meant to be Black. Black Catholics who struggled with the changes instituted by the Council objected to the political strategies and cultural aesthetics of Black Power in the same breath. This made disagreements especially bitter. Black Catholics critical of postconciliar changes or Black Power discovered that their objections might result in withering attacks from coreligionists. What it meant to be both Black and Catholic was now hotly contested.

Father George H. Clements and Black Power in Chicago

The connection between Black Catholics and Black Power in Chicago was neither abstract nor ephemeral. And one man embodied it in an enduring way. Father George Clements played an instrumental role in the early years of the Illinois Chapter of the Black Panther Party as well as the Afro-American Patrolmen's League, two of Chicago's most significant Black Power organizations. Who was this Black priest?

Born in Chicago in 1932, the Catholic roots in George Harold Clements's family ran deep. His father hailed from Lebanon, Kentucky, in the region known as the "Holy Land," named for the Catholic communities founded by Maryland migrants in the eighteenth and nineteenth centuries. Along with New Orleans and Baltimore, the Kentucky Holy Land was one of the earliest Black Catholic communities in the United States, where white Catholics had settled with their baptized slaves. Clements's father was not especially devout. His grandmother, though, devoted herself to maintaining their family faith. The matriarch traveled frequently back and forth between Kentucky and Chicago, growing close with Clements's mother in the process. She convinced George Clements's mother to receive religious instructions, baptize her children, and become active in their local parish, Corpus Christi.

Clements came of age in the golden years of Corpus Christi parish. At his grandmother's insistence, George attended Corpus Christi grammar school where the Sisters of St. Francis educated him. He roamed the streets of Bronzeville with the Franciscan friars. Since he grew up in the heyday of the Living Stations, Clements surely was transported to the passion of Christ on Calvary along with the rest of the parish each Lent. It was in this environment that Clements became interested in the Catholic priesthood at a young age. When it was time to enter high school, he left Corpus Christi for Quigley Preparatory Seminary. He advanced to St. Mary of the Lake Seminary in 1945 and became only the second Black priest ordained by the Archdiocese of Chicago in 1957.

Clements dreamed of becoming a monsignor, perhaps one day even a bishop. As we have seen, the assassination of Martin Luther King on April 4, 1968 altered those dreams. Yet while Clements later marked King's assassination as the moment of his conversion to Black racial consciousness, there were a number of events prior to this watershed moment that established his activist credentials within the Black Catholic community. In 1962 Clements was made an assistant priest at the Black parish of St. Dorothy in the South Side Chatham neighborhood. The pastor at the time, a white priest named Father Gerald Scanlan, was beloved by the St. Dorothy community and encouraged Clements to embrace his Black identity. Clements fondly recalled this older white man as "Blacker" than many of his own African American parishioners.[12] Scanlan mentored Clements into the role of activist-priest, famously renting a train car to transport Clements and parishioners to the 1963 March on Washington for Jobs and Freedom.[13]

Clements continued to follow in his pastor's footsteps over the next few years. He heeded Martin Luther King's nationwide call for religious leaders to march for voting rights in Selma, Alabama, in March 1965.[14] Once back in Chicago, his commitment to protest politics grew. In June that same year he was arrested (along with other priests and sisters) in a demonstration organized by the local civil rights group Co-Ordinating Council on Community Organization. Much like other Black activists in the urban North, he seems to have been increasingly attracted to more militant organizations and was reported to have attended a meeting of the Revolutionary Action Movement, a forerunner of the Black Panther Party.[15]

As King's assassination and subsequent urban uprisings accelerated Father Clements's radicalization, they also accelerated the rise of Black Power in Chicago. Five young Black members of the Chicago Police Department joined together in outrage over Mayor Richard Daley's order that police officers should shoot-to-kill looters during the April uprising. One of those officers, Renault "Reggie" Robinson, was a parishioner at St. Dorothy who knew Clements well. Fearing reprisal from fellow officers, most of whom were Irish Catholics, Father Clements arranged for them to meet in secret in a parish basement.[16] There they founded the Afro-American Patrolmen's League (AAPL). Over the next ten years the AAPL confronted discrimination within the force and fought to transform the image of the Black police officer in African American communities. Their objective was to establish Black control of policing in Black neighborhoods. To further their goal, the AAPL adopted the motto "Black Power through the Law" and pledged support for any efforts that established "respect for Black manhood, Black womanhood and Black pride within the law." They dedicated themselves to fostering a community "where those of us who are Black will be able to live lives of beautiful fulfillment."[17]

Clements also played a surprising role in an even more controversial Black Power organization, the Black Panther Party. Huey P. Newton and Bobby Seale, then students at San Francisco State University, first organized the Black Panther Party for Self-Defense in 1966 to combat police harassment and brutality in Black Bay Area communities. They began by policing the police. Armed with pocket U.S. Constitutions and prepared to defend themselves if necessary, the Panthers shadowed police officers to ensure the protection of Black civil rights. Newton and Seale's Black Panther Party Platform, first published in 1967, combined a nationalist call for Black solidarity and a Marxist critique of American capitalism with an extended repurposing of the U.S. Declaration of Independence. Sometimes referred to by its subtitles "What We Want, What We Believe," the Platform demanded Black social, political, and economic self-determination and exemplified the radical anti-imperialist end of the broader Black Power spectrum. The radical politics and revolutionary swagger of the Black Panthers in Oakland attracted increasingly militant Black activists across the urban North and West.[18] Young Black Chicagoans on the West and South Sides founded the Illinois Chapter of the Black Panther Party in 1968. Led by charismatic leaders like Fred Hampton and Bobby Rush, Chicago's Black Panthers quickly became famous throughout the city for combating police harassment and brutality, providing free meals and social services for those who needed them, and forging an interracial coalition of Black, white, and Latino radicals known as the "Rainbow Coalition."[19] According to Clements, the Panthers called on him to mediate an internal dispute in 1968. When the priest successfully resolved the issue, he came to be known affectionately as their "chaplain" and became friends with Fred Hampton.[20] The connections Clements forged between Black Catholics and Black Power activists would play a critical role in the fight for Black Catholic self-determination in Chicago.

Self-Determination on the South Side of Chicago

On August 1, 1968 the white principal of St. Dorothy Elementary School resigned. Four of her fellow Sisters of Charity of the Blessed Virgin Mary as well as the associate pastor of St. Dorothy, all of them white, resigned in support. (Six other white nuns refused to follow them.) They claimed that Father George Clements had mistreated them because of their race. Clements was a "Black militant separatist," they charged, whose insistence on installing a Black principal at the elementary school had forced the principal, Sister Mary Agnella, to leave.[21]

This was a troubling accusation. A group of "concerned parishioners of St. Dorothy" rallied to support Clements and resented the false accusation that their assistant pastor was a "militant separatist." The accusation was troubling not least of all for Clements himself. He denied being a "Black militant separatist" and sought to clarify his position on school leadership. "Some Black principals would be worse than some white principals," he noted. The larger issue at stake for him was that "Black priests should be in control of [their] own institutions whenever possible."[22] In other words, Clements was trying to make a subtle distinction between crude identity politics and Black self-determination. He was not arguing that Black educators should replace all white ones, regardless of qualification. He was arguing, however, that Black people should be in the position to control predominantly Black institutions, such as St. Dorothy church and school.

This skirmish anticipated the coming crisis that would pit the white Archdiocesan establishment and its allies, both white and Black, against a small but vocal group of activists. It also illuminated growing divisions among Black Catholics themselves that became clearer over the course of the next year. Many Black Catholics remained unsure about the compatibility of Black Power and Catholic life. For some, Black Power's insistence on institutional self-determination and cultural self-definition presented a solution to the problem of racism plaguing the American Church. For others, the increasing entanglement of politics (and the politics of identity) with religious practice threatened much of what they held dear about being Catholic.

Four months after Sister Mary Agnella retired, St. Dorothy's beloved pastor Father Scanlan retired. By the time the retirement letter reached Cardinal Cody on December 18, the archbishop already had received "advice" regarding Scanlan's potential successor from a number of constituencies. Much of this counsel was unsolicited. Lay representatives of St. Dorothy presented Cody with what was effectively an ultimatum days before Scanlan retired. Seven hundred and fifty-eight parishioners signed a statement that demanded "Father George Clements be appointed pastor of St. Dorothy church." They proclaimed that "this Black man has worked diligently, self-sacrificingly, and laboriously in our parish for the past five and one-half years, so we fully realize he is well qualified and that he has a sympathetic understanding of all the intricacies and ramifications of our Black community."[23] (Over two-thirds of the three thousand-member parish either abstained or refused to sign, however. This division foreshadowed the debates to come.)

Father Clements's involvement in Black Chicago was a priority for the signatories. The ultimatum pressed Cody to either make good on his purported racial liberalism or admit the Church's hypocrisy on racial issues. "If Father Clements is not named as pastor or administrator," the letter read, "this will be considered as an affront and a slap in the face to all Black people—and show, in the eyes of the nation that the Catholic religion does not really care about civil rights, but has been just going along so that the name 'Catholicism' was included." The petitioners realized that assistants do not usually become full pastors until they have fifteen to twenty years of experience (a point the archdiocese confirmed). Nevertheless, they insisted that "we need Father Clements now." If Cody refused, nearly eight hundred parishioners threatened to boycott their church and school. Twenty-one priests of "inner-city parishes" joined them in petitioning their archbishop for Clements's promotion.[24] Soon even prominent outsiders such as Rev. Jesse Jackson—the Baptist minister and director of Operation Breadbasket, an organization dedicated to economic justice for African Americans that grew out of Martin Luther King's Southern Christian Leadership Conference—entered the fray.

This situation must have rankled the archbishop. Cardinal John Patrick Cody in many ways embodied the tensions of a Church in transition. He was considered a racial liberal when he was appointed to succeed Cardinal Albert Meyer. But Cody ruled his archdiocese with a strong hand. Historians have come to mixed judgments about the archbishop. Judged against his predecessors who were more open in the administration of their priests, Cody has been described as "dictatorial" and accused of working to dismantle the city's liberal Catholic traditions. According to one journalist at the time, the best way to understand the conflict between Cody and the supporters of Clements was to situate it in the broader struggles over church power and authority. "The church has been in turmoil for several years, most often over precisely the question of the authority of its hierarchy," the author noted, "and Cardinal Cody has a reputation for being a strict authoritarian who seldom communicates his decisions publicly until they are made. In this situation the struggle over his authority has coalesced with Black determinism to become an explosion."[25] In hindsight, Cody seems to have resisted the egalitarian spirit many of Chicago's younger priests and nuns interpreted as the spirit of Vatican II. Cody was neither accustomed to parishes petitioning for their pastors, nor would he abide threats or ultimatums made by parishioners and *his* priests.[26]

So, on the same day he received Father Scanlan's resignation, Cardinal Cody reassigned another Black priest, Father Rollins Lambert, from his pastorate at St. James church to St. Dorothy. Cody may have thought this the perfect solution. Though he refused to be pressured into promoting Clements, he saw merit in assigning the only Black priest with nearly twenty years' experience to lead the South Side parish.[27] Father Lambert was the first Black priest ordained by the archdiocese. But if Cody viewed this as an olive branch, this was not how the concerned parishioners received it. Father Clements's advocates had called on Cody to move beyond tokenism and promote a rising Black Catholic activist to a position of power. The St. Dorothy ultimatum had delivered a pointed threat. "If you [Cardinal Cody] fail to heed our demands," they argued, "you will leave us no other choice than to boycott the church, withdraw our children from St. Dorothy school, and then, use whatever other means we deem necessary to dramatize to the whole world that you did not want to promote Father George Clements because he is Black."[28] Cody's decision to reassign Lambert effectively meant placing one Black priest in supervision over another. It confirmed the suspicions Clements's supporters had about the paternalism of the white Church. While Cody seemed to think the parishioners simply wanted a Black pastor, the petitioners made it clear that Father Clements's activism was at least as important (if not more so) than his identity as a Black man.

In this light, the decision to transfer Lambert appeared to be a political stratagem. Cardinal Cody rebuffed attempts by laypeople to dictate pastorates with one hand and denied charges of discrimination with the other. The archbishop could argue that he had not denied Clements a pastorate because he was Black, because the new pastor was Black as well. In a carefully reasoned and conciliatory letter, Cody acknowledged that "over the past few weeks, a number of the parishioners of St. Dorothy's parish have written and telephoned about the assignment of a new pastor for their parish." After much prayer, Cody said, he had decided to reassign Rev. Rollins Lambert based on the latter's "experience as a pastor" and his service on "many commissions which will assist the Cardinal in the administration of the Archdiocese." Lambert was "more experienced" than Clements, the archbishop said, and had displayed obedience to archdiocesan authority. It should be noted, though, that while Lambert had been a priest eight years longer than Clements, he had spent most of his career in archdiocesan administrative roles. Clements was just as experienced as Lambert in parish leadership, if not more so. Cody acknowledged the parishioners' affection for their assistant pastor, but concluded that "the choosing of pastors is one of the most serious duties of any bishop" and that he was "persuaded that a parish such as St. Dorothy's needs a pastor of longer experience in the priesthood."[29] The archbishop thereby reinforced his own authority over those he took to be *his* priests. Ecclesial authority, meaning who had the power to determine church leadership and control religious institutions, would be thoroughly entangled with issues of race in the coming controversy.[30]

Father Rollins Lambert now found himself in an uncomfortable position. Though he had once served briefly as assistant priest at St. Dorothy, he was reluctant to return. He had been the pastor of St. James church for less than ten months. What is more, it seems he anticipated the role he was being made to play in the dispute. Cardinal Cody insisted, however. The archbishop invoked the vow of obedience all priests take to their bishop, effectively forcing Lambert to choose between his obligations as a Catholic priest and his obligations to the Black community.[31] Lambert took neither lightly and relented only under pressure.[32] (It should be noted that the difficulty of this decision would be later lost on many of Lambert's Black Power detractors.)

One week later the parish council publicly commended Cody for Lambert's assignment. Prominently publicized by the Archdiocesan newspaper the *New World*, they expressed gratitude for the appointment of Rollins Lambert, even going so far as to name Lambert a "beautiful Black Christmas present." Cody may have imagined the issue settled when the council pledged to "meet the Cardinal's generosity by giving ourselves an additional Black Christmas present—a parish firmly and faithfully united behind Father Lambert . . . Father Scanlan . . . and Father Clements."[33] This letter did not note that "half the congregation" stood up and walked out of Father Lambert's inaugural Mass in a show of support for Clements and in defiance of their archbishop. The depth of the divisions that wracked Black Catholic communities in the sixties and seventies become clearer when the original ultimatum made by supporters of Clements is read alongside this show of support for the archbishop. Neither this parish nor the wider Black Catholic community was univocal. In fact, by January 1969 this "beautiful Black Christmas present" devolved into a church controversy that engulfed the entire archdiocese and made national news.[34]

Beginnings of a Black Catholic Revolution

The claim that Black priests should control Black Catholic institutions stemmed directly from Black Power. Black Catholics had begun to draw on the rhetoric and tactics of Black Power by the late 1960s. In doing so, they attempted to effect a revolution in the Church. We are not accustomed to hearing the word "revolution" in the same sentence as "Catholics," certainly not Black Catholics and especially not in regard to the Black Power revolution. A few words of clarification are in order. By "revolution" I do not mean that Black Catholics advocated a radical restructuring of the political and economic order in the sense that the Black Panther Party was at times "revolutionary"—though it is worth noting that some Black Catholics did. Instead, what was latent in the protests over Father Clements's potential pastorate and emergent over the next decade was a comprehensive transformation of the ways Black Catholics understood what it meant to be both Black and Catholic. This transformation operated on an intellectual level, yes, but it also involved changing the ways Black Catholics lived their lives, how they sang and dressed and prayed. By the early 1980s, Black Catholics worshipped and told their history and imagined themselves in ways inconceivable before the onset of the Black Power era. And since Black Catholics often self-consciously juxtaposed this new Black Catholicism with their religious lives prior to Black Power, "revolution" captures the drama of these changes.

This revolution is largely absent in the annals of Catholic history. This absence is due to the conceptualization, chronology, and characters that have defined histories of Catholics and race. The most significant works on the subject focus on the ways the civil rights movement influenced Catholics, while admitting that most Catholics did not themselves contribute much to the movement. The scarcity of Catholics in the civil rights movement seems even starker where Black Catholics are concerned. Historian John T. McGreevy, for instance, points out how "for the most part . . . African American Catholics remained culturally conservative." He even quotes a lament from a liberal white priest who "publicly wished for a 'Catholic version of Martin Luther King.'"[35] Black Catholics do come into view, however, if we think more expansively about the characters and chronology constitutive of Black freedom struggles.

Most historians of U.S. Catholicism have relied on the classic conceptualization of the "civil rights movement" in their assessment of its influence on Catholics and vice versa. The classic concept characterizes civil rights as, more than anything else, a liberal interracial struggle for integration in the postwar period that began with the *Brown v. Board of Education* decision and ended with the assassination of Martin Luther King—beginning in 1954 and ending in 1968. With liberal interracialists as the principal characters and 1954–1968 as the primary chronology, Catholics are only present as notable exceptions such as the Catholic Interracial Councils or women religious committed to the "racial apostolate."[36] Recent works by Timothy Neary and Karen Johnson have expanded the bounds of this chronology, illuminating the pioneering work of Catholic interracialists in the decades preceding *Brown v. Board of Education*. Even here, though, the underlying concept remains unchallenged. Racial justice is presumed to be more or less equivalent to interracial liberalism.[37] African American studies scholars in recent years have not only expanded the chronological scope of Black freedom struggles but also shifted the focus away from liberalism and interracialism. Historian Martha Biondi, for example, argues that Black activism did not collapse in the years after Martin Luther King's death; it peaked. Black student activists, to take Biondi's work as an example, not only flourished in the 1970s, they also criticized the limits of racial liberalism as a governing philosophy and forwarded substantial challenges to the status quo in American higher education.[38] If we turn our attention to the late 1960s and early 1970s and if we shift our focus away from liberal interracialists and toward the fight for Black self-determination, it becomes clear that 1968 marked the beginning of Black Catholic engagement in Black freedom struggles, not the end. The rise of Black Power galvanized Black Catholics and provided a new generation with the tools to transform the Church. There may have been no equivalent of Martin Luther King, but by 1970 there were Black Catholic Malcolm Xs, Stokely Carmichaels, and Angela Davises.

Sister Martin DePorres Grey, then a Black Sister of Mercy, pinpointed April 1968 as the onset of the revolution, the commencement of "Black consciousness for black Catholics."[39] Father Herman Porter, who hailed from the diocese of Rockford, Illinois, convened over sixty Black Catholic priests and brothers on April 16 in Detroit. Grey also attended. This was the inaugural meeting of the Black Catholic Clergy Caucus (BCCC). Clements and Lambert were among its founding members. The BCCC had deep connections to Black Catholic Chicago, born in part of the shock and rage in the wake of Martin Luther King's assassination and Mayor Daley's inflammatory response to the subsequent urban uprising.[40] This meeting produced a statement that exploded across the Catholic press and awoke the nation to the presence of Black Catholics. It began: "[T]he Catholic Church in the United States, primarily a white racist institution, has addressed itself primarily to white society and is definitely a part of that society."[41] According to the BCCC, the Catholic Church "is not cognizant of changing attitudes in the Black community and is not making the necessary, realistic adjustments. The present attitude of the Black community demands that Black people control their own affairs and make decisions for themselves."[42] The BCCC pronounced "nonviolence in the sense of Black nonviolence hoping for concessions after white brutality is dead." Continuing, the priests stated "that the same principles on which we justify legitimate self-defense and just warfare must be applied to violence when it represents Black response to white violence."[43] The BCCC ultimately demanded that Black priests be put in positions of real religious power.

While Sister Grey was present at the founding of the BCCC, the priests prohibited her from fully participating. In response to her exclusion, she spearheaded the founding of the National Black Sisters' Conference (NBSC) that same year.[44] Black women religious pledged themselves "to work unceasingly for the liberation of Black people." They denounced "expressions of individual and institutional racism found in our society and within our Church" and declared them "to be categorically evil and inimical to the freedom of all men everywhere, and particularly destructive of Black people in America."[45] NBSC objectives included the eradication of "the powerlessness, the poverty, and this distorted self image of victimized Black people" and the promotion of a "positive self image among ourselves in our Black folk, especially in our Black youth," as well as the stimulation of "community action aimed at the achievement of social, political, and economic Black power."[46]

These two statements demonstrated the depth to which Black priests and sisters, what could be called the religious elite of the national Black Catholic community, increasingly were influenced by Black Power. In calling for control of Catholic institutions in Black communities, Black priests shared in arguments for self-determination and community control gaining popularity at the time, in large part due to Stokely Carmichael and Charles Hamilton's eloquent defense in *Black Power: The Politics of Liberation* (1967). The BCCC's endorsement of armed self-defense, another key principle for many Black Power activists, is perhaps more surprising. Black priests provided a matter-of-fact critique of principled nonviolence and rather than turn to Martin Luther King, they seemed to paraphrase Malcolm X's famous aphorism, that "I don't call it violence when it's in self-defense; I call it intelligence." Black sisters expanded on many of the points made by Black priests and what is more, directly addressed the psychological wages of institutional racism in the Church. Their attention to improving the Black "self image" bore the influence of Black cultural nationalism, which insisted that social and political liberation were impossible without emancipation from what Elijah Muhammad and Marcus Garvey before him, termed "mental slavery." The BCCC and NBSC were just the first of a number of organizations that initiated a decade of advocacy and activism that came to be known as "the Black Catholic Movement."

Carefully composed for the press—the result of long hours of debate and compromise among priests and sisters—the BCCC and NBSC statements exuded a clarity and unity that did not exist at the local level. Unity did not last on the South Side of Chicago more than a fortnight. St. Dorothy parishioners calling themselves the Concerned Black Catholics (CBC) scheduled a meeting in the gymnasium of St. Martin on January 3, 1969. Fliers circulated beforehand made the night's agenda abundantly clear. "Why—is Fr. Lambert pushed out of St. James after only nine months as pastor? Why is he the only Black pastor among nine Black priests in Chicago? Why is he being replaced by a white pastor? Why does a school 95 per cent Black get a white pastor so fast? Why—didn't Cardinal Cody consult the parishioners at St. James? Why didn't he pay attention to the people at St. Dorothy? Why is this happening so fast?"[47] There, a hundred people listened to Joshua Alvez, a representative of the CBC, defend the cause of Father Clements. He argued that Clements's outspoken Black militancy and "public stance on many controversial racial issues" lay behind Cody's decision.[48] According to Alvez, Cody's decision was calculated to thwart Father Clements's activism by moving Lambert around "like a chess piece," rendering Lambert nothing more than a "pawn" of the white establishment.

Father Kenneth Brigham (the third Black priest ordained by the Chicago archdiocese) spoke next. He thought that Cody had "pitted the big white power structure against Black people." Brigham was especially attentive to the ways in which Cody's political expediency threatened to tear Black Catholics apart:

> I hear people say that something has been gained, but I don't see it. I think we've been nearly torn apart. I don't appreciate the fact that Father Lambert was taken out of St. James. . . . I don't appreciate the fact that he is at St. Dorothy's now. . . . Father Clements has been running the parish for the past three years and it has been progressing all along while other inner city parishes were having great trouble operating. When it came to a point where he could have been made pastor very easily, what did they do?[49]

Another St. Dorothy parishioner and CBC co-chairman, Dr. Pedro Walls, resituated the controversy in the context of Black self-determination.

"Our position is that wherever there is a Black priest available, that priest should be made pastor where he is assigned," Walls said.

The meeting took a turn, however, when some began to question Father Lambert's "authenticity" as a Black man. Thomas Mitchell, another member of the Concerned Black Catholics, grabbed the microphone and shouted, "[T]he meeting is far from over!" Mitchell, also a civilian member of the Afro-American Patrolmen's League, pushed the conversation in a more divisive direction. Disagreements among those present became starker and frustrations began to boil over. "The real issue here," Mitchell argued, "is Father Rollins Lambert, the classic example of an Uncle Tom . . . [He is] the only guy who can spoil our whole campaign (for Father Clements)." Though Mitchell insisted he spoke for eighteen different organizations, including the St. Dorothy parish council, he met vociferous opposition from others present.[50] Mitchell pushed on. He described Father Lambert as a "suave, polished, sophisticated and urbane [Negro], but he's not specifically associated or relevant to the problems of the Black community."[51]

Criticisms of Lambert echoed Black Power discourse on "authentic Blackness" emergent at the time. Mitchell and other critics of Lambert lampooned him not only because of his presumed collaboration with the white archdiocese, but also on the grounds of his background and comportment. A convert educated at the University of Chicago who had worked in the predominantly white archdiocesan establishment since the 1940s, Lambert was characterized as a "polished" and "urbane Negro" whose commitment to the archbishop rendered him aloof and irrelevant to the "real" Black community. In other words, to Mitchell and others Lambert was an Uncle Tom not just because Cody used him, but because he expressed his Blackness and Catholicity in particular ways. This would be a recurrent theme nationwide in the 1970s.

At this point a surprising new participant entered the debate. Black Panther leader Fred Hampton arrived at St. Martin gym accompanied by a cohort of comrades. Hampton berated the audience for their timidity. When one white priest attempted to leave the room, a Black Panther reportedly restrained him. "Several Black and white laymen and priests stood up at this point," according to one account, to come to the departing priest's aid. Though the confrontation passed, emotions were rising to a fever pitch. John Hatch, president of the Catholic Interracial Council, attempted to broker some sort of compromise between the conflicting sides, but he was overpowered by Hampton's vigorous defense of Clements. Soon even Alvez, the speaker who had opened the meeting, declared Father Lambert "a traitor and an Uncle Tom." His accusations echoed Mitchell and Hampton and met with vigorous dissent "of the older Black lay people."

This confrontation captured mounting divisions among Black Catholics. Joshua Alvez, Pedro Walls, Thomas Mitchell, and the Concerned Black Catholics took up the banner of the Black Panthers. They imbued Black Power with deep religious significance that impacted everything from attire and hairstyle to music and movement in Catholic Mass. The reason its consequences were so comprehensive was that Black Power emphasized particular expressions of Black identity at the expense of others. Historian Thomas Sugrue names this as a defining feature of Black Power, which "embraced a cultural politics, one that rested on an understanding of Blackness and that created a set of cultural practices that articulated Blackness, celebrated it, reinforced it, and marginalized those who questioned or rejected it. At the core of Black power was cultural essentialism—the notion that there was a true, identifiable, authentic form of Black racial expression and that movement energies should be directed toward the production and reproduction of it."[52] In other words, the embrace of Black Power involved an embrace of a particular understanding of what it meant to be Black. Black Catholics who did not fit the bill might be criticized as self-hating and escapist, as "Blackfaced white people." As we will see, the CBC and like-minded activists hoped to win over other African Americans to their cause. But in these first years of the Black Power era, Black Catholics like Alves, Walls, and Mitchell remained the exception rather than the rule.

We have seen that African Americans were attracted to Catholic rituals and relationships because of their difference from the religious life prevalent in other Black churches. Many Black Catholics resisted identifying themselves as "Black" and rebuffed attempts to make their worship more "authentically" African and African American. Consequently, fault lines deepened not only between Black activists and the white archdiocese but also among Black Catholics themselves, most of whom remained uneasy about the ways the CBC hoped to bind Black Power to the changes of Vatican II. This conflict between Black

Catholics amounted to a struggle over what it meant to be Black and Catholic in the first place. Thomas Mitchell and other Concerned Black Catholics criticized coreligionists who rejected Black Power as brainwashed, even Uncle Toms. It would not be long before their critics would respond in kind.

Black Unity Masses

The drama unfolding in Black Catholic Chicago took new form two days after the St. Martin's meeting. On Sunday January 5 five Black Panthers occupied the vestibule of St. James church. Over fifty protestors, identified as the Concerned Black Catholics and Whites Concerned about the Black Community, sang and prayed through the service. Regular St. James churchgoers attempted to worship at Mass, protestors prayed their own alternative Mass, and undercover members of the Chicago Police Department (CPD) Tactical Unit known as "the Red Squad" took diligent notes. Reports described the demonstration as a "pray-in." Demonstrators called it a "Black Unity Mass." This was just the first of many Black Unity Masses in the coming months, rituals that attracted the persistent surveillance of the CPD throughout 1969.[53]

This first "Black Unity Mass" was a prayer that doubled as protest. Protestors occupied pews in the parish and prayed forcefully over parishioners. Form is at least as important as content for our analysis here. One prayer illustrates the ways the Concerned Black Catholics creatively combined Vatican II and Black Power.

> That we as Black people may never stop striving for Our place in the sun.
> [*Response: "Hear us Lord."*]
> That we might recognize Our Blackness as a thing of pride and beauty.
> That more of Our Black Brothers and Sisters might be brought into the One Black Fold.
> That we might always have the courage to carry out OUR THING—whatever it may be.
> That the Lord may strengthen Our faith in each other and love for one another.

> That Archbishop Cody might soon come to understand OUR BLACK THING.
> That Father Rollins Lambert might soon return to St. James as pastor.
> That Father George Clements be brought back to St. Dorothy as pastor.
> That ALL of Our Black priests might be put in leadership positions in Our Church.
> That the churches in the Black community might be run by Black people.
> That we might never have dissension among Our Black People.
> That Rev. Dr. Martin Luther King Jr. might be recognized as a saint by all Black People.[54]

This prayer was a version of the General Intercession or common prayer, more generally known as the "prayer of the faithful," which the Concerned Black Catholics in Chicago had adapted to their own intentions. Though the prayer of the faithful had roots in fourth-century Christian communities, it had fallen out of use. Its revival was one piece of the liturgical reforms instituted by the Second Vatican Council in the 1963 "Constitution on the Sacred Liturgy" (*Sacrosanctum Concilium*). The prayer encouraged laypeople to actively engage in the liturgy by praying for the intentions of the congregation. What is more, the Council intended the prayer of the faithful to include not only prayers for the Catholic Church but also "for the civil authorities, for those oppressed by various needs, for all mankind, and for the salvation of the entire world."[55] Even as it challenged the institutional Church in Chicago, then, the Black Unity Mass at St. James exemplified the Council's call for lay participation devoted to the needs of the oppressed.

The prayer articulated two of the most important elements prevalent in Black Power at the time. The first five and final two intentions echoed cultural nationalist calls for Black self-love, unity, and pride. The prayer described African Americans as "Black people" and celebrated the beauty of "Our Blackness." Crucially, the intentions also hinted at divisions among African Americans over Black consciousness. Protesters prayed that "more of Our Black Brothers and Sisters might be brought into the One Black Fold," that there be no "dissension" among them. Activists struggled to convince Black Catholics that they should identify themselves according to Black cultural nationalist terms, a point many Black Catholics resisted.

Meanwhile, the middle five intentions listed the Concerned Black Catholics' demands and expressed its underlying political philosophy. Protestors hoped that Archbishop Cody might have a change of heart and called for the immediate installation of Fathers Lambert and Clements as pastors. Protestors also prayed more expansively for self-determination, "that the churches in the Black community might be run by Black people." The form and content of both these prayers illustrate the mutual influences of Black Power and Vatican II on Black Catholic protest. A martyr of Black freedom struggles, Martin Luther King, was reimagined as a saint; insistence on Black control of institutions in Black communities and affirmation of Black pride were reformulated as prayers in the spirit of Vatican II. This prayer, not to mention the presence of Black Panthers, dramatized the ways the Catholic Mass itself was becoming a charged event. Though Father McDonnell claimed the demonstrators did not disturb him—"they were only praying," he said—one report noted that some parishioners left Mass abruptly in disgust.[56]

One week later, at a public press conference Father Rollins Lambert publicly announced his support for Clements and accused Cardinal Cody of being an "unconscious racist." The press conference featured statements from Lambert now joined by newly allied activists, including the Black Catholic Clergy Caucus, Operation Breadbasket, the Black Consortium, the Afro-American Firemen and Patrolmen Leagues, the Concerned Black Catholics, the Catholic Interracial Council, the Concerned Transit Workers, the Martin Luther King Laymen's League, the Chicago Conference of Laymen, Committee for One Society, the St. Dorothy Parish Council, the Inner City Priests conference, and Alderman William Cousins from the 8th Ward. Lambert said that if Clements was not made a pastor immediately and "if Black pastors are not appointed in Black parishes wherever possible, I will not continue to serve as pastor of St. Dorothy's Church." If the archdiocese refused to relent to their demands, he would consider his ministry at St. Dorothy's "to be a participation in racism."[57] Lambert challenged what he took to be Cardinal Cody's manipulative decision making, saying his "appointment to St. Dorothy's was a purely political move."[58] He joined in calling the archbishop racist, though he did nuance it. "There are two kinds of racism," Lambert proclaimed, "deliberate and unconscious. . . . Cardinal Cody is not a conscious racist but his actions help to perpetuate racism prevalent in the Catholic Church of America."[59]

As we have seen, some of Clements's supporters had characterized Lambert as "the only guy who could spoil our whole campaign."[60] Now his fiercest critics did an about-face. When asked about this dramatic reversal, Thomas Mitchell simply said that Lambert's "recent statements work to the contrary [of any Uncle Tom characterization]." Mitchell credited himself and his fellow Black Power activists for Lambert's transformation.[61] Father Lawrence Lucas, a Black priest in Harlem and a nationally prominent Black Catholic, offered his interpretation in his book *Black Priest/White Church: Catholics and Racism* (1970). Lucas labeled the actions of Cardinal Cody a blatant attempt to "use a Black man to disarm the protest of Black people and their white supporters." Though Lambert may have assented to his archbishop's orders at first, Lucas said, "Father Lambert saw the light . . . encouraged by the Black brothers and sisters."[62] A notion of "authentic Blackness" operates here in the background. Elsewhere in the book Lucas argues, "[T]he most devastating effect of Catholicism on Negroes has been the loss of their minds as Black people."[63] For the CBC and other Black Catholic activists, Lambert's "enlightenment" was a restoration of his authentic "Black mind," whereby he transcended the "Negro" identity foisted on him by the white Church.

The second "Black Unity Mass," just days after this press conference, gave further liturgical expression to the expanding movement of Concerned Black Catholics. Instead of prayer-protest operating in parallel to worship, as at St. James, this service was a full-fledged liturgy designed by Black Catholic laypeople, sisters, and priests. Father Lambert and Father Clements celebrated this Black Unity Mass together in St. Dorothy church, joined by nine other Black priests from across Chicago and the country. If the transformation of worship was one of the most visible consequences of the Second Vatican Council, among one of the most innovative and contentious examples of postconciliar change was the integration of so-called "Black" religious practices into the Catholic Mass—changes initiated by those inspired by Black Power.

Chicago Catholics had already set a precedent for this kind of experimentation a month prior. The Knickerbocker Hotel hosted Chicago's first "African Mass" on December 1, 1968. This service served as the culmination for a meeting of the Chicago Conference of Laymen, an organization dedicated to implementing Vatican II teachings regarding the lay apostolate. When it came time for the presentation of the gifts, a Black man stripped to the waist processed to the altar with the chalice, performing an interpretative dance "to the beat of jungle music" along the way. Musicians dressed in "African robes" provided the music and relied heavily on drums, which led some critics to call this the "Drum Mass."

Father George Clements witnessed the liturgy and spoke with media afterward. He situated the Mass in the context of the Council. "African masses as offered in the jungle village are in keeping with the renewal program of the Roman Catholic church as started by the second Vatican council," Clements argued. He went so far as to suggest that "African masses with jungle music" would soon be offered in Black parishes throughout Chicago and that Black saints would populate their altars. Cardinal Cody, on the contrary, rejected Clements's claim that this represented a logical (or legitimate) consequence of Vatican II. He insisted that "permission has not been granted . . . nor will it be granted to conduct any services not in keeping with the devotional spirit of the liturgy. It is forbidden to introduce nonliturgical elements into the mass at any time."[64] This exchange between Clements and Cody, a precursor to the St. Dorothy controversy, highlighted a growing divide among all Catholics over the legacies of the Council.

The widening divide within Black Catholic communities sharpened after the second Black Unity Mass, hosted in St. Dorothy church on Sunday, January 12, 1969. Thousands of people crammed into the parish, forcing a few hundred more to listen outside to a service that stretched the better part of three hours. Mass featured eleven Black priests garbed in "African-style vestments." Father Lawrence Lucas was among them. Protestant, Jewish, Muslim, and nonreligious African Americans joined Black Catholics. White allies, such as members of the Catholic Interracial Council, were present in support. Black Panthers provided security, "strung out all over the sanctuary." A wide range of activist organizations was represented, including the Afro-American Youth Organization, the Black Consortium, Afro-American Patrolmen's and Firemen's Leagues, and the Concerned Transit Workers.[65] Rev. Jesse Jackson was present and his civil rights organization, Operation Breadbasket, provided the music for the service with an eight-piece band and eighty-voice choir. Gospel hymns like "Down by the Riverside," "Precious Lord," and "I Wish I Knew How It Feels to Be Free" were sung.[66]

The *Los Angeles Times* described the event as "an old-fashioned hymn-singing religious rally and Mass of a kind never seen in a Catholic Church in the city. The congregation was addressed not only by the priests, but by Black militant leaders as well, who urged them to back Father Clements."[67] Father Lambert's sermon restated his decision to resign if Clements was not appointed pastor and called on the congregation to "be proud of their Blackness and to defy the tactics of racists by affirming themselves in Black unity." These statements of pride and self-determination were met with roars of applause.[68]

Different descriptions of the St. Dorothy Black Unity Mass, some skeptical and others celebratory, highlight how explosive Black Catholic liturgical experimentation could be. Anne Getz of the *Chicago Tribune* wrote the most vivid account of the Mass, though her disapproval rings clear. The musicians were "a rock-and-roll band which played Negro spirituals" and the experience was participatory, as "members clapped vigorously and priests and church members swayed to the beat of drums." The music crescendoed during the collection and invocation when a lay reader called for the appointment of Father Clements as pastor. Getz went on to imply the illegitimacy of a service "barely recognizable as a traditional Catholic ceremony" because "Father Clements and Father Lambert were dressed in multi-colored robes," "altar boys wore zebra-striped robes, the altar was adorned with African symbols and a picture of the late Rev. Martin Luther King, Jr., and the ceremony rose to a fever pitch as a priest proclaimed 'unity before God.'" Getz also noted Jesse Jackson's militancy at the press conference after the Mass, when he challenged Cardinal Cody to put "Catholic money into Black banks," employ "Black laborers in Catholic schools," and use "products made by Black persons."[69]

The surveillance report filed by the CPD Tactical Unit echoed Getz's bemusement. From the Red Squad's perspective, the service was virtually illegible as a Catholic Mass. The report describes a liturgy that "differed from the normal Catholic Mass in that it followed the Black Baptist Church services rather than the rituals of the Roman Catholic Mass."

The Red Squad report claimed that the Black Unity Mass did not follow Roman rituals, this in spite of the fact that a program attached to the report enumerated all the essential elements of a Catholic liturgy: the proclamation of the gospel, a homily, prayers of the faithful, and, most crucially, the consecration of bread and wine into the body and blood of Jesus. This discrepancy conveys just how revolutionary it was to incorporate the aesthetics of the Black Power era (African-inspired garb) and Black Protestant musical traditions ("Down by the Riverside," "I Been 'Buked, I Been Scorned," et al.) into the Catholic Mass.[70]

The revolutionary nature of the Black Unity Mass was not lost on Father Lawrence Lucas, who described it as "what Mass is supposed to be—a celebration." Lucas connected this celebration to protest politics. "Black Catholics had come together for a cause, a cause worthy of celebration," he recalled. "They came to tell Cardinal Cody and the entire American Catholic Church that they disagreed that the Church in Chicago had no room in it for a relevant Black man in a position of power." The implications of the Black Unity Mass extended beyond the bounds of one service, in Lucas's eyes. He hoped the Mass might wake up Black Catholics and force them to shout out "'you can't continue to use one of us to shoot another down; you can't continue to misuse and abuse Black people; you can't continue to make Uncle Toms of Black folks.'"[71]

Black Unity Masses reveled in the inseparability of religion and politics, of Black Catholicism and Black Power. Perhaps for this reason, Black Unity Masses became one of the most prevalent and powerful modes of protest in the movement around Clements—whether they were staged as pray-ins concurrent with another Mass, as at St. James, or were standalone celebrations like this one at St. Dorothy. Clements's Red Squad file alone included surveillance reports on Black Unity Masses at St. James (January 19, January 26, February 2), St. Agatha (February 2), Holy Name of Mary School (February 14), and St. George (February 16). It also became customary for weekly meetings of the Concerned Black Catholics to conclude with their own "mini-Black Unity Mass" in the homes of activists. These services brought to life new ways of being both Black and Catholic, drawing freely from an array of aesthetics. Priests wearing the red, black, and green colors of the Black Liberation flag sang songs common in "Black Baptist Church services," as the surveillance report put it, and consecrated the Eucharist on altars bedecked with tiger

Figure 4.1. Father Rollins Lambert (center) concelebrates a Black Unity Mass at St. Agatha Church, Chicago (February 2, 1969). Courtesy of David J. Endres/*U.S. Catholic Historian*.

pelts and African sculptures, shields, and spears. Catholic liturgies thus served as the bedrock for the broader project of building a distinctively Black Catholicism.[72]

Black Catholic Critics of Black Power

By many accounts, the people in the St. Dorothy pews were deeply moved that day. Rollins Lambert reported that most of the reactions to the Black Unity Mass were positive, even if some complained that the service was "unchurch-like." Mrs. Earl Tinsey, a St. Dorothy parishioner, said that the Mass was a "beautiful demonstration that brought tears to my eyes." She stood for the entire service and felt that she "had a God-like spirit." Another parishioner called the service a "beautiful lesson in Christian unity."[73]

But if Black Unity Masses expressed the aspirations of Concerned Black Catholics, they represented the worst fears of many others. Catholics across racial, ethnic, and class spectrums were deeply divided over the meaning and legitimacy of religious life after Vatican II and this conflict was compounded when activists connected liturgical changes with notions of "authentic Blackness." Enthusiastic about both Vatican II and Black Power, some Black Catholic activists hoped to transform what it looked like, felt like, sounded like, and what it meant to be Black and Catholic. Many more resisted this combination, however. These critics feared that activists had embraced racial particularism over and against "true" universal Catholicism. They grew increasingly distressed as saints' statues were painted black, Sunday services began to feature African drumming, and especially as they were ridiculed as not being "Black enough." Conflict among Black Catholics burst into the public following the St. Dorothy Black Unity Mass.

The archdiocesan newspaper the *New World* initially defended the service. The editorial "Time to 'Lay it Down' in St. Dorothy Dispute" reminded readers (presumably white ones) that

> The Black Unity Mass at St. Dorothy's last Sunday with its Afro flourishes, disturbed some whites and Blacks. It should not have been any more disturbing than a Polish Mass or a Spanish Mass. . . . Nor is it surprising that not all Black Catholics liked the kind of liturgy that was celebrated last Sunday. There is a generation gap among Blacks as well as among whites. Not all white Catholics like "guitar" Masses either to draw a parallel. Young Blacks liked the liturgy of the Black Unity Mass. Older middle-class Blacks had their reservations.[74]

Subsequent letters to the editor showed that many Catholics disagreed with this assessment. None were as vociferous in their criticism as Black Catholics and some published those frustrations in the *New World* and the *Chicago Defender*. One writer thought it unfair to assume that all of St. Dorothy is "Black." This anonymous writer had converted to Catholicism in large part for a devotional style, one fading after Vatican II. "The Mass was [once] held as a dignified, reverent, solemn service," the author reflected. It was a "time to retreat, if necessary, to meditate, and hear a lesson sermon that would enlighten, encourage, and inspire one by quoting the words of God." The author rejected outright all this "Black this or the other" that now seemed to invade Catholic sermons, pointing out that "I do not need it repeated for me or to me over and over again to make me know it or to feel proud. Everyone knew I was Black the minute I was born."[75]

Another letter writer, a woman who described herself as one of "the Black parishioners who pay the bills at St. Dorothy," challenged Concerned Black Catholics as outsiders who were not representative of real Catholics and were unable to support their churches. "It was not the parishioners of the church that made the [Black Unity] mass a success," she said, "we hated it." She challenged the legitimacy of those opposed to the archdiocese, arguing that "Cardinal Cody has been good to Black people and these crazy Black priests aren't helping us any."[76] Another disgruntled Black Catholic wrote, "I am a Catholic and have been all my life . . . [and] I am a Negro and cannot see why we have to have a Baptist minister to be on our altar to tell us how to run our church." "We do not need those Black militants to have any part of our religion," this reader lamented. "We always had such a solemn and quiet church, you could meditate, but not any more."[77]

The debate echoed throughout Chicago's parishes, even making its way into the Corpus Christi parish bulletin—further evidence of just how divisive this church controversy had become. On the same day as the St. Dorothy Black Unity Mass, the bulletin featured letters from two of the parish's priests. Father Michael Mooney began by openly declaring his support for "Father Lambert and the Black Caucus." "Unfortunately I will not be at Corpus Christi on Sunday," Mooney lamented. But he wanted parishioners to know that he did not "think that 'telling it like it is' is being disloyal to the church; rather, it is this kind of 'truth' that sets a man free!" Mooney remained "very proud of our Black priests," he intended to "follow their leadership on this issue," and he hoped that "many in Corpus Christi parish feel the same." Recall that Clements himself had once been a member of Corpus Christi, where he celebrated his first Mass as a priest in 1957. Father Mooney did not have the last word, however. Father Vincent Elsen announced that he would be present at Corpus Christi on Sunday, "perhaps also 'unfortunately.'" Elsen insisted that he too was "proud of our Black priests." He wished, indeed, that "we had many, many more" and reported that he had "spent a good part of my life trying to help more Black boys to become priests." Nevertheless, he was in "full support of Cardinal Cody and legitimate authority in the church anywhere and everywhere." He did not "intend to follow [the Concerned Black Catholics'] lead on this issue (because it is all too one-sided) and I hope that most people in Corpus Christi parish will feel the same."[78]

It was finally becoming clear to all that this protest was about more than one pastorate. Supporters of Father Clements had mobilized a challenge to ecclesial authority and asserted Black Catholic self-determination. Once this realization set in, the tone of the *New World* coverage shifted from paternalistic skepticism to outright hostility. A January 24 editorial first acknowledged that "what started out as a rather simple issue to have Father George Clements named to the pastorate of St. Dorothy's parish on the South Side has now been broadened to include a whole host of issues touching Black autonomy within the Catholic Church."[79] The editorial then adopted a conspiratorial tone. "The pleas for a pastorate for Father Clements have been used as a ploy to open up for discussion a whole area of relations between Black Catholics and the Archdiocese," the author argued. He characterized the presumably foreign force of "militant Black power groups" as the problem.[80]

Speculation that "militants" had coerced agreement from their opponents resonated widely with critics, who charged activists with "pressuring" and "intimidating" priests and nuns. This implied that white support for Black Power (which, of course, there was) was motivated by fear or guilt rather than a genuine commitment to the cause. It also portrayed Black Power as an outside influence infiltrating a Church where it did not belong. According to the *New World*, the manipulation of these "Black militant groups who claim to speak for the Black community" was the only plausible explanation for how an internal archdiocesan affair became national news. These groups, with their "strong arm tactics, reminiscent of white gangsterism, have angered or at least unsettled many of the priests now working in the Black community, and leave their future relationship uncertain." The editorial predicted that this attack was "only a beginning assault on all religious denominations, Black and white, in the Black community. Once the white priests have been taken care of, Black priests and ministers will be next. The whole apparatus of Christianity in the Black community is under attack." Black Power challenged "so-called 'white racist' institutions" and now all of "organized religion just happens to be under the gun."[81] As anxious speculations increased, Father Clements's white allies had to insist again and again that their support had not been coerced.[82]

The archdiocesan newspaper was not alone in presuming the machinations of militants. Black Catholic critics soon wrote to the *New World* in gratitude for its clarity. One reader was convinced that Black Catholics had only remained silent in the face of Black Power because they did not fully comprehend the ramifications of the St. Dorothy controversy. Now it was clear that the Church faced nothing short of its complete "take-over" by militants, many of whom were "non-Catholic." The silent Black Catholic majority must be spurred to action, another reader admonished. Otherwise the results could be cataclysmic: "I forsee [*sic*] the day when the bunch of little Hitlers, not content with telling us how, when, and where Holy Mass should be celebrated, will be dictating our manner of dress, of wearing our hair, and choosing our friends lest we be declared 'traitors to the cause.'"[83] Another reader also drew on Nazi imagery to characterize Black Power activists, charging them with having "every characteristic of and us[ing] every tactic of Hitler storm troopers." This concerned Catholic of a different sort speculated, "Father Clements would probably be a pastor today if he had the maturity of patience and had followed the counsel of friends rather than malcontents. One wonders if he is first a racist and second a Christian? For a racist is one who subordinates all judgments to the racial issue, and fails to see any point of view but his own."[84]

The accusation that Concerned Black Catholics were racists first and Christians second—by which I take the author to mean that they subordinated all judgments to a race-based analysis—highlighted an emerging tension within Black Catholic communities. Should Black Catholics be distinctively Catholic, offering their own unique contributions to the broader Church as *Black* people? Or was this sort of distinctiveness antithetical to what it meant to be *Catholic* in the first place? Historian Albert Raboteau notes how Black Catholics have confronted the tension between the ideal of Catholic universalism and the demands of racial particularism again and again throughout their history.[85] Black particularism and Catholic universalism lay at the heart of Black Catholic debates in the 1960s and 1970s. Many African Americans who became Catholic in the first half of the twentieth century understood themselves to be joining the "One True Church," an institution whose bodily disciplines and distinctive practices offered a potential avenue to transcend otherwise inescapable racial particularity. But for advocates of Black Power, racial consciousness functioned not only as identity but also as a critical lens through which social, political, and, in the case of the CBC, even religious institutions could be challenged. The very category of race could become a "political space," in a sense.[86] Black Catholics influenced by Black Power took racial particularity—meaning the unique experience of being Black people in America—to be an essential element for forcing the Church to be truly universal. Rather than accepting a vision of Catholic universalism that emphasized oneness or uniformity, activists in the CBC asserted a catholicity premised on an inclusiveness of difference.

It is impossible to understand just how revolutionary this argument was without coming to terms with its forceful critics. Debates about Vatican II became inseparable from debates about Black Power for Black Catholics in the late 1960s and 1970s, largely as a result of organizations like the Concerned Black Catholics and protests like Black Unity Masses.[87] The CBC interpreted the Council as an opportunity to incorporate African and African American cultural traditions into Catholic liturgy, as a call to enter into struggles for Black liberation. They interpreted conciliar changes in the context of Black Power's self-determination and self-definition. But other Black Catholics remained deeply skeptical of both. They scoffed at the infiltration of "Black stuff" into their churches and lamented the diminishing quiet of once reverent worship services. They criticized Black Power and the ways in which it was entangled with the changes in Catholic practice. Critics rejected an emphasis on the particularity of "Blackness," taking it to be contradictory to the universalism for which they had converted. They yearned instead for the "quiet dignity" of the Latin Mass that they feared was being replaced by a vernacular, "Protestantized" one. And they were increasingly anxious about connecting religious life with political action, expressing disgust with "crazy Black priests." These anxieties, shared by many whites, were particularly potent when linked with ideas about Black authenticity.

Redeeming the Church through Black Power

The controversy surrounding St. Dorothy church expanded yet again on January 20 when the Concerned Black Catholics "crashed" a meeting of Chicago's Inner City Priests Conference (ICPC). The ICPC was a group of fifty-one priests working in predominantly African American neighborhoods on the South and West Sides of Chicago. Almost entirely white, ICPC constituents embodied an array of Catholic approaches to Black communities. Some priests remained committed to the "convert-making" apostolate which had been popular since the 1930s. Others had begun to engage in struggles for racial justice. This group had suggested that Cardinal Cody promote Father Clements to pastor back in December 1968. Now the CBC leveled demands on them. Activists insisted that the inner-city priests arrange CBC meetings in their parishes, publicly support recent statements that called Cody an unconscious racist, and sign a statement of support for the CBC. One of the more vocal leaders of the CBC insisted that "Black people had to have hegemony over their own 'Black turf.'" "Before we leave," he urged, "we would like to know the names of those pastors living on our turf (inner city parishes) who can't support us." When every pastor stood up in support, they were dismissed incredulously. "I don't trust you just standing up, so put an asterisk on a list beside your name if you want a Black unity Mass and if you'll agree to a statement of support of the CBC in a press conference."[88]

Fifteen representatives of the ICPC spoke to the press the next day and announced ICPC endorsement of the Concerned Black Catholics. The group declared that Catholic schools must continue to serve Black neighborhoods and that they should be controlled by Black people. They pressed the archdiocese to appoint a Black coordinator of "inner city diocesan affairs." Reporters failed, though, to goad the priests into calling Cody racist. Instead, ICPC representatives hoped Cody had "gained a much clearer perspective and appreciation of the issues," expressing a cautious optimism that a resolution might yet be reached.[89]

This insistence that Black Catholics be given leadership roles within the archdiocese, shared by the CBC and the ICPC, illuminates an important point. In the wider constellation of Black Power activists and organizations, Black Catholics and their allies were distinguished by their desire to remain part of a majority-white institution even as they struggled for Black self-determination in the confines of specific institutions such as churches and schools. Priests like Lambert and Clements might threaten to leave if their demands were not met. But their ultimate objective was a transformation of Catholicism from within.

Father George Clements remembers his indignant response to Black radicals and white Catholics who, back in the 1960s and 1970s, rejected the possibility of being both Black and Catholic. To both "the Blacker than Blacks who say 'how can you stay in that racist white church?' and the whites who say 'if you don't like what's going on in our church, why don't you just get out [and] stop screaming about it?'" he responded "I'm not going to go anywhere, I'm going to stay right here, because this is where I feel Christ wants me to be. . . . You didn't put me in [the Catholic Church] and you can't put me out!" Clements recalled Father Lawrence Lucas reacting in a similar fashion when challenged by white Catholics. When people would ask him "Why don't you just leave?" he was known to swiftly retort "Why don't *you* leave!? This is my Church, not yours!"[90] Black Catholics fought for power and self-determination within the institutional Church. They did not seek separation—at least not for the most part.[91] On the contrary, they understood themselves to be representatives of the *true* Church. Black Power awakened Black Catholic activists to a new sense of racial consciousness. Vatican II provided the tools to bring that consciousness into the life of the Church.

It certainly was shocking to hear Catholics call their Church a "white racist institution." Yet the vast majority of Black Catholics were not separatists or schismatics. One priest put it this way. Black Catholic activists articulated "what has always been for many an unresolved tension: the determination to be Black and Catholic while remaining within a 'white racist institution.'"[92] The whole point of the larger movement—of which the protests surrounding Father Clements were but an early example—was to incorporate Black Power into Catholicism in order to ultimately redeem an institution of its endemic white supremacy, to transform it into the Body of Christ as it was meant to be. Sister Mary Roger Thibodeaux, a Black Sister of the Blessed Sacrament, used poetry to make this point in 1972. *A Black Nun Looks at Black Power* pleads with the Church to incorporate Black Power for its own sake: "the Catholic Church would do well to absorb / some of the courage displayed / during the beginning stages / of the Black Power movement. / We must at times / risk everything / to gain a greater good."[93] Black Catholics like Thibodeaux and Clements dreamed of transforming the Church, not destroying it.

In many ways the Second Vatican Council made this possible. As Mc-Greevy has demonstrated, the Council promoted a new conception of ecclesial authority that was especially important for "American Catholics interested in racial issues." Vatican II "reframed conceptions of the nature of the church," replacing hierarchical and institutional definitions with the biblical image of "the people of God." It emphasized the need for laypeople to work toward social justice in the world. This was especially clear in *Gaudium et Spes*, or "The Pastoral Constitution on the Modern World," which famously declared "the joys and the hopes, the griefs and the anxieties of the man of this age, especially those who are poor or in any way afflicted, these two are the joys and hopes, the griefs and anxieties of the followers of Christ." And with "the abandonment of Latin" and the "unprecedented tolerance of new liturgical forms," the Council further gestured toward "the formation of a global church."[94] McGreevy went on to show how, when Vatican II intersected with the civil rights movement, white Catholic liberals rushed to embrace it.[95] For Black Catholics it was the convergence of Vatican II with Black Power that spurred at least some of them to action. And, as evident in the work of the Concerned Black Catholics, this convergence took shape in struggle. If Black priests, sisters, and laypeople wanted control of Catholic institutions in Chicago, they were going to have to fight for it.

The Controversy Concludes, the Movement Continues

Concerned Black Catholics and other supporters of Father Clements received resolution on June 13, 1969, nearly six months after the protests began. Cardinal Cody announced the promotion of three Black priests to pastorates in Chicago. Rollins Lambert remained pastor of St. Dorothy while George Clements was made pastor of Holy Angels church. Kenneth Brigham was assigned to administrate Our Lady of Perpetual Help and Divine Word priest Dominic Carmon became the first Black pastor of St. Elizabeth church, the "mother church" of Black Catholic Chicago where another Black Divine Word priest, James LaChapelle, would assist.

On hearing the news, Clements was quick to claim the success for the entire Black community. He hailed the decision as "a great victory for the Black community in general and groups such as the Afro-American Patrolmen and Firemen's leagues, the Concerned Black Catholics, and Operation Breadbasket in particular." What is more, from Clements's perspective this was a crucial victory for an ongoing struggle. The promotion of Black priests to positions of power across the city, the beginnings of Black Catholic self-determination in Chicago, was not just a direct response to "the legitimate demands of the Black community." It may be "the only hope for the Catholic church in the Black community."[96]

Lambert, Clements, and Carmon led a fitting celebration on June 30. Together with eleven other Black priests, the three Black pastors led the first Black Unity Mass at Holy Angels, just the first of many. With a tiger skin draped over the altar and "assorted African" symbols (spears, swords, masks, shields, and sculptures) behind him, Father Lawrence Lucas declared in his sermon that Black Power had won the day; that Cardinal Cody had tried to make Lambert a "house nigger"—had tried to divide the Black community—and failed.[97]

The appointment of four Black priests to positions of power in Chicago parishes represented the first major victory for a movement that soon spread across the country. Father Clarence Williams, himself a Black priest in Chicago, argued that the success of the protest movement supporting Father Clements served as "the impetus for the national black Catholic Church movement and in the organization that came into being." The coalition of Catholics, Black and white, and Black Power organizations such as the Black Panthers and AAPL had demonstrated "the effectiveness of black Catholic's [sic] challenge to the Church for determining their destiny."[98] Black Power continued its rise in currency in the Black freedom struggles as the 1970s began and as it did, Lucas and Clements and like-minded Catholics became the dominant voices in a national Black Catholic Movement. If the Catholic Church were to survive at all in Black communities awash in Black Power, they argued, Black people had to gain control over the Catholic institutions in their neighborhoods. Catholic churches had to be made *Black*. But as we will see, to accomplish this ambitious goal activists would have to win over their critics. Catholics would have to become Black.

5

Becoming Black Catholics

The Black Catholic Movement and the Rise of Black Catholicism

Mere months after George Clements became pastor of Holy Angels parish the Chicago Police Department and the Federal Bureau of Investigation conspired to kill charismatic Black Panther Party leader Fred Hampton. Drugged by an informant who had infiltrated the Chicago chapter and provided the police with the layout of the apartment, Hampton was gunned down as he slept in bed beside his pregnant girlfriend in December 1969.[1] The Panthers had been directly involved in the movement to promote Clements and Clements had grown close with Fred Hampton in the process.[2] With Hampton now dead, the remaining Chicago Panthers feared further assassinations. Police raided the apartment of Chicago Panther's second-in-command, Bobby Rush, the following day, but by this point he was already safely in hiding.[3] As Father Clements later recalled in the *New World*, he played a role in protecting Panthers sought by the police. "Everyone knew that Bobby was next on the list. And he fled," said Clements. Where did he go? The new pastor of Holy Angels had introduced Rush to "a little known thing in the Middle Ages called the 'right of sanctuary,'" encouraging Rush to hide at Holy Angels.[4]

As he hid in this South Side Chicago parish, Bobby Rush may have taken solace in one of the side altars of the church. There he would have found himself face to face with an unlikely saint's shrine. Among Father Clements's first acts as pastor was overseeing the removal of St. Anthony of Padua from his place in the sanctuary. A portrait of the late Rev. Dr. King took his place. The side altar was rededicated as the "Shrine of St. Martin Luther King Jr." Needless to say, this rededication was controversial. King did not meet the criteria for canonization in the Catholic Church for a whole host of reasons, not least of which was the fact that he was not Catholic in the first place. This fact did not stop Father Clements, though. Nor was this a unilateral decision by the newly installed pastor. Instead, Clements acted according to the will of his parishioners and justified the decision by citing the Catholic tradition known as "acclamatio populorum"—King was a saint because the "people acclaimed" him as such.[5] Here Holy Angels parishioners with the help of Clements asserted their self-determination as a Black religious community at the same time that they invoked long-standing Catholic traditions. They creatively combined Black Power with elements from the Catholic past.

When Rush eventually surrendered himself, he did so under escort by Black Catholic police officer and ally Renault "Reggie" Robinson.[6] Robinson, as we have seen, was a founder of the Afro-American Patrolmen's League (AAPL), which was, along with the Black Panthers, among those Black Power organizations instrumental in achieving Clements's appointment. Once a St. Dorothy parishioner, Robinson and his family joined Holy Angels when Clements became pastor. He was among the many parishioners who made Holy Angels a self-determined Black religious community over the next decade.

Father George Clements paid tribute to Fred Hampton at his funeral. At the request of Hampton's family, Clements read Fred's obituary and closed his brief eulogy with a "refrain familiar to those who knew Fred":

> You can kill the revolutionary, but you can't kill the revolution. You can jail the liberator, but you can't jail the liberation. You can run the freedom fighter all around the country, but you can't stop freedom fighting. So believed Fred—so said Fred—so say we all.[7]

Shortly thereafter, the Black Catholic pastor organized a memorial Mass for Hampton at Holy Angels in an attempt to channel the grief and outrage of the community. Hundreds of students from Holy Angels grammar school attended as well. A portrait of Hampton rested against the altar and looked out over those present. As Clements tried to convey the significance of Hampton's life, he abruptly broke down in tears. "I was just shattered, I was devastated," Clements remembered. But in the quiet of Clements's tears, an eighth-grade boy stood up and shouted, "I am Fred Hampton!" He was joined by declarations from other girls and boys who celebrated Hampton as a hero.[8] Soon after this memorial Father Clements commissioned a local artist, Louis Boyd, to paint a five-foot by thirty-foot "Wall of Black Saints." Visitors would now be greeted by portraits of "slain Black heroes," including Fred Hampton, Medgar Evers, Martin Luther King, Malcolm X, the students killed at Jackson State College, and other martyrs to the cause. A mural memorializing "the pain and agony that Black folks encounter daily in white America" now joined the Shrine of St. Martin Luther King on the walls of this iconoclastic Black Catholic church.[9]

Over the next decade Holy Angels became nationally renowned as the biggest "Blackest" Catholic church in the city. In this they were the exemplars of a national movement on the rise. In the years following Martin Luther King and Fred Hampton's assassinations, a growing group of Black Catholic activists across the United States established a network of organizations that advocated not only Black control of Catholic institutions but also the incorporation of "authentic Black" practices into Catholic religious life. Vocational associations of priests and sisters, the Black Catholic Clergy Caucus and the National Black Sisters' Conference, sparked these efforts in 1968. Laypeople, brothers, and seminarians soon joined them. Black Catholic activists referred to themselves and their organizations collectively as the "Black Catholic Movement."[10]

It was not long before the Movement developed a robust critique of the Church in the United States as well as a defense of a distinctive Black Catholicism. Informed by the Black Power prevalent in the late 1960s and early 1970s, activists argued that Black Catholics were first and foremost a *Black* people—as much inheritors of "the Black Church" tradition as they were Catholic. From this perspective, the Catholic Church in the United States was a "white racist institution" not just because white people occupied positions of institutional power but even more so because Black Catholics had been coerced to conform to white religious norms.[11] At the heart of their challenge lay a cutting criticism of the very missionaries who had been so instrumental in the conversion of thousands of African Americans decades earlier. As we have seen, missionaries introduced African Americans to what they took to be the universal "One True Church." Activists in the 1970s reinterpreted this mode of evangelization as cultural imperialism. They argued that missionaries had, in fact, inculcated African Americans in *white*, European Catholicism.[12] Black Catholics had been forcibly removed from their true religious heritage, they insisted. They had become Black-faced white people. Movement activists hoped to change this.

The Black Catholic Movement revolutionized Black Catholic life. As with all revolutions, the results were neither inevitable nor uncontroversial. Activists demanded that Black Catholics control their own institutions and insisted that those Catholics be free to worship in ways that they understood to be distinctively Black—the motto of Chicago's Concerned Black Catholics was "Concerned Black Catholics Will Control Black Communities."[13] Activists fought fiercely to remain Catholic and identified Black Power as the key to saving their Church from the sin of white supremacy. But as we have already seen, in Chicago Black Catholics themselves were among those most skeptical of this cause. Activists strove to convince their fellow Black Catholics that theirs was the most authentic way to be Black and Catholic. They attempted to persuade their coreligionists to become *Black* Catholics, which meant in part to incorporate distinctive African diasporic and African American traditions into their Catholic practices. They fought against the idea that the Catholicism instituted by missionaries in the first half of the twentieth century—its sensorium, its habits of devotion, its way of being in the world—was the only legitimate expression of Catholicism. And as we will see, the Black Catholic Movement largely succeeded at transforming Black Catholic identity and practice. The rise of Black Catholicism, the relative success of their revolution, was the fruit of activists' labors.

There were two notable ironies of their revolution, though. A sharp critique of the Catholic Church's "missionary mentality" with regard to African Americans rested at the heart of the Black Catholic Movement. Activists argued—rightly, as we have seen—that missionaries had imagined Black people to be foreigners in their midst who must be "made" into good Catholics. The missionary Catholicism that contributed to tens of thousands of conversions was regarded by Black Catholic activists, to borrow phrases from the Black Catholic Clergy Caucus's 1968 statement, as "enlightened paternalism" at best and "white racism" at worst. The first irony of the Black Catholic Movement was that, when faced with opposition from fellow Black Catholics, these activist critics of missionary Catholicism were forced to become missionaries of a sort themselves. They labored to convert coreligionists to a distinctively *Black* Catholicism, to help them become Black Catholics rather than just Catholics who happened to be Black. While the Black Catholic

Movement embraced Black Power and rejected the "whiteness" of the American Church, they embraced methods reminiscent of the very missionaries against whom they set themselves. And by the 1980s they had largely succeeded in convincing people that one could be both "authentically Black and truly Catholic."

A second irony specific to Chicago was that Holy Angels achieved self-determination as a Black Catholic community—as a parish that, to paraphrase its pastor, did not apologize either for being Black or for being Catholic—not because they cut their ties with missionary Catholicism, but precisely because they preserved its methods. Readers will recall that missionaries explicitly linked evangelization with education in parochial schools and emphasized the exclusivity of Catholic truth claims. Non-Catholic students and parents were required to attend religious instruction classes and there they learned how to be members of "the One True Church." This approach to parochial education came under fire on multiple fronts by the 1970s. Both Black Catholic activists and liberal Catholics rejected the emphasis on conversion in education, albeit for different reasons. But just when religious instruction classes and mandatory Mass attendance for non-Catholic families began to look antiquated, if not reactionary, Father George Clements maintained them as the bedrock of the Holy Angels parish and school. Holy Angels became one of the most remarkable success stories of Black Catholics in the United States in the 1970s. While commentators wondered why Black conversions to Catholicism had slowed and why membership was dropping for the first time in decades, Holy Angels grew in size and stature. And so another irony of the Black Catholic revolution, at least as it played out in the idiosyncrasies of this particular community on the South Side of Chicago, is that it was accomplished not by overturning missionary Catholicism but by incorporating it in creative tension with Black Power.

The "Inner City" in Crisis

Journalists never failed to note that Father George Clements's new parish was located in the middle of "Chicago's worst ghetto." Low-income federal housing projects surrounded Holy Angels parish and school, which sat south of the Ida B. Wells Homes and east of the Robert Taylor

Homes. Father Clements informed the *Chicago Tribune* in 1971 that 80 percent of Holy Angels students lived in public housing projects and "at least half the children come from families receiving public aid."[14] The Grand Boulevard neighborhood was called an "inner city" or "ghetto" community by journalists and community members alike, as were most urban Black neighborhoods in Chicago and other American cities at the time.[15] Inner-city communities like that of Holy Angels found themselves in the midst of a crisis in the 1970s, one not of their own making.

Until recently narratives of urban "ghetto formation" have emphasized restrictive covenants, white flight to the suburbs, and deindustrialization as the collective causes that led to the divestment and decline of Black communities in American cities. Scholars conceived of Black ghettoes as the products of de facto segregation and poverty, the legacies of racism and slavery. Scholars have complicated this narrative over the past decade, however.[16] Robert O. Self argues that while terms like "white flight" and "urban decline" gesture toward historical realities, they also "mask volatile and protracted social and political struggles over land, taxes, jobs, and public policy in the thirty years between 1945 and the late 1970s."[17] Historical narratives of impoverished Black people abandoned by white flight and deindustrialization fail to account for the ways in which racist real estate practices and the overdevelopment of white suburbs occurred at the expense of urban Black communities. They also do not account for local resistance to the divestment of Black communities. The Federal Housing Administration (FHA), for example, literally subsidized white suburbs, effectively forcing Black families to pay more money for inferior housing. Ghettoes did not emerge simply because Black people could not afford or were not allowed to purchase suburban homes. Rather, there were significant economic incentives for the construction of white enclaves outside the city.[18]

The Holy Angels community was a product of these processes, as were many Black parishes across urban America. As we have seen, Black Catholics typically worshipped in churches originally built and financed by European immigrants and their children. In the middle years of the twentieth century many white Catholics had begun to move away from their childhood parishes and into white suburban enclaves. This white migration to the suburbs was encouraged and incentivized by predatory real estate agents, who bought up sections of neighborhoods, sold them to Black families, and then circulated fears that poverty and crime necessarily followed these Black migrants. This process, known as "blockbusting," was highly lucrative for real estate agents and devastating for white and Black homeowners alike. Though not all white Catholics left their old parish neighborhoods, those that did were also drawn by federally subsidized housing and tax incentives into the suburbs. This financial aid made suburbanization not only viable but also advantageous.[19]

Black Catholics in the postwar United States, the majority of whom lived in urban areas, experienced the deterioration of predominantly Black neighborhoods firsthand. Black Catholics faced a related crisis as well, one that threatened the survival of Black Catholicism itself. The growth of Black Catholic communities through conversion had ground to a halt by the late 1960s and African Americans were beginning to leave Catholic churches in rising numbers. The Black Catholic Clergy Caucus (BCCC) took note of this trend in April 1968. "The Catholic Church is rapidly dying in the Black community," read their inaugural statement.[20] This crisis was shocking because it followed decades of unprecedented Black Catholic growth. African American conversions to the Catholic Church had reached record highs in the 1940s and 1950s. The national Black Catholic population grew from a little under 300,000 to over 900,000 members from 1940 to 1975, a 208 percent increase.[21] But by 1974 the Black Catholic population in Chicago had begun to shrink. Between 1971 and 1974, 115,000 of the 1 million Black Catholics in the United States left. Vocations were also falling; one hundred and fifty Black women religious left their orders in 1973 alone.[22] The crisis appeared so stark that one Black Catholic activist bluntly asked, "[W]ill there be an urban Catholic Church? Will there be a Catholic Church for Black People?"[23]

Black Catholic Movement activists as well as journalists echoed this observation throughout the 1970s. When Brother Joseph M. Davis, a Black Catholic activist from Cincinnati who served as the executive director of the National Office for Black Catholics in the 1970s, reflected on the "position of the Catholic Church in the Black community" in 1969, he said the future of Black Catholicism "looks bleak."[24] Two years later, speaking to a conference of Josephite priests in Baltimore, Davis described the "diminishing returns" of Black Catholic communities nationwide faced with departing youth, lack of conversions, and aging communities.²⁵ *Newsweek* reported on Black Catholic decline in 1974.²⁶ Robert McClory wrote a series of articles for the *National Catholic Reporter* in 1977 investigating how the Church was "losing ground" among Black Catholics. "Old white liberals from the interracial movement, and young, militant Blacks into liberation theology," according to McClory, agreed on the "loss of Catholic influence in the Black community."²⁷ That same year Father Clarence Williams discussed Black Catholic "decline," describing how "many young Blacks who are now starting families are no longer participating in the church."²⁸

The Birth of the Black Catholic Movement

The different organizations Black Catholics founded in the late 1960s attempted to address these crises. The Black Catholic Clergy Caucus (BCCC) and the National Black Sisters' Conference organized in 1968, as we have seen. The National Convention of Black Lay Catholics followed suit in 1969. Many Black Catholic activists aspired to establish an official institution that might centralize these separate organizations and advocate on behalf of all Black Catholics, though even activists were not unanimous on this count. Father Lawrence Lucas recalled how difficult it was for the Black Catholic Clergy Caucus to retain the language declaring the U.S. Church a "white racist institution" in the BCCC inaugural statement.²⁹ Black priests, brothers, and women religious were further divided over how best to unite their different organizations, with Black sisters preferring the diffuse authority and relative autonomy of a "National Alliance of Black Catholics" to more centralized models.³⁰ Over the objections of women religious, a coalition of Black Catholic priests, sisters, and laypeople sent a joint proposal to the National Conference of Catholic Bishops (NCCB) in November 1969. The coalition proposed a "central office for Black Catholicism" that would be underwritten and supported financially by the NCCB. It would serve as the "secretariat for Black Catholicism, consisting of priests, brothers, religious women and lay people, with authority to formulate programs for action in the Black community." The NCCB approved the formation of the National Office for Black Catholics (NOBC), though the budget the bishops provided fell well short of Black Catholic demands. The first act of the NOBC, then, was their decision not to accept "one penny of the racist money."[31] Beginning with this act of defiance and continuing throughout the 1970s the NOBC hoped to transform Black Catholics into a self-sustaining, empowered Catholic community.

In their attempt to explain why Black Catholicism was declining in American cities, activists in the Black Catholic Movement consistently identified two causes. The first cause was economic and the second was cultural and psychological. On the economic front, activists argued that the white Catholic Church was abandoning urban Black Catholic communities. One of the most drastic consequences of this material abandonment was the collapse of Catholic schools that had long been highly valued institutions in Black communities. They had represented one of the scarce alternatives to the public school system available to Black people, a public school system that was practically "non-functional" in 1970s urban America. Catholic schools across the United States faced financial problems at this moment in history, but the problems were even more acute in urban Black communities. The typical Church response to the financial strain of ailing schools was to consolidate or close schools, many of which served predominantly Black communities. As historian John T. McGreevy put it, "[A] standard tableau of the late 1960s was the initial decision of archdiocesan administrators to close inner-city schools awash in a sea of red ink." The decision to close inner-city schools was often followed by "heroic efforts of parents to save the school and tense negotiations between administrators and local African-American Catholics," but they were frequently unsuccessful.[32] Church authorities explained this tendency as a financial necessity as well as a response to the high percentage of non-Catholics attending these predominantly Black schools. Black priest and activist Father Clarence Williams, on the other hand, characterized the policy as a "withdrawal of the Catholic Church from the Black community"—"CCC ... consolidate, cluster, and close," as he called it.[33]

Black Catholics were further outraged that inner-city schools were being allowed to collapse while suburban Catholicism simultaneously expanded. Black Catholics witnessed parishes closing in Black communities at the same time as larger and more affluent white congregations opened new parishes and schools in the suburbs that catered exclusively to white Catholic communities. Religious orders of priests and sisters often followed their white Catholic congregations out of the city, with some less inclined to serve in places they increasingly perceived to be undesirable and even dangerous. Black Catholic activists interpreted this as the overdevelopment of the white Catholic suburbs and the underdevelopment of the Black Catholic inner city. Father George Clements in Chicago railed against the subsidization of effectively all-white suburban Catholic schools when Black Catholic schools in the city struggled to remain open.[34] Father Paul Smith, a Black priest who worked with Clements at Holy Angels parish on Chicago's South Side, lambasted the "gradual 'pullout' of the church from the inner city to the [white] suburbs."[35] This "pullout" posed a grave existential threat to the Black Catholic community. The Black Catholic Movement should be understood in part as a direct response to this economic divestment of Black Catholic communities.[36]

Following extensive research and consultation, the National Office for Black Catholics published an official statement in January 1976 addressing "The Crisis of Catholic Education in the Black Community." The statement detailed "the *collapse* of Catholic schools in the Black community." What is more, the NOBC identified the issue underlying the archdiocesan withdrawal from Black communities, namely, "whether 'Catholic' money should be used to educate 'non-Catholic' children."[37] The NOBC stated forcefully that "when Catholic officials say that there will be Catholic schools 'where parishes can pay for them,' they are stating obliquely that there will be Catholic schools in the white community." When white Catholics established new schools in the affluent suburbs, they effectively heaped more "Catholic schools onto an already more-than-adequate suburban system, to provide a highly selective opportunity to communities that already have more than average opportunity, and to deprive Black people totally of one of the most essential services they could have."[38] The NOBC proposed instead that the Church invest in Black communities as part of the broader reorientation of the Church following Vatican II. The Second Vatican Council's "Declaration on Christian Education," *Gravissimum Educationis*, had reiterated the special role Catholic schools played in preaching the gospel and serving the poor. Now the NOBC called on the Church in the United States to live up to this mandate, literally lining the margins of their special statement with quotes from the declaration. "In refusing to abandon the Black neighborhood," they insisted, "the Catholic school evidences the value it places in the people." What is more, "in an atmosphere in which it is obvious that so many believe that young Black people cannot be educated, the Catholic school is a constant witness to the talented and creative potential Black youth possess."[39] Closing Catholic schools to non-Catholics in the inner city amounted to putting up a "for Catholics only" sign and this sign gave an "unmistakably clear notice to *all* Black people—Catholics and non-Catholics—where its priorities are: the white suburban population."[40] If the Church were to survive in Black communities at all, it would have to invest in them.

The second cause Black Catholic Movement activists identified to explain the crisis facing urban Black Catholic communities was cultural and psychological. Urban Black communities had increasingly embraced Black self-determination and cultural nationalism associated with Black Power in the late 1960s. But, according to the BCCC inaugural statement, "the Catholic Church apparently is not cognizant of changing attitudes in the Black community and is not making the necessary, realistic adjustments."[41] Charles Burns, a Divine Word missionary, put it another way in a 1976 essay "Catholicism and Black Americans." "The reason for the dying state of Catholicism among Blacks," Burns asserted, "is that it has yet to become a truly 'Black institution'—that is, one that truly belongs to the people."[42]

Black Catholic activists argued that African Americans occupied a second-class status in the predominantly white Catholic Church. They employed an anticolonialist logic in their critique, reinterpreting Black Catholics as an internally colonized people. The executive director of the National Office for Black Catholics, Brother Joseph Davis, developed a sophisticated argument for what he understood as a spiritual colonialism. According to Davis, the Church in the United States had long understood African Americans as a foreign people. This was precisely why the Church had consistently relegated their care to specialized missionaries rather than diocesan clergy. This practice had produced a "missionary mentality," as Davis termed it. The Church had established a "psychological *difference* between the regular parish and the Negro mission." The use of psychological language to characterize Black Catholics as an "internally colonized" people pervades much of Davis's writings and was clearly influenced by the thought of anticolonial psychiatrist and revolutionary Franz Fanon, whose writings served as some of the most significant theoretical foundations for Black Power activists.[43] Since missionary work in the "Negro apostolate" called for the courageous sacrifice of missionaries on behalf of a spiritually impoverished people, the Black community had effectively become "an outlet for practicing the Works of Mercy and for the heroic dedication of clerics and religious who felt called to go a step beyond the sacrifices called for in normal service to the church."[44] Missionaries gained spiritual strength by condescending to serve Black "heathens" and reinforced a sense of Black religious inferiority as a result. From this vantage point, conversion itself became an act of cultural imperialism. Missionaries "converted [Black people] away from something, from a culture, tradition and heritage that was not of itself significant, valid or civilizing."[45] Missionaries endorsed Euro-American Catholicism as normative (even if they did so inadvertently) and degraded the distinctive cultural values of the African Americans they served.[46]

As we have seen, Father Lawrence Lucas also took aim at this spiritual crisis in his 1970 book *Black Priest/White Church: Catholics and Racism*, which served as an explosive manifesto for the Movement writ large. Lucas was a Black Catholic priest from Harlem who wrote openly of the heavy price Catholicism had cost him as a Black man. The book begins with a familiar figure for all those struggling with racial consciousness at the time, Malcolm X. Lucas recounted his first encounter with Malcolm. They ran into each other one morning in Harlem, Lucas "dressed in the Black-suit, Black-tie and white-shirt uniform of seminarians." Malcolm asked Lucas what he was about. Lucas said he was studying to be a Roman Catholic priest. Malcolm's reply changed Lucas's life. "Are you out of your God damned mind?"[47] This anecdote introduced the central theme of the book, namely the psychological toll of Catholicism. Lucas asserted that "the Church wrecks Black minds," by which he meant that "the Church encouraged [him] to think about [himself] and Black people the way white people think about Black people."[48] Lucas drew directly on Malcolm X and indirectly on the anticolonial psychoanalytical arguments of Fanon, arguing that "Catholicism has so bleached Negro Catholics that many of them today are whiter than white Catholics."[49] From Lucas's perspective, the only way to adequately address this spiritual crisis was to confront it head on. To this end he advocated developing a "theology that can justify what the Black Panthers are doing."[50]

In this way, the Black Catholic Movement was firmly situated in what contemporaries were beginning to call "Black Theology."[51]

The organizations and activists of the Black Catholic Movement primarily addressed themselves to these two problems, responding to white Catholic economic withdrawal from the inner city and the failure of the Church to embrace cultural (and psychological) Blackness. Yet to these two we could add a third explanation for the sudden waning of Black Catholic growth. The convergence of Vatican II with Black Power contributed to a number of changes in Black Catholic life and practice, as we have seen, launching a significant debate about what it meant to be Black and Catholic by the early 1970s. Many African Americans joined the Church in the first half of the twentieth century because they found Catholic ritual life compelling. But by the late 1960s, this ritual life was undergoing a significant transformation. This rapid shift in religious life seems to have been a contributing factor in declining Black Catholic growth and increasing departures from the Church. It was rarely mentioned in official Movement publications, perhaps because it conflicted with activists' attempt to integrate Black Power more fully into Catholic life. It was, however, recorded in journalistic treatments of the crisis.

Newsweek's 1974 article discussed how the attempt by some Black Catholics to incorporate African American Protestant practices in Catholic liturgical life led to the dissatisfaction and departure of others. The article reported that African Americans had converted to Catholicism in order to distance themselves from an "evangelical Protestant past." In this context, "imposing a Black flavor on their new church seems to cancel out the move." A white pastor from Atlanta was quoted saying that his Black parishioners had left "more demonstrative backgrounds . . . for a quieter form of worship."[52] In the 1977 *National Catholic Reporter* article titled "Black Catholics: Church Losing Ground," Robert McClory expanded this point to include Black Catholics in cities such as Chicago. He quoted John McDermott, the chairman of the Chicago-based National Catholic Conference on Interracial Justice, who noted an inadvertent consequence of the "ecumenical spirit and the call for openness [in the late 1960s]." "Black people perceived they could be somebody without joining the Catholic Church," he said. This would have directly undercut the arguments of Catholic missionaries who attempted to convert African Americans to the "One True Church." Father George Clements confirmed this point. "We have had a fantastic leakage [of Black Catholics]," Clements reflected.

> The people who were attracted [to the Church] years ago have gone their way. It wasn't so much racism that turned them off, it was change. They joined the church because it seemed a stable, timeless rock in a swirling sea. Suddenly the old traditions, including the Latin liturgy vanished.

"The anchor was gone," Clements concluded.[53]

All three of these explanations are necessary to understand the crisis facing Black Catholic communities across the country. Black Catholic parishes across the country experienced a decline due to a combination of white Catholic divestment from Black Catholic communities, the apparent unwillingness of a predominantly white Church to allow for "authentic Black" representations of Catholic life, and ironically, the dissatisfaction of some Black Catholics with the "authentic Black" rituals championed by the Black Catholic Movement. Recognition of these three simultaneous causes of the crisis helps to explain why Father Clements's parish thrived on the South Side of Chicago when so many other Black Catholic communities failed. Holy Angels embraced Black Power and exemplified the successes of the Black Catholic Movement at the same time that the parish maintained legacies of missionary Catholicism that were increasingly the subject of sharp criticisms. David Sutor, writing for *U.S. Catholic* in 1972, noted that "while Catholicism seems to be dying a slow death in the other Black communities in Chicago, George Clements and Paul Smith are keeping it alive in Grand Boulevard—with methods that liberal Catholics would describe as 'pre-Vatican II.'"[54]

Holy Angels and Black Catholic Self-Determination

Father George Clements assumed the pastorate of Holy Angels just as the national Black Catholic Movement emerged as a religious and political force in the U.S. Church. Controversy followed Clements wherever he went and, as we have seen, his inaugural controversy as Holy Angels pastor began in his first full year when he consecrated a shrine to St. Martin Luther King Jr. Cardinal Cody strongly objected to the shrine, as might be expected. From the archbishop's perspective, replacing a

Catholic saint with a Protestant minister was sacrilegious. Cody ordered Clements and his parishioners to return St. Anthony of Padua to his rightful place. Failure to comply, the archbishop threatened, would lead to Clements's suspension and the elimination of archdiocesan funding for Holy Angels School.[55] Unforeseen by Cardinal Cody, his ultimatum inadvertently set Father Clements and the Holy Angels parish community on the path to self-determination.

In response to the archbishop's threat, the new pastor convened a meeting that included not only Holy Angels parishioners but also parents and children from the school, many of whom were not Catholic. Clements read them Cody's letter and laid out the options available to the parish. The community decided not to comply with their archbishop's request. In fact, the community transformed the ultimatum into a teaching moment for Holy Angels schoolchildren. Students learned about civil disobedience and read speeches by Black heroes like Frederick Douglass. They discussed the necessity of conflict and struggle for securing civil rights in a democratic society. Teachers especially stressed the significance of economic independence for maintaining those rights.[56] Father Clements informed Cody that they would not move St. Martin Luther King from their parish shrine. If Cody wanted the portrait removed, Clements challenged, he would have to send someone to remove it, though Clements provocatively claimed that he could not guarantee the person's safety.[57] The archbishop canceled archdiocesan funding to the parish and school, but Holy Angels was prepared. The parish immediately launched a massive fund-raising campaign, gaining national fame and unexpected allies in the process.

The eventual success of Holy Angels School was rooted in this economic independence from the Archdiocese of Chicago. When Cardinal Cody reluctantly made Clements the pastor of Holy Angels in 1969, the parish and school were over $60,000 in debt. Clements later speculated that this was why Cody had assigned him there. The archbishop assumed the parish would collapse and close in the foreseeable future, which mitigated his misgivings about assigning this controversial activist-priest. Clements took the challenge in stride. His first goal was to cajole his parishioners to take ownership of their community, something Clements fondly remembers. After an offertory collection one Sunday Mass, the pastor received the baskets carrying the community's weekly donations.

Clements shook his head and shouted, "Not good enough!" He knew his parishioners struggled to support their families, but Holy Angels would only survive if they kept it alive. Clements instructed his ushers to lock the doors and said, "No one is leaving until we've raised enough money to keep our church afloat!" The baskets went around a second time. "This is good, but I know you can do better," Clements admonished again. The proceeds from a third and fourth collection eventually satisfied the pastor.[58] This pastor had a flair for the dramatic, but he was also skilled at more ordinary fund-raising. He organized benefits and took out advertisements in newspapers explaining the dire financial situation facing Holy Angels School. Hundreds responded. An Irish Catholic woman admitted she "did not understand some of the militancy of the Black movement, but did believe in equal rights." A hospitalized war veteran sent what little money he could "because he believes in Black self-determination."[59] Clements even received a letter of support from President Richard Nixon and arranged a benefit concert with the "Little Angels" kindergarten choir featuring Barbara Streisand.[60]

From one vantage point, this newfound economic independence at Holy Angels could certainly be understood as an inheritance of the Irish American parishioners who had preceded them. In the 1880s, a group of immigrant Irish Catholics moved into the Oakland neighborhood on the South Side of Chicago. The area was predominantly white, middle class, and Protestant at the time, so the newcomers to the neighborhood first worshipped secretly in an apartment above a furniture store. Faced with significant opposition from nativist Protestants who refused to sell land for the establishment of a Catholic parish, the growing congregation purchased small parcels of land in secret until they had acquired enough territory to found their parish.[61] Father Clements came across this story while searching the parish archives for inspiration. He discovered the original parish motto, "We Got It Together By Ourselves," and adopted it as a mantra for Black Catholic self-determination.

More directly, though, a particular tradition within the broader constellation of Black Power influenced Holy Angels in this regard. One of the most prevalent ideas connecting Black Power activists was that of "self-determination." Black communities would only gain social, political, and economic power, many activists argued, by banding together, much as the Irish, Poles, and Italians once had done. Elijah Muhammad and the Nation of Islam had exemplified this model of Black self-sufficiency for decades. Stokely Carmichael and Charles Hamilton made this argument in *Black Power* (1967). "Black Power recognizes—it must recognize—the ethnic basis of American politics as well as the power-oriented nature of American politics," they argued. "Black Power therefore calls for Black people to consolidate behind their own, so that they can bargain from a position of strength."[62] Father Clements directly made this comparison in 1973 when he admonished Black Catholics to "get up . . . and work!" Chicago was "filled with big fancy churches, big Catholic schools, orphanages and hospitals" because "poor immigrants . . . decided to get up in the morning and go to work." Black Muslims had produced so much for the same reason. Now it was time for Black Catholics to accomplish the same.[63]

The ultimate objective of community ownership extended beyond material benefits. Clements and other Black Catholic activists hoped to instill pride among Black Catholics. Black communities often viewed Catholic churches as white institutions. Even if congregations were entirely Black, those administrating the churches were almost always white priests and sisters. Once Black Catholic priests and laypeople controlled Holy Angels the church became theirs; it became a Black church in a new way. Holy Angels came to be known as the "Blackest" Catholic church in Chicago. This church "radiated Black Pride" in part due to its abundance of Black leadership: four Black priests and one Black religious brother served there by 1972.[64] But pride in Black ownership was fostered even more by the direct involvement of parishioners, students, and parents in the daily administration of the church and school. Students were expected to raise money for the day-to-day maintenance of the school each year. Parents participated in these fund-raisers and invested their time in a variety of ways. "Everyone pays something," one article noted in 1971. "A blind man answers the telephone in the school office to pay the tuition for his children. Mothers work as teachers' aides or in the school cafeteria or day care center if they can't afford tuition." A banner hung in the church proclaimed "we are called to create our own future" and this was borne out in the life of the church and school.[65] By Clements' fifth year as pastor, Holy Angels parish and school boasted financial self-sufficiency, a remarkable feat considering the social and economic circumstances of this "inner city" parish community.

Making Holy Angels "Relevant"

Holy Angels stood as a testament to what was possible when Black Catholic communities became self-sufficient. By rejecting archdiocesan subsidies, Holy Angels secured the freedom to make its own religious, political, and social decisions with minimal interference. Parishioners decided which saints they would honor, whether Baptist ministers could speak at church functions, and which political organizations they would support, regardless of whether or not the archbishop deemed them too radical. This allowed Holy Angels to assert their "relevance" in the Black community surrounding them.

"Relevance" was a buzzword for Black Catholic communities in this period. Black Catholics who embraced Black Power in the late 1960s and 1970s increasingly understood "relevance" as *the* attribute that determined whether any given priest or sister was fit to serve in a Black community. To quote Rosemary Jackson, the president of Chicago's Black Lay Catholic Caucus in 1976, Black Catholics sought to build "a church that is responsive to the people."[66] Regardless of whether they were Black or white, a religious leader was relevant if he or she stood on the side of racial justice and actively engaged the Black freedom struggles. This was evident in the protests surrounding Father Clements's promotion, when supporters claimed he was relevant to the Black community in ways Father Rollins Lambert could never be. This particular conception of relevance contrasted sharply with what many Black Catholics had experienced in the first half of the twentieth century. For decades missionaries emphasized the importance of the spiritual and eternal over the material and temporal. As the Midwest Clergy Conference on Negro Welfare reiterated in their literature as late as 1963, fighting for integration or a living wage paled in comparison to saving your immortal soul.[67] Providing social, economic, and political services for African Americans might provide a fruitful ground for conversions, but social activism and the struggle for racial justice were not ends in themselves. A significant minority contingent of liberal Catholics was committed to interracial cooperation as early as the 1930s, but most Catholics (white and Black) were not actively involved in ongoing Black freedom struggles. From the perspective of Black Catholic activists like Clements, it was time for the Church to enter Black freedom struggles and enter on the side of Black Power.

The Holy Angels community made sure to make their church relevant. Their pastor, of course, had encouraged this since he had been involved in Black Chicago's social and political struggles for years now. Clements had already demonstrated his willingness to engage in struggles for civil rights and Black Power prior to his pastorate and this only intensified during his tenure at Holy Angels. His continuous involvement with the Afro-American Patrolmen's League (AAPL) demonstrated as much. Police harassment and brutality were among the most pressing issues facing African American urban communities in the late 1960s and 1970s. Police violence sparked riots in cities across the United States and catalyzed political mobilization.[68] The Chicago Police Department (CPD) was particularly infamous in regard to overt racist practices. Historian Jakobi Williams notes, for example, that thirty-nine Black Chicagoans were killed by police officers in 1969 alone without a single case brought to court or indictment filed. One study of the CPD's use of force in 1969–1970 revealed that African Americans were "six times more likely to be killed by a police officer than were whites."[69] We have already seen how Father Clements aided the efforts of Black police officers in their establishment of the AAPL, supporting them in their mission to establish "respect for Black manhood, Black womanhood and Black pride within the law."[70] Father Clements, speaking for the AAPL in 1969, even dreamed that one day Black police might "operate in the community unarmed."[71]

The activism of the Afro-American Patrolmen's League soon brought Black police officers and their allies like Clements into direct confrontation with Irish American Catholics who dominated the force (not to mention city governance). The AAPL hoped to establish Black self-determination in policing by, in part, challenging white Catholic power. The AAPL began to directly confront Chicago's "Irish Conspiracy," as they called it, in early 1970. Father Clements publicly condemned the Irish monopoly "on 'key' city and county governmental posts."[72] "Black policemen have no hostility to the Irish," Clements clarified. But they did wish to "share more equally in power. . . . As long as one ethnic group is in virtually complete control of the city, all the other groups will remain powerless." Here Clements echoed the interpretation of Black Power as a politics of ethnic solidarity, the one popularized by Carmichael and Hamilton in their book *Black Power*.[73] With the support of a Black priest who had already demonstrated a knack for Catholic iconoclasm, the AAPL protested this Irish Catholic monopoly with a St. Patrick's Day protest. Father Clements and Reggie Robinson designed a Black St. Patrick's Day celebration, one that would be "more or less diametrically opposed" to the city's famous State Street parade.[74] With a keen sense of symbolism, an AAPL patrolman helped dye the South Side Washington Park lagoon black at the same time the Chicago River was dyed green. This Black St. Patrick celebration was meant to illuminate "the corrupt, naked power of the Irish people in Chicago" and demonstrate that "green is beautiful but Black is beautiful, too."[75]

The alliance between Father George Clements and Reggie Robinson, Holy Angels pastor and parishioner, and the Afro-American Patrolmen's League exemplified the Black Catholic ideal of "relevance." For Clements and Robinson, Black freedom struggles were not merely "compatible" with Black Catholic life, they were essential elements in it. Robinson remained an active Holy Angels parishioner and a member of the Holy Angels school board throughout his political and legal struggles with the Chicago Police Department. Both Robinson and Clements served as liaisons connecting the Holy Angels community to the broader social and political struggles of Black Chicago.[76]

The assertion of Black Catholic relevance to the broader Black community extended beyond ostensibly "political" organizations as well. As he had already demonstrated dramatically with his shrine to a Baptist minister, Father Clements was committed to reorienting the relationship between Holy Angels and other (non-Catholic) Black religious institutions. Clements thought Black Catholic churches ought not to be considered Black enclaves in a white church but rather as part of "the Black Church." Clements had already marched alongside Black Baptists and Methodists in civil rights protests. As pastor of Holy Angels he now set about resituating the parish in Chicago's wider Black religious community. He participated in a panel discussion at St. Philip Lutheran Church in December 1969 on the "Revolution in the Black Church," for instance. He joined the renowned Black Baptist preacher and author, Rev. D. E. King, for the dedication of his new Monumental Baptist church in 1970, a service that brought Black Catholics and Black Baptists together in a historic ecumenical gathering, with choirs joined together in song and a Catholic priest preaching from a Baptist pulpit.[77] Clements joined

Figure 5.1. Portrait of Father George H. Clements, Pastor of Holy Angels Catholic Church. Courtesy of the Celano Archives of the Sisters of St. Francis, Dubuque, Iowa.

various Black Protestant ministers for ecumenical services at St. John Church-Baptist, which hosted the Interdenominational Ministers Alliance in 1974.[78] Clements's willingness to go beyond Catholic boundaries to forge alliances with other religious leaders was not limited to ecumenical services. Holy Angels often honored Black leaders who were not Catholic. Most famously, a likeness of the Honorable Elijah Muhammad stood before the altar in February 1975 as Holy Angels parish paid homage to the passing of the Nation of Islam's founder.[79] When parishioners celebrated Black Baptist ministers and civil rights leaders such as Jesse Jackson, not to mention Black Muslims like Elijah Muhammad and Malcolm X, they signaled a new sense of Black Catholic identity and how Black Catholics related to other Black religious traditions.

Making the Church "Black"

This impetus to make Holy Angels relevant to the wider Black community, to remake it as a Black parish rather than a Catholic parish that happened to be Black, was one the Chicago community shared with the national movement. The Black Catholic Movement hoped to make the Catholic Church in the United States relevant to Black people. From the perspective of the National Office for Black Catholics and other activist organizations, Catholic churches had to become "Black" if they were to survive in Black communities at all. But this begged a question. What did it mean to be "Black" in the first place? Black Catholic activists, as we will see, had a very specific understanding of Blackness, one that drew heavily on the Black cultural nationalist and pan-Africanist traditions prevailing in the Black Power era. They argued that African Americans shared a cultural heritage, ways of knowing and living in the world, that connected them to Black people across Africa and the Americas. The founder of the National Black Sisters' Conference, Sister Martin De Porres Grey, attempted to explain this to a conference of mostly white Josephite priests in 1971. Citing scholar Theresa Perry, Grey said, "Black people understand Blackness as that unique manner of speaking, writing, dancing, singing, cooking, dressing, drawing, acting and behaving, which is innate to Black people in American [sic] and characteristic of people of African descent living anywhere in the West." "Blackness," Grey concluded, "is the sum total of all the ideas, attitudes, actions and creations that stem from the African's attempt to accommodate himself to, dig this, to integrate into, co-exist with, and separate from the West."[80]

The Black Catholic Movement stressed the religious content of "Blackness." Activists argued that African Americans were a spiritual people who were spiritual in specific ways passed on by their ancestors. Brother Davis called this special attunement to the sacred "SOUL." This one word provided Davis with "a concise description of [the] fundamental world-view and life style of Black people, as it has been retained from our African heritage."[81] "Black people came to this country as a *spiritual* people ... [who] had formulated a clear and precise philosophical/theological construct of life which integrated the physical and spiritual, the sacred and secular."[82] SOUL also identified the fundamental differences between Black African and white European spiritualities, at least from the perspective of Black cultural nationalists. Juxtaposed with cold and cerebral white religion, Black spirituality was experienced "with the fullness of one's being: the head, the heart, the body, the hands, the feet, the SOUL."[83]

Activists laid claim to a distinctive Black cultural heritage and argued that Black Catholic life should be situated firmly in it. This represented a direct response to the "missionary mentality" addressed above. Black Catholics in the Black Catholic Movement asserted that practices long understood to be "universal" were, in fact, rooted in the cultural specificity of Euro-American Catholic communities. Sister Jamie Phelps, a Black Dominican sister and Black Catholic theologian, illustrates this point. Reflecting back on her experiences as a sister in Chicago, Phelps recalls how white priests left Black churches for the suburbs in the late 1960s and 1970s. They fled because "that's where they were comfortable and that's where they thought they had 'real' Catholicism.... [In other words, they] did not realize that their Catholicism was Irish. It was so natural." And it had been naturalized for African Americans as well. Phelps remembered being aware that Irish, Italian, German, and Polish practices surrounded her growing up. But, as a child, she never thought, "Well, wait a moment, I'm African American.... What about my culture?" Instead, she constantly met "the idea that it was strange for me to be Black and Catholic. There was always the assumption, by the Catholics, that I was probably Baptist and if I weren't, then, what was wrong with you? Why aren't you Baptist?" This served as a subtle form of alienation and racism. In this sense, Black Catholic activists like Sister Jamie Phelps simply demanded the same thing the Irish and other white Catholics already had: the freedom to express their unique religious heritage.[84]

The Black Catholic Movement connected this unique heritage to "the Black Church" as a tradition. Activists argued that Black Catholics needed to conceive of themselves as part of the Black Church, regardless of the fact that they were members of an institution that, at least in the United States, was largely white. Over the course of the 1970s, Movement activists developed their own interpretation of the Black Church that connected the cultural heritage of the Black Church with Africa and the legacies of African religion. Their particular interpretation was shaped by the relationship the National Office for Black Catholics forged with a new program in Black Church Studies at Colgate Rochester Divinity School. This program was born in the wave of student revolutions that swept college campuses in the late 1960s and early 1970s.[85] In 1969 Black seminarians occupied buildings at Rochester Seminary and demanded the establishment of "Black Church Studies."[86] When the seminary relented, they hired Rev. Dr. Henry H. Mitchell, a Black Baptist minister, as the inaugural professor and director of the Martin Luther King Program in Black Church Studies. The program aspired to train a generation of "master pastors" skilled in the preaching, praying, and singing traditions of the Black Church.

It is worth pausing here to note that this Black Church Studies program reminds us that concerns over the compatibility of "authentic Blackness" and Christianity were by no means limited to Catholics. Black Protestants who engaged Black Power, Mitchell among them, also had to confront the Black nationalist critique that Christianity was "the white man's religion." Scholar-activists responded to this critique by reimagining the history and nature of Black religion in the United States and across the African diaspora. Ministers and theologians such as Albert Cleage and James Cone articulated an explicitly "Black" theology, which reinterpreted Jesus as a Black revolutionary and challenged Black churches to engage in political struggle on the side of the oppressed. The "Black Manifesto" published by the Black National Economic Conference in 1969, which identified Christian and Jewish complicity in white supremacy and demanded reparations from white churches and synagogues, was one of the most famous examples of this broad Black theological impetus.[87] Religious historians including Vincent Harding, Charles Long, Lawrence Levine, Albert Raboteau, and Gayraud Wilmore further contributed to this historical-theological project, writing landmark studies that directly linked African and African American religious cultures. Mitchell was part of this wider context and developed the Martin Luther King Program in direct consultation with Harding and Long, rooting his conception of the Black Church in West Africa. He argued that West Africans had distinctive ways of being religious that they brought with them across the Middle Passage and into the Americas. These practices had survived the holocaust of slavery and contributed to the formation of the Black Church. As a result, fellows in the program were expected to travel to Western Nigeria and Ghana, and to the Sea Islands off the coast of South Carolina, as well as to Jamaica and Haiti in search of firsthand experience of the origins of Black religion.[88]

This particular historical-theological conception of "the Black Church" remained highly influential for Black Catholics over the next decades, especially as Mitchell played an important advisory role for the National Office for Black Catholics. In the process of understanding these Black Church legacies, Black Catholic activists forged relationships not only with Black Protestants like Mitchell, but also with Black Catholics across what could be called a Black Catholic diaspora. These relationships came alive in the pages of *Freeing the Spirit*, the magazine of Black liturgy published by the National Office for Black Catholics. This quarterly publication created space for theoretical and practical conversations about the nature of African and African diasporic religion as well as how to introduce Black Catholic churches to their Black Church heritage. The first issue featured a dialogue between the NOBC editors and three African priests: the Tanzanian Father Alkuin Chinguku and the Nigerian Fathers J. Kunirum Osia and Chris Edema Boyo. These priests were involved in efforts on the African continent to integrate African religious expressions into African Catholic churches. They collectively criticized the Catholic colonialism of European missionaries and insisted on the fact that Africans were "basically a spiritual and religious people."[89] They then went on to discuss specific ways to Africanize Christianity. Another issue featured research by a Haitian Jesuit, Michael

Figure 5.2. The cover of *Freeing the Spirit: The Magazine of Black Liturgy Published by the National Office for Black Catholics* 1, no. 2 (Spring 1972). Courtesy of David J. Endres/*U.S. Catholic Historian.*

Laguerre, on the subject of drums and dance in Haitian Christian liturgies. "Most indigenous African religions are dancing religions," Laguerre argued, and the drum plays a critical role in communicating the "cosmic rhythm."[90] While he admitted that drum dance served a very different purpose in diasporic religions like Vodou (such as inducing "rapture" or a "trance-like state"), he also identified the numerous Church precedents for drums and dance in religious celebrations, arguing for the recovery of religious choreography in Catholic worship.[91] These conversations between priests and scholars across the Black Catholic diaspora profoundly shaped the ways the Black Catholic Movement imagined African religion, the Black Church, and the relationship Black Catholics had with both.

Black Power Meets Missionary Catholicism in Chicago

On the glossy pages of publications it might appear that the Black Catholic Movement endorsed Blackness over and against the whiteness of Catholicism—in fact, some Black Catholic activists even said as much. However, the degree of separation between Black Power on the one hand and the legacies of missionary-era Catholicism on the other were never quite that clear in the lives of local Black Catholic communities like Holy Angels. This South Side Chicago community exemplified Black Catholic self-determination and asserted its relevance to the broader Black community. Parishioners and pastor alike understood their community to be a *Black* church. But Holy Angels also challenged widely held assumptions about what Black Power was supposed to look like. The success of Holy Angels, its school in particular, was predicated precisely on the combination of Black Power contemporaries and the missionary Catholic past.

From the early 1970s into the 1980s, Holy Angels succeeded in educating young Black people in the "inner city" where numerous public and private schools failed on a regular basis. Students at Holy Angels performed at or above national averages for reading and mathematics, prepared for the challenge of elite high schools and colleges. The school accomplished this with the help of strategies that challenged reigning educational norms. David Sutor took note of this in his six-part special report on "The Church and Inner City Schools" for the archdiocesan

New World in 1972. Sutor described Holy Angels as "a Catholic school of a kind that some people think no longer exists: strongly orthodox with rigid rules laid down to govern student conduct, parental involvement, and religious participation by students and parents."[92] The majority of Holy Angels students were not Catholic, yet Holy Angels School insisted that non-Catholic students and parents attend instructions and participate in Mass. Compulsory religious instructions appeared increasingly discordant with the ecumenical impulse among many Catholics in the years following the Second Vatican Council.[93] Nevertheless, requisite religious education for both students and parents was often one of the aspects of Catholic education most valued by Black parents.[94] In this way Holy Angels School represented a creative negotiation of Black nationalism with the "Chicago Plan," inspired by Black Power and Catholic missionaries alike. The school grew in fame for integrating Black pride into the entire curriculum at the same time it gained the reputation of being "the most conservative school in the Archdiocese."[95]

The school's methods for success became the primary talking point for contemporary commentators. Jack Slater, writing for *Ebony*, remarked in his article "The School That Beat the Odds" that "several strains of old-fashioned conservatism have been blended ingeniously with a dash of Black militancy."[96] Both Slater and David Sutor took note of Clements's use of "radical methods" to maintain what was described as one of the most conservative Catholic schools in the archdiocese.[97] Journalists struggled to explain just how a "militant" Black Power priest established such a traditional Catholic school, not to mention how the school succeeded in educating poor Black children where so many others had failed. This combination and its success had as much to do with the dynamic leadership of the school's principal and assistant principal as it did with the parish's pastor. Father Clements spearheaded the financial self-sufficiency of Holy Angels that established the conditions for Black Catholic self-determination. But it was a Black priest and a white sister who successfully combined Black Power with Catholic pedagogy to produce one of the highest performing Catholic schools in the country.

When Clements assumed control of Holy Angels he replaced the school's white principal, a School Sister of St. Francis, with Black layman Eldridge Freeman. Clements thought Black youth needed to experience strong Black male leadership. His initial choice proved a dismal failure, however. The school declined in discipline and academic performance and by March 1970 was on the verge of financial collapse. It was clear to all involved, especially the sisters who taught at Holy Angels, that Freeman was not qualified.[98] Clements set about securing a replacement, eventually offering the position to Father Paul Smith. Born and raised Catholic in Baltimore, Maryland, in 1931, Smith bore the brunt of Catholic segregation and racism throughout his life. He maintained an interest in becoming a priest, despite being rejected by all three Catholic high schools in the area because he was Black. He went on to become one of the first Black graduates of Loyola College in Baltimore and after numerous rejections the bishop of Alexandria, Louisiana, accepted his application to the priesthood. In 1962 he was the first Black man from Baltimore to be ordained a priest and eventually he earned a Master's Degree in English and Administration from the University of Scranton. Despite the support of his bishop, Smith continued to meet resistance from white Catholics. When Smith was assigned as principal of a recently integrated high school in 1969 in Alexandria, Louisiana, white parents fiercely objected. It was at this point that Father Clements approached Smith about the possibility of leading Holy Angels School. The pastor "pulled no punches" with Smith, explaining that the school was situated in an "inner-city ghetto." This was precisely why Clements sought a principal capable of instilling a sense of Black pride, strict discipline, and high academic performance among the students. Smith accepted and served the Holy Angels community for the rest of his life.[99]

Smith freely admitted that his educational philosophy was "unabashedly old-fashioned," as was his personal practice of Catholicism.[100] He refused to apologize to critics who claimed Holy Angels School was far too conservative in an age of liberalizing education. "The philosophy and goal of Holy Angels School," he once told a reporter, "is to proclaim the dignity and intrinsic worth of every human being, believing that, through the operation of the intellect, a person is able to achieve one's ultimate self; is able to love God, one's self and others; is able to choose the Good that makes for a full and wholesome life benefiting one's self and those one may encounter." These goals were especially critical for the needs of the inner city. One way Smith attempted to instill Black pride and dignity was through the enforcement of strict discipline. Students formed lines to move through the halls of the school. He insisted that students use "the King's English" when speaking. Teachers demanded silence and cleanliness in the classroom, enforced by corporal punishment and expulsion. All students, even kindergarteners, received daily homework assignments. Smith worked to further extend this discipline by instituting a twelve-month school year in 1972, so that there would be no month in the calendar when students were not under the supervision of the school at some time.[101]

Sister Helen Strueder implemented this philosophy. Strueder, a descendant of German immigrants, was born in a farm community outside Milwaukee in 1939. When she was a young student she attended a school administered by the School Sisters of St. Francis. She joined the community in 1957 with the firm desire to serve in a Black community. After earning a Master's Degree in Counseling and Administration from DePaul University, Strueder was assigned to Holy Angels in 1960 and quickly became indispensible to the school under the leadership of Father Joseph Richards and Sister Hortensia.[102] She maintained a strictly disciplined classroom, even with the older students, and won the affection of the parish. Her reputation preceded her and one of Father Paul Smith's first acts as principal was to request that she serve as his assistant principal, a position she held until she became principal herself in 1995. Smith and Strueder worked well throughout their twenty-four-year tenure as principal and assistant. Strueder described the relationship between them as "hand-in-glove"; they had a high level of trust in each other, often holding meetings with parents and children together.[103] She also helped to recruit qualified teachers from across the country. The numbers of women religious had dwindled and many sought to move out of the inner city. In response, Father Smith and Sister Strueder appealed to a variety of religious and secular teachers. They invited teachers from Canada and Ireland, appealed to priests and women religious across the country, and encouraged all interested and qualified teachers to apply. The result was a diverse staff, made up of Black and white, lay and religious teachers.[104]

Together the Black priest and white sister managed to incorporate Black Power into the daily routines of Holy Angels School. They did not employ any "special Black Studies." Instead, Black pride became "a way of life." Children learned Black history and talked about being Black in every class.[105] Each day students sang the Black national anthem and saluted the Black liberation flag alongside the American flag.[106] The school hosted a Black Panther rally for community control of the police and the students elected to offer a memorial service for Panther leader Fred Hampton after his assassination. Father George Clements maintained an unapologetic stance when it came to the school's commitment to Black Power. He paraphrased Malcolm X, saying, "we don't catch hell because we are Catholics . . . but because we are *Black*."[107]

Clements, Smith, and Strueder successfully demonstrated, however, that this emphasis on Black pride was not mutually exclusive with a Catholic education. Clements insisted, for example, "no one here ever apologizes for being Black or Catholic."[108] This was borne out in the daily curriculum of the school. Every morning students composed answers to two questions, one about a famous Black person and one about Catholicism. "Who is Angela Davis?" and "What is a Sacrament?" "Who was Mahalia Jackson?" and "What is the Trinity?"[109] Both Black and Catholic content were integrated into the daily curriculum.

At the same time as Black pride was a way of life, then, Holy Angels School also remained committed to a particular style of Catholic parochial education. Smith and Strueder's educational philosophy was often labeled "conservative" or "old-school" because they resisted the liberalizing trends sweeping across public and private schools in the United States. The school embraced large class sizes, rote memorization, and corporal punishment when educational theorists had long abandoned them as antiquated and ineffective.[110] The teachers taught large classrooms of thirty or forty students with a "chalk-and-talk" style reminiscent of the religious instruction classes of missionaries, combining chalkboard lectures with "a relentless series of drills both in reading and math." Teachers imposed strict discipline, which included mandatory uniforms, "expulsion for disrespect to teachers, fines for tardiness and even paddling."[111] By the end of the decade, Holy Angels was famous as a "school that blends perhaps the toughest disciplinary standards in town—for both pupils and parents—with pride, insistence on order, high academic standards, parental involvement, and a 220-day classroom year."[112] This sometimes provoked criticism from local educators, who argued that Holy Angels "repress[ed] the children's freedom." But from the perspective of Holy Angels' pastor and principals, comprehensive order and discipline were a requisite for their Black students whose lives outside school were defined by "turmoil almost constantly—muggings, disorder, and confusion." Holy Angels represented one place where parents could send their children and expect "some kind of order, some kind of discipline." It served as an "oasis in the midst of turmoil."[113]

Holy Angels School bore the unique legacies of missionary Catholicism beyond these disciplinary and pedagogical approaches as well. Parents of non-Catholic students were obligated to attend religious instructions and Sunday Mass weekly. The rationale behind this arrangement was that Catholic schools educated families, not just children. As we have seen, the "Chicago Plan" contributed to tens of thousands of African American conversions in the 1940s and 1950s. Vatican II posed a serious challenge to this requirement, however. The Chicago Plan was designed as a missionary strategy to convert African Americans to the "One True Church," premised on the widespread Catholic belief that their Church was the only path to eternal salvation. The Second Vatican Council's "Decree on Ecumenism," *Unitatis Redintegratio*, contradicted this claim and stated that "the separated [Protestant and Orthodox Christian] Churches and Communities as such, though . . . deficient in some respects, have been by no means deprived of significance and importance in the mystery of salvation."[114] This decree encouraged Catholics to forge relationships with other Christian communities in the late 1960s and 1970s. In this context, requiring non-Catholic parents to attend Mass and religious instruction increasingly appeared out of step with the ecumenical spirit of the Council. Nevertheless, while Holy Angels parish and school remained under the leadership of Father Clements, Father Smith, and Sister Strueder, "every parent and student is required to attend church on Sunday [and] all non-Catholic parents with children in school are required to take instructions in the Catholic tradition."[115] More notable still, Catholic and non-Catholic African Americans in Holy Angels' Grand Boulevard neighborhood both embraced the Catholic identity of their school. They wanted sisters teaching in their children's classrooms ("sister's rooms," as they were called) and they wanted the sisters to wear habits.

Liberal Catholics would probably label these requirements "pre-Vatican II," as David Sutor noted. But this community disrupted attempts to categorize Catholicism neatly as either "pre–" or "post–Vatican

II," as either "conservative" or "liberal Catholic." On the one hand, the Second Vatican Council allowed for the very possibility of a school like Holy Angels. Vatican II permitted Catholics to take on active roles in the modern world and encouraged Catholics to form relationships across denominational boundaries. This allowed Black Catholics to enter into Black Power activism, collaborate with Protestants, and draw inspiration from the Nation of Islam. On the other hand, the Black Catholic Movement posed significant challenges to the postconciliar Church in the United States as well. Many Black Catholic activists remained deeply skeptical of white Catholic liberalism. Father Paul Smith was no exception. He argued, "[T]he church is still trying to impose a white-style church, with all its liberalism, freedom from rules and obligations, and freedom to choose." All that accomplished, according to Smith, was the emptying of churches. Smith argued that obligations sustained Black Catholic communities. He pointed to the young men and women who joined the Black Panthers and Black Muslims precisely because these groups made "severe demands on their followers" and expected "unswerving obedience."[116] Father Clements shared Smith's appraisal. Clements claimed that both conservative and liberal Catholics failed to grasp the real reasons for Holy Angels' success. Conservatives approved of the school for "all the wrong reasons." "You like us because we don't take handouts and because you see us as pulling ourselves up by the bootstraps," Clements said, "yet many of you are still denying the human rights and dignity of Black people." Meanwhile, he interpreted liberal Catholic calls for integration as veiled attempts to control Black communities. "I've taken my oath of allegiance," Clements proclaimed, "and that's to the Black community—not to our oppressors."[117]

There were other ways Black Catholics and the Holy Angels community fit uneasily onto the liberal-conservative Catholic spectrum emerging in the wake of the Second Vatican Council. The central role religious sisters maintained in the Holy Angels community served as yet another legacy of the parish's missionary past that persisted alongside Black Power. The School Sisters of St. Francis still staffed Holy Angels School in 1969 when Father Clements arrived, but the lives of religious sisters underwent dramatic changes in the 1960s. Regulations on clothing, housing, and the role of sisters in the parish had changed. For the first time in their lives, Black schoolchildren saw the hair and necks and arms and legs of these sisters whose habits, till that point, had contributed to an aura of mystery and authority. Sisters had also gained greater independence from the life of the parish. Many of the sisters at Holy Angels moved out of their convent and into apartments in the 1970s, sometimes commuting from other areas of the city to teach at Holy Angels. This posed significant problems for Fathers Clements and Smith, who had a particular vision for the role of women religious in the parish.

These Black Catholic priests envisioned a school staffed by "faith-filled" sisters and habits played a substantive role in establishing the presence of "faith," as Clements and Smith conceived it. Habits moreover established the role of sisters in the Black community, another legacy of the Catholic missionary past. "Blacks want the Sisters in habits," Smith insisted. "A white nun with a habit can safely walk through sections [of the community] that even I might hesitate to walk in," Smith continued. "People know who she is and know that she's part of the community."[118] More than just habits, Clements insisted that sisters attend Sunday Mass at Holy Angels even when they lived in apartments close to an hour's drive away. From Sister Helen Strueder's perspective, this was one of the things that made Clements so "traditional." She worked to reconcile Father Clements's progressive (one could even say radical) political positions with his religious perspective that was clearly influenced by both preconciliar and postconciliar Catholicism. She insisted that Clements was "traditional," not "conservative," resisting the attempt to position him on one or the other end of the liberal-conservative binary."[119] One thing is certain. Clements saw no contradiction between his political and cultural commitments to Black Power and his more "traditional" personal practice of Catholicism, rooted in his experiences as a boy in the Corpus Christi parish that built the Living Stations of the Cross into a national phenomenon.[120]

Another alignment between Black Power and missionary Catholicism was on the subject of masculinity, patriarchy, and the place of the family in the Black community. Enrollment in Holy Angels School involved the entire family. Parents were expected to attend Mass with their children on Sundays, to raise money for the school through candy drives and banquets, to take religious instruction courses, to attend regular Parent-Teacher Association meetings, and to supervise their children's homework, among other responsibilities. Failure to comply with these requirements resulted first in fines and eventually in the expulsion of their children from the school. This vision of familial education was deeply engrained in the Catholic educational tradition. Missionaries insisted that non-Catholic parents attend religious instruction, lest their ignorance and negligence at home undo the work of priests and sisters. Moreover, familial education took on added meaning in urban Black communities. The "Black family" had become a politically charged concept by the 1970s. In an attempt to explain the impoverishment of urban Black communities, Assistant Secretary of Labor Daniel Patrick Moynihan, a Catholic raised in New York City's poor Hell's Kitchen neighborhood, published a study titled *The Negro Family: The Case for National Action* in 1965. "The Moynihan Report" argued that the legacies of slavery and Jim Crow left Black families bereft of father figures, leaving them ill-equipped to overcome the obstacles on the path to economic and political opportunity.[121] This report sparked a vociferous debate over whether Moynihan was effectively blaming Black women for the plight of Black families. A number of Black Power leaders articulated an analogous argument in those same years. They argued that white supremacy had disempowered and emasculated Black men. One prominent objective for some Black Power activists was the restoration of Black men to their rightful place as the leaders of Black families and communities.[122]

Father Clements and Father Smith's commitment to educating the entire family had, at its heart, this Black Power impetus to restore Black manhood to what they perceived to be its rightful place of power.[123] Their insistence on the centrality of the family—and the significance of the father within it—was evident in the Holy Angels School rules and regulations, which included a subsection on "Fathers & Male Guardians." The school aimed to "build the Black Community and consequently the family unit," which involved "the head of the household." If there was "a father or male guardian in the home," this man was "responsible for all school business." Students facing disciplinary action could not "return to school except [if] the father brings them."[124]

This "daddy-policy" reinforced gender norms regarding the proper roles of men and women in the family, reflecting the Catholic theological tradition known as gender "complementarity" that many Black nationalists shared. But more than that, this masculinist and patriarchal policy showed striking disrespect for working single mothers who struggled to enroll their children in private Catholic school. It characterized Black women as irrational and incapable of properly raising disciplined, high-achieving children. If a student was suspended, "Daddy has to take off from work, so he's mad at me when he comes. Mother emotes and dawdles and talks about 'her baby' being suspended. Daddy is no-nonsense. We have no further trouble with the child."[125] This policy echoed arguments employed by the Moynihan Report as well as some Black Power activists insofar as it insinuated that Black men must take control of their families in order for African Americans to overcome adversity. It also resonated with the early-twentieth-century missionary policy that good Catholic education is necessarily familial, one that involved and educated entire families, not just children. In these family policies, as well as in the daily curriculum and pedagogy, Holy Angels School represented the creative negotiation of Black Power with the legacies of missionary Catholicism.

Black Catholic Missionaries and the Rise of Black Catholicism

The national Black Catholic Movement was not without its own ironies. Black Catholic activists hoped to Africanize and African Americanize Black Catholic life across the United States in the 1970s. Their insistence that Black Catholics worship in "authentic Black" ways opened with a comprehensive reinterpretation and critique of the practices reigning in Black Catholic churches as "white." For decades missionaries had inculcated African American converts in traditional devotional practices such as the Latin Mass and Eucharistic adoration, the rosary and the stations of the cross. Influenced by Black Power, activists now argued that these disciplines had accomplished "the acculturation of Black Catholics to white Catholic religious expression as the right Catholic way." Brother Joseph Davis and the nationally renowned Black Catholic liturgist Father Clarence Joseph Rivers both noted that Black converts had been chastised if they "spontaneously answered 'Amen!' 'Yes, Lord!' 'Praise God!' to a moving sermon by the priest preacher." Missionaries admonished converts when they expressed emotions "in the Protestant way."[126]

These, at least, were the remembrances of Black Catholic activists. But as we have seen, not all Black Catholics agreed with Davis and Rivers's assessment. The perceived "quiet" of the Catholic Mass and the emotional resonance of Catholic devotionalism led tens of thousands of African Americans to become Catholic. Black Catholics enthusiastically embraced the Living Stations of the Cross, to take one especially dramatic example, and performed it annually for thirty years not in spite of but because it expressed a different way of being Black and religious in the United States, different at least from the evangelical Protestant practices more prevalent in Black communities. The legacies left behind by Catholic missionaries posed a serious problem for the Black Catholic Movement quite simply because many Black Catholics resisted the Movement's insistence that there was one way of being Black and religious that could be considered "authentic," or that one could be Catholic and worship in a Protestant manner.

Father Lawrence Lucas captures the conflict between these two positions in a passage in *Black Priest/White Church* (1970). No one was more withering in his attack on the "whiteness" of Catholic practices than Lucas. He argued that the price African Americans had to pay to become Catholic was to "become a reincarnation of a white middle-class American."[127] "Negro Catholics" had been "bleached," "whitewashed," and imprisoned in self-hatred. One anecdote Lucas offered was that of a Black Divine Word missionary, Father James LaChapelle, who served St. Elizabeth parish on the South Side of Chicago and had actively participated in the movement supporting Father George Clements in 1969. When he preached on the Black freedom struggles, however, he often faced criticism from his Black parishioners. Lucas reported that on one occasion, a parishioner pulled him aside after Sunday Mass. "Father, you speak well. You lift us up to the heavens," the parishioner began. "But talk to us of sanctification. Talk to us about Jesus Christ and heaven. Don't tell us about being Black. Every time you say the word 'Black,' you bring way down all those beautiful things you are talking about."[128] When LaChapelle conducted a survey at St. Elizabeth, he found that the elders of St. Elizabeth associated Black Power and Black pride with:

> Disrespect and vulgar language.... To rob, rape, murder Black and white indiscriminately. To bust whites over the head because they are white. To loot and burn Black and white stores indiscriminately.... To be dirty and stinky. To wear the natural. To be loud and undisciplined.[129]

For many Black Catholics, especially those raised in the heyday of convert communities of the 1940s and 1950s, Black Power politics and Black nationalist practices had no place in Catholic churches. The vast majority of Black Catholics were not convinced that the cultural nationalism of Black Power was entirely compatible with Catholic life. Many resisted the cultural turn toward "Blackness" and concomitant attempts to incorporate Black church practices into Catholic worship, in large part because they had converted to Catholicism to distance themselves from these very practices.

Activists in the Black Catholic Movement, Lucas among them, consistently cited the absence of Black cultural nationalism in Catholic churches as a prime cause for Black Catholic decline. They made a generational argument, insisting that young Black men and women hoped to root their religious lives in distinctively "Black" traditions and, finding that Catholic churches had little to offer in this regard, began to leave in droves.[130] This was one reason activists offered in defense of their mission to make churches Black. In other words, alongside the struggle for Black Catholic self-determination, the Black Catholic Movement pursued a more elusive objective.

Throughout the 1970s, the NOBC and others in the Black Catholic Movement worked to convince Black Catholics that Black distinctiveness did not contradict Catholic universality. This point recurred throughout publications, documents, and anecdotes. For instance, the first issue of *Freeing the Spirit* was dedicated to "those Blacks who still have not found themselves; who have not discovered their *Beautiful Black Self.*"[131] Brother Joseph M. Davis acknowledged his frustration with these resistant Black Catholics. He reflected on the many times he was asked "why [do Black Catholics need] a Black Catholic organization?" Another question usually followed swiftly: "Are you advocating a separate, Black, Catholic, Church?" Davis had come to expect this accusation from white Catholics, but these questions came just as forcefully from Black Catholics.[132]

The National Office for Black Catholics consequently devoted much of its energy to evangelizing within Black Catholic communities. Activists hoped to convert Black Catholics to their own understanding of "Blackness." The Black Catholic Movement proselytized a particular understanding of Black identity in Black Catholic communities. Critical of the claim that Euro-American Catholic norms represented "real" Catholicism, the Black Catholic Movement promulgated its own conception of what comprised "real" Blackness, drawing on the Black cultural nationalism prevalent at the time. This missionary impetus was evident in the NOBC's 1974 pastoral letter "Black Perspectives on Evangelization of the Modern World." The NOBC insisted that evangelization among African Americans must "start where revelation begins—in the culture and ethos of the people."[133] This letter challenged the "distorted perspective" of missionaries who "confused the proclamation of the Gospel with promulgation of their own [white] culture."[134] The NOBC sought to root evangelization in Black communities in Black cultural heritage, even if many Black Catholics did not necessarily identify with that heritage. The irony of this position, of course, was that it effectively made the Black Catholic Movement a missionary movement. Activists challenged what they understood to be the white cultural imperialism of Catholic missionaries at the same time that they promoted their own essential conception of "Blackness."

As the National Office for Black Catholics worked to spread Black religious identity and practices in Black Catholic communities across the United States, the missionary efforts of the Black Catholic Movement were among its most enduring legacies. The NOBC established a Department of Culture and Worship which served as the clearinghouse for the transformation of Black Catholic liturgy and worship across the country throughout the 1970s. *Freeing the Spirit* offered academic articles on the history of African religions, the Black Church, and the Black Catholic community as well as sample "Black liturgies" and suggestions for introducing the parish to Black religious practices. The Department of Culture and Worship provided direct liturgical consultation for parishes across the country from prominent Black Catholics trained in liturgy and worship, such as Father Clarence Rivers and jazz pianist Mary Lou Williams. The pointed title of one of Father Rivers's essays gives a pithy summary of his perspective both on the state of the liturgy in the Black Catholic community in the midst of its transformation and on liturgical practices prevalent prior to the Second Vatican Council and Black Power: "Thank God We Ain't What We Was."[135]

The Department of Culture and Worship also developed workshops on Black religious culture and Catholic liturgy. Some of these workshops were intended to provide Black Catholics with the tools to make their own parishes Black. One proposed course on "liturgy and liturgical practice in the Black community" illustrated the ways the NOBC hoped to make Catholic churches Black.[136] The 1976 proposal argued that more and more Black people wanted to root the significant aspects of their lives in African and Afro-American heritages. Worship played a unique role in this process since "worship has been the vivifying, and centralizing force in the Black church," in and of itself an argument about the distinctive nature of Black religiosity. Catholic worship, on the contrary, had historically been "characteristically more European in orientation." If Catholic churches in Black communities were to survive, they needed to reverse this trend and root their worship services in African and African American traditions if they were going to survive at all. The summer course offered to do just that by introducing participants to African American religious history and practical workshops on Black worship.[137] The NOBC also strove to produce "Black-thinking" white priests and sisters with similar workshops, one tellingly titled "White Priest/Black Church."[138] The impact of these efforts over the course of the decade increasingly legitimized these practices in Black Catholic churches and the larger transformation of Black Catholic identity.

"What We Have Seen and Heard," the pastoral letter readers will recall from the Introduction, was one fruit of the labors of these Black Catholic activists and institutions. If priests, sisters, and laypeople birthed the Black Catholic Movement amidst the street protests of the late sixties, the ten Black bishops of the United States announced its culmination in the pastoral letter on evangelization they issued on September 9, 1984, the feast day of St. Peter Claver—the seventeenth-century Spanish Jesuit missionary, once the patron saint of slaves and now a patron saint of African Americans. Nothing better demonstrated the success of Movement activists than the fact that these bishops, ten Black men now counted among the highest ranking Catholics in the United States, could state with institutional authority and without controversy that one could and should be both "authentically Black and truly Catholic." Writing to "our Black Catholic brothers and sisters in the United States," they noted that "to be Catholic is to be universal. To be universal is not to be uniform." Sharing the gifts of Blackness would be "our part in the building up of the whole Church."[139]

What gifts did Black Catholics have to share? Here the bishops illustrated the influence Black Catholic activists such as Brother Davis, Sister Grey, Father Lucas, and Sister Phelps had sown since 1968. The bishops championed "Black Spirituality." We can hear in their definition of the term the impact of all the workshops, publications, and assorted missionary work of the National Office for Black Catholics. Black Spirituality "is contemplative. It is holistic. It is joyful. It is communitarian." By "contemplative," the bishops meant "prayer is spontaneous and pervasive in the Black tradition. Every place is a place for prayer because God's presence is heard and felt in every place." "Holistic" indicated the absence of the Cartesian spirit-body split. Black people "are not ashamed of our emotions," they stated. "For us, the religious experience is an experience of the whole human being—both the feelings and the intellect, the heart as well as the head."[140] Joy served as another "hallmark of Black Spirituality," a celebration of "movement and song, rhythm and feeling, color and sensation, exultation and thanksgiving."[141] Lastly, the bishops affirmed Black Christianity as "eminently a social reality," as an inherently communal religion born of "African culture" where "the 'I' takes its meaning in the 'we.'"[142] In other words, without being any less Catholic, Black Catholics were the inheritors of their own unique tradition, one that stood in contrast "with much of the Western tradition."[143]

"Through the liturgy," the bishops insisted, "Black people will come to realize that the Catholic Church is a homeland for Black believers just as she is for people of other cultural and ethnic traditions."[144] The liturgy thus "should be authentically Black. It should be truly Catholic. And it should be well prepared and well executed."[145] Two Chicagoans among those ten bishops, James P. Lyke and Wilton D. Gregory, were instrumental to the project that aided and ensured that this well-prepared and well-executed Black Catholic worship became a reality. Alongside liturgists, musicians, educators, and theologians—together with laywomen and men, sisters, priests, brothers, and seminarians—Lyke and Gregory helped produce *Lead Me, Guide Me: The African American Catholic Hymnal*. Published in 1987, the hymnal was meticulously curated to include everything from gospel hymns and sorrow songs to Latin chants and popular postconciliar tunes. Opening with essays that situated Black Catholic music in the rich traditions of African American sacred song and the liturgy of the Roman Rite, this was more than simply a songbook. It served as another defense of an "authentically Black, truly Catholic" Catholicism. As Bishop Lyke put it in the preface, *Lead Me, Guide Me* was "born of the needs and aspirations of Black Catholics for music that reflects both our African American heritage and our Catholic faith"—needs felt "for a long time, but particularly within the last two decades."[146]

Both James Lyke and Wilton Gregory were the sons of Black migrants born on the South Side of Chicago. Neither were Catholic when their parents enrolled them in parochial schools but both left with the desire not just to become Catholic but to become priests. And first as priests and later as bishops, both Lyke and Gregory contributed to the revolution that forever changed what it meant to be Black and Catholic in the United States. So we end with one final irony, one last unintended consequence of the work of missionaries who converted entire neighborhoods into foreign mission fields. Neither of these Black men would have been Catholic if not for white sisters and priests who introduced them to what was then known as the One True Church. And yet once it was in their hands, and in the hands of hundreds of thousands of Black children, women, and men like them, the struggle for Black Catholic self-determination and power would ensure that their Church would never be the same again.

Conclusion

Forty-seven years after Father George Clements became pastor of Holy Angels, the South Side of Chicago remains home to the most famous Black Catholic church in the United States. Turning off 79th Street onto South Racine Avenue in the middle of Chicago's Auburn Gresham neighborhood, it is impossible to miss the presence of a parish plant that looks as if it belongs to an earlier era in the Catholic Metropolis. A sign at the intersection identifies the redbrick apartment complex as St. Sabina Elders Village, a home run by Catholic Charities since 1977. Other storefront signs name the neighborhood as the Faith Community of St. Sabina. There is St. Sabina Academy, a Catholic school that serves students from preschool through the eighth grade. There is the ARK of Saint Sabina, a community youth center that serves as a "safe haven for youth to escape from the storms of the world," the St. Sabina Employment Resource Center, and an office for Catholic Charities Social Services. At the heart of the block towers a gray stone belfry.

Upon entering the church sanctuary one is immediately struck by the evidence of two different communities. Stained-glass, stations of the cross, side altars, and a majestic rose window have changed little since the church was dedicated in 1933, when St. Sabina served as a virtual cathedral for the Irish South Side and the birthplace of Chicago's St. Patrick's Day parade. Porcelain white statues and traditional bronze stations are overshadowed today, though, by new additions. A platform rises in front of the old altar rail in the midst of the congregation, occupied by lay ministers, altar servers, musicians, and priests. Ministers sit on a throne made of black walnut carved into images of African men, arms upraised and clasped in unity. Statues of Black women pouring water stand sentinel in front of the right side altar, a Black Madonna in front of the left one. Kente cloth hangs from the walls and drapes over the altar, which is shaped like an African drum. Suspended above the altar is a yellow neon sign that proclaims, quite simply, JESUS. And where the original altar once stood now hangs an enormous twenty-foot-high painting of a Black Christ, arms outstretched with God's hands enlarged and inviting the congregation into a warm embrace.

Sunday Mass begins in vibrant song and dance. A cantor leads the congregation in a roaring call-and-response rendition of "*Alleluia*." After about a half-hour the pastor processes in, swaying and clapping with the percussive cadence of the choir, and opens the service with extended extemporaneous prayer. He calls the congregation to worship God by God's many names and they respond in kind with shouts of "Hallelujah!" and "Praise Him!" The service accelerates toward its climax when the pastor will proclaim his sermon. This is definitely not a typical Catholic homily. Father Michael L. Pfleger's sermons draw heavily on the rhythm and rhetorical flourishes of the Black preaching tradition, regularly call on the congregation to interact with him and one another in the pews, and, depending on the day, can stretch well over an hour. Perhaps even more striking than the sermon itself, though, is the man delivering it. To quote Cathleen Falsani, a journalist who has followed his career for decades, "No one is whiter than [Michael Louis] Pfleger; no one is whiter than this blond, blue-eyed, movie-star-handsome Catholic priest raised on the white South Side of Chicago."[1]

* * *

One of the most prominent Black churches in Chicago today is a Catholic church pastored by a white priest. This book has illustrated how this is possible. The Faith Community of St. Sabina is a living testament to the rise of Black Catholicism. First of all, St. Sabina's story bears a striking resemblance to many of the parishes we have studied. St. Sabina was an emblem of Irish Catholic triumph that, much like Corpus Christi and Holy Angels before it, found itself in crisis just decades after its dedication. As Black Chicagoans attempted to escape the confines of the Black Belt, they moved into white Catholic parish neighborhoods hostile to their presence. A brief, albeit ambitious, experiment in parish integration failed. In 1964 about three thousand families, mostly white, were registered parishioners. Three years later the parish claimed only 530 families. By 1971, the parish and the school were majority Black.[2] But as Cardinal Cody prepared the church for closure, a charismatic white priest set about repopulating the pews with Auburn Gresham's Black residents.

Ordained in 1975, Michael Pfleger bears comparison with both his white missionary and Black activist predecessors. Just as Fathers Martin Farrell and Joseph Richards before him, Pfleger was a white priest who uncharacteristically requested an assignment in a transitioning parish and once there, worked to save a dying white parish by transforming it into a vibrant Black one. Unlike the "convert makers," though, Pfleger succeeded in making himself and the parish relevant to the surrounding Black community. In this he took more after one of his mentors, Father George H. Clements. Pfleger installed a bronze bust of Martin Luther King, Jr., in the church—he had been inspired to enter the priesthood in part by the Chicago Freedom Movement and, like Clements, had been radicalized by King's assassination. Pfleger employed African and African American aesthetics in the sanctuary in order to encourage Black ownership of the church, commissioning West African-inspired wood-carved furnishings as well as the portrait of the Black Christ titled *For God So Loved the World* by the Mexican-born Jesuit Fernando Arizti. The parish became famous—and more than a little controversial—for its invited guest speaker series, which has included over the years Coretta Scott King, Harry Belafonte, Cornel West, Minister Louis Farrakhan, and Rev. Jeremiah Wright.[3]

This South Side community has achieved—and could be said to achieve anew each day—self-determination of a kind the Black Catholic Movement aspired to in the 1970s. Under the leadership of Dr. Kimberly M. Lymore, who has been a member of St. Sabina since the early 1980s and full-time pastoral associate since 2000, weekly worship integrates praise practices common in Black evangelical churches with the Catholic Eucharistic liturgy as well as African-inspired liturgical dance. St. Sabina Academy has thrived as a highly rated majority-Black school that incorporates both "the gospel of Jesus Christ and African values."[4] Parishioners have organized protests and spearheaded campaigns on every issue that has plagued the local community. They fought to remove cigarette and alcohol advertisements from neighborhood billboards, they fought for the closure of stores selling drug paraphernalia, and perhaps most famously, they led struggles against gang warfare and gun violence. The Faith Community of St. Sabina has even asserted its own self-determination in the face of open resistance from two different Chicago archbishops, first Cody and more recently the late Cardinal Francis George who attempted (unsuccessfully) to remove Father Pfleger as pastor of the parish.

* * *

St. Sabina is clearly unlike your ordinary Catholic church. Viewed from another vantage point, though, St. Sabina—and Holy Angels, Corpus Christi, and St. Malachy before it—illuminates the new stories that can be written and the new conclusions that become possible when Black Catholics are centered in our scholarship. Without diminishing the significance of Catholic interracial activism, we can safely say that missionaries dedicated to the conversion of African American migrants were more important to the making of Black Catholic Chicago and, by extension, Black Catholic America than the liberal interracialists who have so dominated the study of Catholics and race in the United States. If we listen to converts themselves, it is clear that becoming Catholic was neither an expedient choice nor a matter of coercion but an educative process that many thousands of children, women, and men found compelling. White missionary priests and sisters inculcated ways of being religious that set Black Catholics apart from the Black Christian communities proliferating around them. Such conversion often came at great cost. Focusing on Black Catholics allows us to glimpse the unforeseen consequences of the fraught relationships forged between migrants and missionaries. Thus, for instance, Black Catholic converts shared an impulse with Black Muslims and Black Hebrews to fashion new ways of being Black and religious amidst the upheavals of the Great Migrations.

Mary Dolores Gadpaille's love of the Latin Mass, the strife a child's conversion could cause in a family, Mary Howard's experience of "living" the stations of the cross—the intricacies of these ordinary lives are lost when we rely on comfortable (and comforting) narratives of Black religiosity. So much of what is written about Black religion is oriented around the struggle for civil rights that it can seem as if Black religion matters only insofar as it is progressive, political, and Protestant. This is no less the case with regard to scholarship on Catholics and race, in which African Americans are often absent unless and until racial justice is discussed. Scholars should not ignore interracialism, but we would be wise to restore it to its proper place: as a remarkable exception rather than the rule. When we shift our attention from liberal interracialists to convert-making missionaries, and more importantly to the tens of thousands of converts in relationship with them, we begin to see Black Catholic life for what it was rather than what we wish it would be. The creativity of the migrations era comes to the fore as we witness Black Catholics engaged in the art of self-transformation alongside Black Muslims, Hebrews, and Moors. Uncomfortable truths also arise; such as the fact that white missionaries were often more concerned with spiritual salvation than social liberation, or that Black converts denigrated what they took to be the uncouth emotionalism of "the Black Church." But if we hope to understand what it means to be Black and religious—or, to put it more simply, what it means to be human—we need to be willing to wrestle with the contradictions and complexities of life as it is lived.

The intersection of Black Catholics and Black Power poses an even more direct challenge to the ways in which scholars have studied race and religion. The rise of a distinctively *Black* Catholicism represents an unexpected aftereffect of the "foreign mission fields" on the South Side of Chicago, one that missionaries could never have predicted. If we take white Catholic encounters with Black people, or even interracial work, as our subject the stories we tell naturally tend toward topics such as "civil rights" and "integration." But the Black Catholic struggle for racial justice did not end with Martin Luther King's death in 1968. It was born of Black Power. As a growing number of Black Catholic activists embraced the anticolonial arguments of the Black Panthers and Stokely Carmichael's call for self-determination, the very missionary mentality that initiated Black Catholic Chicago's rise became the focal point for a comprehensive critique of the Church as a "white racist institution." The rhetoric and aesthetics of Black Power revolutionized what it meant to be Black and Catholic when it was taken up by the laypeople, sisters, and priests who gave birth to what they understood be an "authentic Black" Catholicism. The goal of twentieth-century interracialists had been to make the Church whole by lifting Catholics up above the color line. Their mantra, that all people were members of the "One Mystical Body of Christ," dreamed of a day when race would be erased, a day when there would not be Black and Irish and Italian and Polish churches but one Catholic Church. The Black Catholic Movement flipped this aspiration on its head. Racial justice for Black Catholics would stem not from the embrace of an "unhyphenated Catholicism," as it were, but from unapologetically Black communities with the power to determine their own destinies.

Black Catholicism thus emerged out of a confrontation with U.S. Catholicism as a whole. For decades Black converts had been sold Catholic universalism and been told that their new religion "knew no race." When activists declared the U.S. Church a "white racist institution," they named something that had long gone unacknowledged. The so-called "universal Church" preached, in practice, its own brand of racial particularism. Though interracialists liked to separate the Church's ideals from the actions of individual Catholics, Black Power activists collapsed this distinction as immaterial. Instead, to paraphrase the Holy Angels parish motto, they insisted that they would get it together by themselves. The study of Black Catholics and Black Power helps us to better understand this particular historical moment. It moves white Catholics to the margins and allows us to recognize the ways in which Black nationalism—an embrace of Blackness rather than its dissolution—empowered activists and sparked the most significant Catholic contribution to racial justice movements in the twentieth century. There is a historiographical challenge here as well, however. When Black Catholics are centered in our studies of Catholicism in America, they force a reckoning with the limitations of our own concepts. For too long scholars have treated "American Catholicism" as an innocent term and assumed that it is a race-neutral category. The Black Catholics who took up Black Power in the 1960s revealed the hypocrisy of that presumption. Their embrace of racial consciousness—by naming the whiteness of the Church and struggling to create a Black one—illuminates what remains hidden in plain sight, namely, that Catholicism, as with all things in America, is ineluctably entangled with race.

Finally, if this book highlights the creative accomplishments of the Black Catholic Movement, it also shows that Black Catholics were never unanimous in their embrace of this revolution, nor are they now uniform in their identity and practice. Attentiveness to the lives of Black Catholics in the turbulent middle decades of the twentieth century makes clear just how controversial the idea of a distinctively Black Catholicism was, especially for Black Catholics. Activists founded new institutions, articulated diverse ways of expressing Catholic identity, made and remade Black liturgies, and became missionaries in their own parishes as they sought to convince Black coreligionists that one could be both "authentically Black" and "truly Catholic." By the 1980s they had succeeded in establishing a new norm for what it meant to be Black and Catholic in the United States, even if it remains true today that "there is no one way to be Black and Catholic." To say as much, to acknowledge the contingency of this way of being in the world, does not belittle Black Catholicism. It testifies to the joys and struggles of Black Catholics and to the "uncommon faithfulness" they share.[5]

NOTES

INTRODUCTION

1. "What We Have Seen and Heard: A Pastoral Letter on Evangelization from the Black Bishops of the United States" (September 9, 1984), 2.
2. Pope Paul VI, "To the Heart of Africa" (Address to the Bishops of the African Continent at the Closing Session of a Symposium Held in Kampala, Uganda), *The Pope Speaks*, vol. 14 (1969): 219. Quoted in "What We Have Seen and Heard," 3.
3. "What We Have Seen and Heard," 3.
4. Ibid., 4.
5. Ibid., 8.
6. Ibid., 15.
7. Ibid., 30.
8. Ibid., 31.
9. Edward K. Braxton, "Black Catholics in America: Authentically Black, Truly Catholic," *Commonweal* 112 (February 1985): 73–77. A more recent use of this phrase is in C. Vanessa White, "Authentically Black and Truly Catholic," *CNN Special: Black in America* (September 5, 2010): www.cnn.com. Bryan Massingale's current research returns to what was an open question in the midst of the Black Power era, namely, whether it is possible to be "authentically Black and truly Catholic." See Bryan Massingale, "Malcolm X and the Limits of 'Authentically Black and Truly Catholic': A Research Project on Black Radicalism and Black Catholic Faith," *Journal of the Black Catholic Theological Symposium* 5 (2011): 7–23.
10. "Mary Dolores Gadpaille to Very Rev. Pius Barth, O.F.M. (3 April and 23 April, 1958)," Franciscan Province of the Sacred Heart Archives (OFM), Corpus Christi Correspondence 1957–1988, IR03010.
11. Albert J. Raboteau, "Minority within a Minority: The History of Black Catholics in America," in *A Fire in the Bones: Reflections on African-American Religious History* (Boston: Beacon Press, 1995), 133.
12. Demographics drawn from the United States Conference of Catholic Bishops (www.usccb.org) and the World Council of Churches (www.oikoumene.org).
13. "What We Have Seen and Heard," 17.
14. Cyprian Davis, *The History of Black Catholics in the United States* (New York: Crossroad Publishing Company, 1995), 28–29.
15. John K. Thornton and Linda M. Heywood, "A Forgotten African Catholic Kingdom," *The Root* (August 12, 2011): www.theroot.com. See also Linda M. Heywood

and John K. Thornton, *Central Africans, Atlantic Creoles, and the Foundation of the Americas, 1585–1660* (Cambridge: Cambridge University Press, 2007).
16 Sylvester A. Johnson, *African American Religions, 1500–2000: Colonialism, Democracy, and Freedom* (Cambridge: Cambridge University Press, 2015), 136.
17 "Gadpaille to Barth (23 April, 1958)."
18 See Matthew J. Cressler, ed., "Forum: Race, White Supremacy, and the Making of American Catholicism," *American Catholic Studies* 127, no. 3 (Fall 2016): 1–33.
19 Malcolm X, "Speech in Los Angeles (May 5, 1962)": www.youtube.com.
20 Beryl Satter, *Family Properties: How the Struggle over Race and Real Estate Transformed Chicago and Urban America* (New York: Metropolitan Books, 2009).
21 Arnold R. Hirsch, *Making the Second Ghetto: Race and Housing in Chicago, 1940–1960* (Chicago: University of Chicago Press, 1983).
22 Allan H. Spear, *Black Chicago: The Making of a Negro Ghetto, 1890–1920* (Chicago: University of Chicago Press, 1967).
23 Adam Green, *Selling the Race: Community, Culture, and Black Chicago, 1940–1955* (Chicago: University of Chicago Press, 2009); Davarian Baldwin, *Chicago's New Negro Movement: Modernity, the Great Migration, and Black Urban Life* (Chapel Hill: University of North Carolina Press, 2007).
24 "Spoke for His Race: Father Tolton, the Colored Priest, Lectures on 'The Catholic Church the True Liberator of the Race,'" *Boston Daily Globe* (June 6, 1892), 3.
25 I directly address the often unspoken racial dynamics at the heart of the story of Catholic immigrants "becoming American" in my Introduction to "Forum: Race, White Supremacy, and the Making of American Catholicism," 1–5. See also Matthew J. Cressler, "What White Catholics Owe Black Americans," *Slate* (September 2, 2016): www.slate.com.
26 Jonathan Z. Smith, *The Map Is Not the Territory: Studies in the History of Religions* (Chicago: University of Chicago Press, 1993).
27 John T. McGreevy, *Parish Boundaries: The Catholic Encounter with Race in the Twentieth-Century Urban North* (Chicago: University of Chicago Press, 1996), 90.
28 Jacquelyn Dowd Hall, "The Long Civil Rights Movement and the Political Uses of the Past," *Journal of American History* 91, no. 4 (March 2005): 1233–1263.
29 David W. Southern, *John LaFarge and the Limits of Catholic Interracialism, 1911–1963* (Baton Rouge: Louisiana State University Press, 1996); Amy L. Koehlinger, *The New Nuns: Racial Justice and Religious Reform in the 1960s* (Cambridge, Mass.: Harvard University Press, 2007); Suellen Hoy, *Good Hearts: Catholic Sisters in Chicago's Past* (Champaign: University of Illinois Press, 2006); R. Bentley Anderson, S.J., *Black, White, and Catholic: New Orleans Interracialism, 1947–1956* (Nashville, Tenn.: Vanderbilt University Press, 2008); Karen Johnson, "The Universal Church in the Segregated City: Catholic Interracialism in Chicago, 1928–1963" (Ph.D. dissertation, University of Illinois at Chicago, 2012); Timothy B. Neary, *Crossing Parish Boundaries: Race, Sports, and Catholic Youth in Chicago, 1914–1954* (Chicago: University of Chicago Press, 2016).

30 This point is inspired in large part by the work of Barbara Dianne Savage. She argues that, contrary to the popular myth about the progressive politics of "the Black Church," the central role Black churches played in mid-twentieth-century civil rights struggles proved the exception rather than the rule in African American religious history. Barbara Dianne Savage, *Your Spirits Walk beside Us: The Politics of Black Religion* (Cambridge, Mass.: Belknap Press of Harvard University Press, 2008).

31 Martin Luther King, Jr., *Stride toward Freedom: The Montgomery Story*, reprint (Boston: Beacon Press, [1958] 2010), 202.

32 Johnson, "Universal Church"; and Neary, *Crossing Parish Boundaries*.

33 McGreevy, *Parish Boundaries*, 162.

34 Ibid., 227.

35 Ibid., 225.

36 The convergence of Black Power with Vatican II changed the course of Black Catholic history. But this was, of course, not the first time Black Catholics championed the cause of African Americans in the Church. The Afro-American Catholic Congress movement of the 1890s gathered lay black Catholics together to announce their presence and name their grievances. The early-twentieth-century Federated Colored Catholics (originally named the Committee for the Advancement of Colored Catholics), founded and led by Thomas Wyatt Turner, understood itself to be "an action group led by black Catholics and for black Catholics that would ensure that the black Catholic community take a responsible and leadership role in American Catholicism and American society." For more on these earlier instances of Black Catholic activism, see *Three Afro-American Catholic Congresses* (Cincinnati, Ohio: American Catholic Tribune, 1898); and Marilyn W. Nickels, *Black Catholic Protest and the Federated Colored Catholics: 1917–1933: Three Perspectives on Racial Justice* (New York: Garland, 1988).

37 Nikhil Pal Singh, *Black Is a Country: Race and the Unfinished Struggle for Democracy* (Cambridge, Mass.: Harvard University Press, 2004).

38 See Martha Biondi, *To Stand and Fight: The Struggle for Civil Rights in Postwar New York City* (Cambridge, Mass.: Harvard University Press, 2003); and Thomas J. Sugrue, *Sweet Land of Liberty: The Forgotten Struggle for Civil Rights in the North* (New York: Random House, 2008).

39 See Timothy B. Tyson, *Radio Free Dixie: Robert F. Williams and the Roots of Black Power* (Chapel Hill: University of North Carolina Press, 2001); and Charles E. Cobb, Jr., *This Nonviolent Stuff'll Get You Killed: How Guns Made the Civil Rights Movement Possible* (Durham, N.C.: Duke University Press, 2015).

40 See Barbara Ransby, *Ella Baker and the Black Freedom Movement: A Radical Democratic Vision* (Chapel Hill: University of North Carolina Press, 2006); and Danielle L. McGuire, *At the Dark End of the Street: Black Women, Rape, and Resistance—A New History of the Civil Rights Movement from Rosa Parks to the Rise of Black Power* (New York: Vintage Books, 2011).

41 See Robert O. Self, *American Babylon: Race and the Struggle for Postwar Oakland* (Princeton, N.J.: Princeton University Press, 2003); Martha Biondi, *The Black Revolution on Campus* (Berkeley: University of California Press, 2012); and Matthew J. Countryman, *Up South: Civil Rights and Black Power in Philadelphia* (Philadelphia: University of Pennsylvania Press, 2007).
42 See Angela D. Dillard, *Faith in the City: Preaching Radical Social Change in Detroit* (Ann Arbor, Mich.: University of Michigan Press, 2007); and Kerry Pimblott, *Faith in Black Power: Religion, Race, and Resistance in Cairo, Illinois* (Lexington: University of Kentucky Press, 2017).
43 This literature includes Anthony B. Pinn, *Varieties of African American Religious Experience* (Minneapolis, Minn.: Augsburg Fortress Publishers, 1998); Savage, *Your Spirits Walk beside Us*; Curtis J. Evans, *The Burden of Black Religion* (Oxford: Oxford University Press, 2008); Edward E. Curtis IV and Danielle Brune Sigler, ed., *The New Black Gods: Arthur Huff Fauset and the Study of African American Religions* (Bloomington, Ind.: Indiana University Press, 2009); Jacob S. Dorman, *Chosen People: The Rise of American Black Israelite Religions* (Oxford: Oxford University Press, 2013); Johnson, *African American Religions*; and Judith Weisenfeld, *New World A-Coming: Black Religion and Racial Identity during the Great Migration* (New York: NYU Press, 2016).
44 Evans, *Burden of Black Religion*, 272.
45 Biography courtesy of Andrew Lyke, the nephew of James P. Lyke. Andrew eulogized his uncle at a local Chicago memorial service in 1993 and became a nationally renowned Black Catholic leader in his own right, in part thanks to the spiritual mentorship of his uncle.
46 Archbishop Wilton D. Gregory, interview with author (June 6, 2012).

CHAPTER 1. MIGRANTS AND MISSIONARIES

1 Nicholas Lemann, *The Promised Land: The Great Black Migration and How It Changed America* (New York: Alfred A. Knopf, 1991), 6.
2 Wallace D. Best borrows this phrase from the African American author and educator Charles S. Johnson in *Passionately Human, No Less Divine: Religion and Culture in Black Chicago, 1915–1952* (Princeton, N.J.: Princeton University Press, 2005), 13, 21.
3 *Corpus Christi Parish: A Hundred Years of Faith* (Chicago: Parish Publication, 2001), 2–3.
4 Maren Stange, *Bronzeville: Black Chicago in Pictures, 1941–1943* (New York: New Press, 2003), 7, 189. Corpus Christi's parish boundaries were from 45th to 53rd Streets (north-south) and from Wentworth to Cottage Grove Avenues (west-east); Rev. Harry C. Koenig, *A History of the Parishes of the Archdiocese of Chicago: Published in Observance of the Centenary of the Archdiocese*, 2 vols. (Chicago: Archdiocese of Chicago, 1980).
5 Mary Howard, interview with author (December 11, 2011).

6 George Shuster, S.S.J., and Robert M. Kearns, S.S.J., *Statistical Profile of Black Catholics* (Washington, D.C.: Josephite Pastoral Center, 1976).
7 Raboteau, "Minority within a Minority," 133.
8 "Annals of Corpus Christi Convent (1932–1940)," Celano Archives of the Sisters of St. Francis, Dubuque, Iowa (OSF), Illinois, Corpus Christi 1f.
9 James N. Gregory, *The Southern Diaspora: How the Great Migrations of Black and White Southerners Transformed America* (Chapel Hill: University of North Carolina Press, 2005), 330.
10 Ibid., 18.
11 For more on the violence migrants faced upon arrival, see C. Vann Woodward, *The Strange Career of Jim Crow*, 2nd rev. ed. (Oxford: Oxford University Press, 1966), 114; Spear, *Black Chicago*; Hirsch, *Making the Second Ghetto*.
12 James R. Grossman, *Land of Hope: Chicago, Black Southerners, and the Great Migration* (Chicago: University of Chicago Press, 1989), 99.
13 John M. Giggie, *After Redemption: Jim Crow and the Transformation of African American Religion in the Delta, 1875–1915* (Oxford: Oxford University Press, 2005), 6–7; John M. Giggie, "The Mississippi River and the Transformation of Black Religion in the Delta, 1877–1915," in *Gods of the Mississippi*, Michael Pasquier, ed. (Bloomington, Ind.: Indiana University Press, 2013), 114.
14 Giggie, *After Redemption*, 179.
15 See Evelyn Brooks Higginbotham, *Righteous Discontent: The Women's Movement in the Black Baptist Church, 1880–1920* (Cambridge, Mass.: Harvard University Press, 1993).
16 Giggie, *After Redemption*, 179.
17 Giggie, "Mississippi River," 124; Giggie, *After Redemption*, 176–180.
18 Ibid.
19 For histories of Holiness and Pentecostalism, see Harvey Cox, *Fire from Heaven: The Rise of Pentecostal Spirituality and the Reshaping of Religion in the Twenty-First Century* (Reading, Mass.: Addison-Wesley, 1995); and Randall J. Stephens, *The Fire Spreads: Holiness and Pentecostalism in the American South* (Cambridge, Mass.: Harvard University Press, 2008). For a history of African American Pentecostalism in particular, see Estrelda Y. Alexander, *Black Fire: One Hundred Years of African American Pentecostalism* (Downers Grove, Ill.: IVP Academic, 2011).
20 Best, *Passionately Human, No Less Divine*, 2.
21 See Best, *Passionately Human, No Less Divine*, 94–117. W. E. B. Du Bois, *The Souls of Black Folk* (New York: Signet Classic, [1903], 1995), 212.
22 St. Clair Drake and Horace R. Cayton, *Black Metropolis: A Study of Negro Life in a Northern City* (Chicago: University of Chicago Press, 1945), 611.
23 McGreevy, *Parish Boundaries*, 15. See also Eileen M. McMahon, *What Parish Are You From? A Chicago Irish Community and Race Relations* (Lexington: University Press of Kentucky, 1996); Timothy B. Neary, "Black-Belt Catholic Space: African-American Parishes in Interwar Chicago," *U.S. Catholic Historian* 18, no. 4 (Fall 2000): 76–91.

24 McGreevy, *Parish Boundaries*, 17.
25 McGreevy, *Parish Boundaries*; Neary, *Crossing Parish Boundaries*; Colleen McDannell, *Picturing Faith: Photography and the Great Depression* (New Haven, Conn.: Yale University Press, 2004).
26 Koenig, *History of the Parishes*; and Neary, *Crossing Parish Boundaries*, vi.
27 Neary, *Crossing Parish Boundaries*, 37.
28 For more on the Chicago race riot of 1919, see Spear, *Black Chicago*; William M. Tuttle, Jr., *Race Riot: Chicago in the Red Summer of 1919* (Champaign: University of Illinois Press, 1970); Hirsch, *Making the Second Ghetto*.
29 For more on the bombing of Black homes in Chicago, see Hirsch, *Making the Second Ghetto*, 40–99; Will Cooley, "Moving On Out: Black Pioneering in Chicago, 1915–1950," *Journal of Urban History* 36, no. 4 (July 2010): 485–506. For more on white Catholic resistance to Black migrants, see McGreevy, *Parish Boundaries*, 94–97; and McMahon, *What Parish Are You From?* 116–129. For more on the language of "invasion," see Grossman, *Land of Hope*, 127; Gregory, *Southern Diaspora*, 47–49.
30 See Robert A. Orsi, *Thank You, St. Jude: Women's Devotions to the Patron Saint of Hopeless Causes* (New Haven, Conn.: Yale University Press, 1996), 40–69; Robert A. Orsi, "Introduction: Crossing the City Line," and "The Religious Boundaries of an In-Between People: Street *Feste* and the Problem of the Dark-Skinned Other in Italian Harlem, 1920–1990," in *Gods of the City: Religion and the American Urban Landscape*, Robert A. Orsi, ed. (Bloomington, Ind.: Indiana University Press, 1999), 1–78 and 257–288. For more on why white Catholics often stayed in changing urban neighborhoods much longer than other white communities, see McGreevy, *Parish Boundaries*, 20; Gerald Gamm, *Urban Exodus: Why the Jews Left Boston and the Catholics Stayed* (Cambridge, Mass.: Harvard University Press, 2001); John C. Seitz, *No Closure: Catholic Practice and Boston's Parish Shutdowns* (Cambridge, Mass.: Harvard University Press, 2011), 81–130.
31 "The Catholic Church and the Negro in the Archdiocese of Chicago, Clergy Conference, September 20–21, 1960," Archdiocese of Chicago Joseph Cardinal Bernardin Archives and Records Center (AAC).
32 "St. Anselm, Summaries of Annals (1941–1952)," Sisters of the Blessed Sacrament Archives (SBS), H40 B2 IL: Chicago St. Anselm, Box 1, Folder 1.
33 Anthony J. Vader, "Mission to Black America," *Chicago Studies* 23 (August 1984), 169–181; Capistran J. Haas, O.F.M., *History of Midwest Clergy Conference on Negro Welfare* (1963); "The Catholic Church and the Negro (1960)," AAC.
34 For a general history of the missionary movements in American Catholic history, see Angelyn Dries, *The Missionary Movement in American Catholic History* (Maryknoll, N.Y.: Orbis Books, 1998).
35 For more on these arguments for Catholic exceptionalism in American history, see Robert A. Orsi, "U.S. Catholics between Memory and Modernity: How Catholics Are American," in *Catholics in the American Century: Recasting Narratives of U.S. History*, R. Scott Appleby and Kathleen Sprows Cummings, ed. (Ithaca,

N.Y.: Cornell University Press, 2012). For more on Bishop Noll, see Leon Hutton, "Catholicity and Civility: John Francis Noll and the Origins of 'Our Sunday Visitor,'" *U.S. Catholic Historian* 15, no. 3 (Summer 1997): 1–22.

36 For more on Catholic Action in American history, see Jeremy Bonner, Mary Beth Fraser Connolly, and Christopher Denny, ed., *Empowering the People of God: Catholic Action before and after Vatican II* (New York: Fordham University Press, 2014).

37 Anne Tansey, "Through Highways and Byways," *Christian Family and Our Missions* (March 1949), 104. See also "How to Win a Convert," *Time Magazine*, July 12, 1948.

38 "No Dull Season in CMOA; Laymen's Plan Prospers," *New World*, July 2, 1948, 14.

39 George Cardinal Mundelein, quoted in *New World*, October 21, 1938, 8.

40 Most Rev. Joseph Rummel, "Negro Is America's First Mission Responsibility," *New World*, March 12, 1943, 1.

41 Pius XII, Encyclical Letter, *Sertum Laetitiae*, November 1, 1939. Quoted in *New World*, November 17, 1939, 1.

42 "Catholics Baptize Record Class of Converts," *Chicago Defender*, May 14, 1927, 4. For another example of the *Defender*'s documentation of mass baptism, see "Accepting the Catholic Faith," *Chicago Defender*, December 25, 1937, 7; "Harlem Catholics Launch Drive for Converts," September 22, 1934, 5; "Cardinal Hayes Blesses Largest Class of Converts," January 20, 1934, 4; "Eighty-Six Converts Join Roman Catholic Church," February 2, 1935, 3; "Jersey Catholics Start Drive for New Converts," October 29, 1938, 20.

43 "Believes Race Is Fast Turning to Catholicism," *Chicago Defender*, November 29, 1941, 12; "Third of Million Negroes in America Are Catholic," February 14, 1948, 6.

44 Claude McKay, "Why I Became a Catholic" and "Converts of Color," *Ebony* 1, issue 5, March 1946, 28–31.

45 "Catholics & Color," 21. See also Harold E. Fey, "Can Catholicism Win America? A Series of Eight Articles Reprinted from *The Christian Century*" (1945).

46 Dries, *The Missionary Movement*, 27.

47 Most Rev. George William Mundelein, "Letter in Favor of the Negro Parish of St. Monica, Chicago," in *Two Crowded Years: Being Selected Speeches, Pastorals, and Letters Issued in the First Twenty-Four Months of Episcopate* (Chicago: Extension Press, 1918), 291–300.

48 Ernest Brandewie, *In the Light of the Word: Divine Word Missionaries of North America* (Maryknoll, N.Y.: Orbis Books, 2000), 9.

49 Ibid., 153.

50 Ibid., 154.

51 Ibid., 155.

52 Ibid., 156.

53 John Evans, "Negro Catholic Converts Build Up Old Parish," *Chicago Daily Tribune*, May 5, 1929, 5.

54 Joseph Eckert, S.V.D., "Methods of Convert-Making among the Negroes of Chicago," in *The White Harvest: A Symposium on Methods of Convert Making*, Rev.

John A. O'Brien, ed. (New York: Longmans, Green and Co., 1927), 96. Emphasis in the original.
55 "Nicholas Christoffel, O.F.M. to Mother M. Theodore, S.S.F., Oct. 25, 1932," OSF, Illinois, Corpus Christi 1f.
56 Robert A. Orsi, *History and Presence* (Cambridge, Mass.: Belknap Press of Harvard University Press, 2016), 3.
57 Sylvester A. Johnson, *The Myth of Ham in Nineteenth-Century American Christianity: Race, Heathens, and the People of God* (New York: Palgrave Macmillan, 2004), 24.
58 John Tracy Ellis, *Documents in American Catholic History* (Milwaukee, Wis.: Bruce Publishing Company, 1962), 571.
59 Hoy, *Good Hearts*, 89.
60 Ibid.
61 Dries, *The Missionary Movement*, 31; and Hoy, *Good Hearts*, 87. For more on the SBS in Chicago, see Hoy, *Good Hearts*, 87–91. For a history of the Sisters of the Blessed Sacrament, see Patricia Lynch, S.B.S., *Sharing the Bread in Service: Sisters of the Blessed Sacrament, 1891–1991* (Bensalem, Pa.: Sisters of the Blessed Sacrament, 1998). Mother Katharine Drexel was canonized by the Catholic Church on October 1, 2000.
62 Neary, *Crossing Parish Boundaries*, 31–34.
63 Hoy, *Good Hearts*, 91.
64 Ibid., 92.
65 Ibid.
66 For more on the missionary project as a colonialist and civilizing project, see Jean Comaroff and John Comaroff, *Of Revelation and Revolution: Christianity, Colonialism, and Consciousness in South Africa*, Vol. 1 (Chicago: University of Chicago Press, 1991); Joel Robbins, *Becoming Sinners: Christianity and Moral Torment in a Papua New Guinea Society* (Berkeley: University of California Press, 2004); Johnson, *African American Religions*. For more on the civilizing project of Catholic missionaries among enslaved African Americans, see Michael Pasquier, "'Though Their Skin Remains Brown, I Hope Their Souls Will Soon Be White': Slavery, French Missionaries, and the Roman Catholic Priesthood in the American South, 1789–1865," *Church History* 77, no. 2 (June 2008): 337–370.
67 Ryan Dunch, "Beyond Cultural Imperialism: Cultural Theory, Christian Missions, and Global Modernity," *History and Theory* 41, no. 3 (October 2002): 324. For more on the new history of missions, see Andrew F. Walls, *The Missionary Movement in Christian History: Studies in the Transmission of Faith* (Maryknoll, N.Y.: Orbis Books, 1996); Mark Noll, "The New History of Missions," *Books and Culture* 30, no. 2 (2004): 30; Paul Kollman, "The Promise of Mission History for U.S. Catholic History," *U.S. Catholic Historian* 24, no. 3 (Summer 2006): 1–18; Dana L. Robert, *Christian Mission: How Christianity Became a World Religion* (Oxford: Wiley-Blackwell, 2009).

68 "Anecdotes: The Biggs Family," 1, SBS, H40 B2 IL: Chicago St. Anselm, Box 1, Folder 1.
69 Ibid.
70 Ibid., 2.
71 Biography courtesy of Dr. Stephanie Morris, Archivist, SBS. Prior to her arrival in Chicago, where she served in Black parishes from 1933 until 1948, Sister Mary Frances Therese served in Pennsylvania, Arizona, and Louisiana.
72 Sr. M. Frances Therese, S.B.S., "Despite the Sisters," *Mission Fields at Home* 12, no. 6 (November 1945): 12–13.
73 "St. Anselm, Annals (1941–1952)," SBS; and "St. Elizabeth, Annals (1950–1959)," H40 B2 IL: Chicago St. Elizabeth, Box 1, Folder 8; "Corpus Christi, Annals (1940–1967)," OSF, Illinois, Corpus Christi 2f.
74 Other examples are collected in "Christmas Letters," Correspondence (1937–1949), SBS, H40 B2 IL: Chicago St. Anselm, Box 1, Folder 12.
75 Ibid.
76 "Sisters of St. Francis Open Colored School in Chicago," OSF, Illinois, Corpus Christi 5f.
77 Shannen Dee Williams, "The Color of Christ's Brides," in "Forum: Race, White Supremacy, and the Making of American Catholicism," *American Catholic Studies* 127, no. 3 (2016): 14–21.
78 See Dries, *The Missionary Movement*, 28–29. Cyprian Davis has written on the tension between the U.S. Catholic Church and Catholic authorities in Rome on the issue of the pastoral care of African Americans. See Cyprian Davis, "The Holy See and American Black Catholics: A Forgotten Chapter in the History of the American Church," *U.S. Catholic Historian* 7, nos. 2–3 (Spring/Summer 1988): 157–181.
79 Davis, *History of Black Catholics*, 133.
80 For more on the Josephite Fathers, see Stephen Ochs, *Desegregating the Altar: The Josephites and the Struggle for Black Priests, 1871–1960* (Baton Rouge: Louisiana State University Press, 1993).
81 Archbishop Wilton D. Gregory spoke extensively about these "exceptional priests"; interview with author.
82 Brandewie, *In the Light of the Word*, 201.
83 Ibid., 152.
84 Joseph F. Eckert, S.V.D., "Autobiography of Father Joseph Eckert S.V.D." (unpublished manuscript), 23, Robert Meyers Archives, Chicago Province of the Society of the Divine Word (SVD).
85 Eckert, "Autobiography," 23, SVD.
86 Eckert, "Methods of Convert-Making," 109.
87 Brandewie, *In the Light of the Word*, 201; and "Around the Negro World," in *Christian Family and Our Missions* (Techny, Ill.: October 1940), 397.
88 Joseph F. Eckert, S.V.D., "How Our Society Was Given St. Anselm's Parish, Chicago (a Factual Account by Rev. Joseph F. Eckert, S.V.D.)," SVD, 9.

89 Eckert, "Autobiography," 24, SVD.
90 Eckert, "Methods of Convert-Making," 96.
91 Ibid., 98. Emphasis in the original.
92 Ibid., 99.
93 Eckert, "Autobiography," 25, SVD.
94 Eckert, "Methods of Convert-Making," 99.
95 Eckert, "Autobiography," 25, SVD.
96 Eckert, "Methods of Convert-Making," 103.
97 Eckert, "Autobiography," 26, SVD.
98 Eckert, "St. Anselm," 13–14, SVD.
99 Eckert, "Methods of Convert-Making," 104.
100 Ibid., 105.
101 Evans, *Burden of Black Religion*, 10.
102 Andrew M. Greeley, *The Catholic Imagination* (Berkeley: University of California Press, 2000).
103 Eckert, "Methods of Convert-Making," 105–106.
104 Ibid., 106.
105 Ibid. Emphasis in the original.
106 Ibid., 107.
107 Ibid., 108.
108 Haas, *History of the Midwest Conference*, 3.
109 Ibid., 15.
110 Steven M. Avella speaks at length about the distinction between interracialists and convert-makers. Steven M. Avella, *This Confident Church: Catholic Leadership and Life in Chicago, 1940–1965* (Notre Dame: University of Notre Dame Press, 1992).
111 "'A CATHOLIC Church in America, Or, One Priest to Another,' Compiled by Clergy Conference of the Mid-West on Negro Welfare, Directed Exclusively to Priests" (Milwaukee: St. Benedict's Press, 1942), 29, University of Notre Dame Archives (UND), Msgr. Reynold Hillenbrand Papers, Box 67, Folder 47.
112 Haas, *History of the Midwest Conference*, 13.
113 "A CATHOLIC Church in America," 12.
114 Ibid.
115 Arthur Huff Fauset, *Black Gods of the Metropolis: Negro Religious Cults of the Urban North* (Philadelphia: University of Pennsylvania Press, 1944), 1.
116 Ibid., 97.
117 Fauset's approach to the study of African American religion has been reinvigorated recently, most notably by Curtis and Sigler's edited *New Black Gods* and Weisenfeld's *New World A-Coming*.
118 John T. Gillard, S.S.J., *The Catholic Church and the American Negro* (Baltimore, Md.: St. Joseph's Society Press, 1929), 4. Patrick Curran also emphasized the missionary potential of African Americans who were not regular churchgoers; Patrick Curran, "Missionary Apostolate among the Non-Catholic Negroes in Chicago," *Christ to the World*, Vol. 5 (1960), 308.

119 John T. Gillard, S.S.J., *Colored Catholics in the United States* (Baltimore, Md.: Josephite Press, 1941), 255. Fey also cites this in "Can Catholicism Win America?" 11.
120 "A CATHOLIC Church in America", 19.
121 Ibid., 24.
122 On the origins of this dispute in early modern debates between Catholics and Protestants, see Orsi, *History and Presence*.

CHAPTER 2. BECOMING CATHOLIC

1 Randolph's story is drawn from details one particular convert recounted in a letter written for his religious instruction class at St. Elizabeth in 1945: "Letters from Converts," SBS, H40 B2 IL: Chicago St. Elizabeth, Box 4, Folder 4 ("Letters from Converts," SBS). I have also drawn on more general characteristics of Catholic devotional habits prevalent at the time. See James M. O'Toole, ed., *Habits of Devotion: Catholic Religious Practices in Twentieth Century America* (Ithaca, N.Y.: Cornell University Press, 2004); Orsi, *Thank You, St. Jude*.
2 For more on classic slave conversion narratives, see Clifton H. Johnson, ed., *God Struck Me Dead: Voices of Ex-Slaves*, William Bradford Collection edition (Cleveland, Ohio: Pilgrim Press, 1993).
3 The concept of "conversion" that took shape in the modern study of religion emphasized personal transformation and individual agency as the authors of religious change. This conceptualization spanned methodological boundaries from the psychological to the theological and sociological: see, respectively, William James, *The Varieties of Religious Experience, a Study in Human Nature* (New York, London: Longmans, Green, and Co., 1902); Rudolf Otto, *The Idea of the Holy: An Inquiry into the Non-Rational Factor in the Idea of the Divine and Its Relation to the Rational* (London: Oxford University Press, 1923); John Lofland and Rodney Stark, "Becoming a World-Saver: A Theory of Conversion to a Deviant Perspective," *American Sociological Review* 30 (1965): 862–875. Contemporary scholarship has moved toward models that provide space for the consideration of conversion as a gradual process influenced by factors that extend beyond the individual agent. See, most notably, Lewis R. Rambo and Charles E. Farhadian, *The Oxford Handbook of Religious Conversion* (Oxford: Oxford University Press, 2014).
4 Fr. Robert Miller, interview with author (October 21, 2012); V. P. Franklin, "First Came the School: Catholic Evangelization among African Americans in the United States, 1827 to the Present," in *Growing Up African American in Catholic Schools*, Jacqueline Jordan Irvine and Michèle Foster, ed. (New York: Teachers College Press, 1996), 47–61; McGreevy, *Parish Boundaries*; Cecilia A. Moore, "Keeping Harlem Catholic: African American Catholics in Harlem, 1920–1960," *American Catholic Studies* 114, no. 3 (2003): 3–21; Neary, *Crossing Parish Boundaries*.
5 Koenig, *History of the Parishes*, 972. See McGreevy, *Parish Boundaries*, 94–97, 134–136.

6. Rev. Steven Avella Oral History Project (1982–1983), "Fr. Martin Farrell interview transcript," 2, AAC.
7. Avella, *This Confident Church*, 284.
8. Ibid., 283. Avella discusses "convert work" among Chicago's African Americans in some detail on pp. 281–288.
9. Avella Oral History, "Farrell interview," 6–7.
10. Ibid., 8.
11. Gregory, interview with author.
12. James W. Sanders, *Education of an Urban Minority: Catholics in Chicago, 1833–1965* (Oxford: Oxford University Press, 1977), 213; Julia Wally Rath, "Faith, Hope, and Education: African American Parents of Children in Catholic Schools and Their Social and Religious Accommodation to Catholicism" (Ph.D. dissertation, University of Chicago, 1995), 109.
13. Vader, "Mission to Black America," 172; Avella, *This Confident Church*, 284. It is likely that Farrell and Richards were also influenced by the missionary efforts of the priests and sisters at St. Charles Borromeo parish in Harlem. For more on missionary efforts in Harlem, see Moore, "Keeping Harlem Catholic."
14. Avella, *This Confident Church*, 284.
15. Ibid., 286; Haas, *History of the Midwest Conference*, 10, 24; "The Catholic Church and the Negro (1960)," AAC; Eckert, "Methods of Convert-Making," 100–101.
16. St. Malachy Catholic Church (Chicago, Ill.), Baptismal Records.
17. Koenig, *History of the Parishes*, 459.
18. Mary Clarice Sobczyk, O.S.F., "A Survey of Catholic Education for the Negro of Five Parishes in Chicago" (Ph.D. dissertation, De Paul University, 1954), 49. For more on the success of evangelization at Holy Angels, see Suellen Hoy, "Lives on the Color Line: Catholic Sisters and African Americans in Chicago, 1890s–1960s," *U.S. Catholic Historian* 22, no. 1 (Winter 2004): 67–91; McGreevy, *Parish Boundaries*, 57–59.
19. Curran, "Missionary Apostolate," 298.
20. "September 1946," OFM, Corpus Christi Parish Bulletins (1943–1947, 1957–1959), IR00513.
21. St. Elizabeth Catholic Church (Chicago, Ill.), Baptismal Records. Curran cites "50 other parishes of the Archdiocese . . . engaged in the work of the apostolate among the Negroes," Curran, "Missionary Apostolate," 295.
22. McGreevy, *Parish Boundaries*, 57.
23. Haas, *History of the Midwest Clergy Conference*, 25.
24. Ibid., 9, 24.
25. "The Catholic Church and the Negro (1960)," AAC.
26. Ibid., 13.
27. Most of the little that has been written on Black Catholic conversion from the African American perspective has been written by Cecilia A. Moore, including "African American Catholic Conversion," *Sacred Rock* (Summer 1999), 1–6; "Conversion Narratives: The Dual Experiences and Voices of African American

Catholic Converts," *U.S. Catholic Historian* 28, no. 1 (Winter 2010): 27–40; "Writing Black Catholic Lives: Black Catholic Biographies and Autobiographies," *U.S. Catholic Historian* 29, no. 3 (Summer 2011): 43–58.

28 Sociological scholarship on Black Catholic conversion experienced a brief heyday in the 1970s. Scholars stressed different motivating factors, but shared a functionalist approach to conversion. Even when arriving at different conclusions, functionalists conceptualized "conversion" as a decision that fulfilled specific social, economic, and/or political functions for the convert. See Joe R. Feagin, "Black Catholics in the United States: An Exploratory Analysis," *Sociological Analysis* 29, no. 4 (1968): 246–254; Hart M. Nelsen and Lynda Dickson, "Attitudes of Black Catholics and Protestants: Evidence for Religious Identity," *Sociological Analysis* 33, no. 3 (Autumn 1972): 152–65; Jon P. Alston, Letitia T. Alston, and Emory Warrick, "Black Catholics: Social and Cultural Characteristics," *Journal of Black Studies* 2, no. 2 (December 1971): 245–255; Larry L. Hunt and Janet G. Hunt, "Black Catholicism and the Spirit of Weber," *Sociological Quarterly* 17, no. 3 (Summer 1976): 369–377; and Larry Hunt, "Black Catholicism and Secular Status: Integration, Conversion, and Consolidation," *Social Science Quarterly* 77, no. 4 (1996): 842–859.

29 This identitarian conception of conversion presumed that different modes of religious life directly corresponded to particular racial or ethnic identities. The Catholic Church in the United States, in this formulation, was understood to be a white religion. An identitarian interpretation of Black Catholic conversion, then, assumed that African Americans became Catholic because of either a conscious or subconscious desire to be white. This line of reasoning was particularly popular amidst the rise of Black racial consciousness in the 1960s and 1970s, often among Black Catholics themselves. I encountered this critique most frequently in interviews and oral historical records. Father George H. Clements, interview with author (January 30, 2012); Clarence Earl Williams, CPPS, "The Growth of Black Catholicism in Chicago since World War II: An Oral History" (July 2, 1976), Tapes in possession of Dr. Larry Murphy, Garrett Evangelical Seminary (Evanston, Ill.). It also features prominently throughout Lawrence Lucas, *Black Priest/White Church: Catholics and Racism* (New York: Random House, 1970).

30 Conversation with author (November 6, 2011). This off-the-cuff response from a prominent parishioner at St. Malachy parish proved invaluable for my research and served as the initial impetus for my approach to the study of Black Catholic conversion that centers the experiences of Black Catholics rather than always attempting to translate them into a sociological, psychological, or economic register.

31 Moore, "Conversion Narratives," 33.

32 "Reflections of a Negro Convert," *Interracial Review* 9, no. 12 (December 1936): 183.

33 James O'Toole, *The Faithful: A History of Catholics in America* (Cambridge, Mass.: Belknap Press of Harvard University Press, 2008), 104–105. For more on the his-

tory of women religious in the United States generally, see Margaret M. McGuinness, *Called to Serve: A History of Nuns in America* (New York: NYU Press, 2013). Special thanks to Mary Beth Fraser Connolly for directing me toward these U.S. women religious statistics.

34 McGuinness, *Called to Serve*, 8.
35 Hoy, *Good Hearts*, 86.
36 "Letters from Converts," SBS.
37 Ellen Tarry, *The Third Door: The Autobiography of an American Negro Woman* (Westport, Conn.: Negro Universities Press, 1955), 43–44.
38 Martin W. Farrell, *The Parish Catechism* (Chicago: United Book Service, 1954), 57; Sobczyk, "A Survey of Catholic Education," 21–22; "The Catholic Church and the Negro (1960)," 12, AAC.
39 Talal Asad, *Genealogies of Religion: Discipline and Reasons of Power in Christianity and Islam* (Baltimore, Md.: John Hopkins University Press, 1993), 45. Catherine Bell similarly de-centers belief in the study of religion. Bell focuses on processes of "ritualization," challenging scholarship that assumes that ritual action is an aftereffect of belief. Catherine Bell, *Ritual Theory, Ritual Practice* (Oxford: Oxford University Press, 1992).
40 Adam B. Seligman, Robert P. Weller, Michael J. Puett, and Bennett Simon, *Ritual and Its Consequences: An Essay on the Limits of Sincerity* (Oxford: Oxford University Press, 2008), 10.
41 Talal Asad engages in a similar critique of sincerity and religious belief in his essay, "Thinking about Religion, Belief, and Politics," in *The Cambridge Companion to Religious Studies*, Robert A. Orsi, ed. (Cambridge: Cambridge University Press, 2012), 43.
42 Asad, *Genealogies of Religion*, 33.
43 Kathryn M. Neckerman offers the most comprehensive study of the segregation and subsequent failure of public schools in "inner-city Chicago" in *Schools Betrayed: Roots of Failure in Inner-City Education* (Chicago: University of Chicago Press, 2007).
44 Drake and Cayton, *Black Metropolis*, 413–414.
45 Neary, *Crossing Parish Boundaries*, 50.
46 Michèle Foster discusses the attraction Catholic moral training had for Black parents, Catholic and non-Catholic alike, in "Mea Culpa, Mea Culpa, Mea Maxima Culpa: The French Catholic School Experience," in *Growing Up African American in Catholic Schools*, Irvine and Foster, ed., 103. Neary likewise discusses the appeal of the sisters' brand of disciplinary education, echoing observations Drake and Cayton made in their 1945 study of Bronzeville. Drake and Cayton, *Black Metropolis*, 412–415; Neary, *Crossing Parish Boundaries*, 49–51.
47 John T. McGreevy situates the rise of a comprehensive Catholic alternative to American public education in the broader trans-Atlantic Catholic revival known as "ultramontanism," which emphasized central authority in Rome over national variations within Catholicism and remained deeply suspicious of liberal modern-

ism. See John T. McGreevy, *Catholicism and American Freedom: A History* (New York: W. W. Norton, 2003), 7–42.
48 Harold A. Buetow, *Of Singular Benefit: The Story of Catholic Education in the United States* (New York: MacMillan, 1970), 227.
49 Ibid., 229.
50 Ibid., 231.
51 Ibid., 238.
52 Orsi, *History and Presence*, 124–125.
53 Ibid., 126.
54 Jacqueline Jordan Irvine, "Segregation and Academic Excellence: African American Catholic Schools in the South," in *Growing Up African American in Catholic Schools*, Irvine and Foster, ed., 87.
55 Ibid., 90.
56 Ibid., 102–103.
57 For more on Catholics and anti-communism, see Richard Gid Powers, "American Catholics and Catholic Americans: The Rise and Fall of Catholic Anti-Communism," *U.S. Catholic Historian* 22, no. 4 (Fall 2004): 17–35; Colleen Doody, *Detroit's Cold War: The Origins of Postwar Conservatism* (Champaign: University of Illinois Press, 2013); Orsi, "U.S. Catholics between Memory and Modernity," 11–42.
58 "St. Elizabeth, Summaries of the Annals (1952–1959)," SBS, H40 B2 IL: Chicago St. Elizabeth, Box 1, Folder 1. These practices were recorded by Sisters of the Blessed Sacrament at St. Anselm as well; see "St. Anselm Annals (1953–1970)," SBS, H40 B2 IL: Chicago St. Anselm, Box 1, Folder 2.
59 Irvine, "Segregation and Academic Excellence," 87.
60 Orsi, *History and Presence*, 135. Emphasis in the original.
61 Unpublished poems in possession of the author, courtesy the late Sister Mary Lou (Roman) Bigler, OSF.
62 Orsi, *History and Presence*, 128.
63 Tarry, *The Third Door*, 46. Elizabeth Laura Adams, a Black Californian convert who published the first major Black Catholic autobiography, also wrote about her initial encounters with the real presence of Christ in the Eucharist. Elizabeth Laura Adams, "The Finding of a Soul," *Sentinel of the Blessed Sacrament* (February 1930): 97–101. See also Moore, "Writing Black Catholic Lives."
64 "Corpus Christi, Annals (1940–1967)," OSF.
65 Sobczyk, "A Survey of Catholic Education," 20–21.
66 Ibid., 16. See also Sanders, *Education of an Urban Minority*, 219–221.
67 Sobczyk, "A Survey of Catholic Education," 21.
68 Ibid., 30.
69 Ibid., 38.
70 Farrell, *Parish Catechism*, 46–47.
71 Ibid., 27.
72 Ibid., 46.

73 See OFM, Corpus Christi Parish Bulletins. For more on the formation of Catholic bodies through devotional disciplines, see Robert A. Orsi, "Material Children: Making God's Presence Real for Catholic Boys and Girls and for the Adults in Relation to Them," in *Between Heaven and Earth: The Religious Worlds People Make and the Scholars Who Study Them* (Princeton, N.J.: Princeton University Press, 2005), 73–109.

74 "Letters from Converts," SBS.

75 "August 1945," 14–15, OFM, Corpus Christi Parish Bulletins.

76 "Converts of Color," 29.

77 "Letters from Converts," SBS.

78 Anthony Burke Smith writes at length on *The Song of Bernadette* and its impact on popular American Catholic devotional culture in *The Look of Catholics: Portrayals in Popular Culture from the Great Depression to the Cold War* (Lawrence: University Press of Kansas, 2010), 56–64. Sobczyk mentions this film being used in religious instruction classes; see Sobczyk, "A Survey of Catholic Education."

79 "Letters from Converts," SBS.

80 Ibid. For more on the Chicago-based devotion to St. Jude, see Orsi, *Thank You, St. Jude*.

81 For more on the revival and flourishing of American Catholic devotionalism in the first half of the twentieth century, see Joseph P. Chinnici, O.F.M., "The Catholic Community at Prayer, 1926–1976," in *Habits of Devotion*, O'Toole, ed., 52–70.

82 "Letters from Converts," SBS.

83 Ibid. Other stories confirm the influence ritual practices had on eventual converts. A sister at St. Anselm, for instance, described a convert who had "been in the habit of spending from one to two hours a day in the Catholic Church . . . to rest and to pray" for fifteen years before she joined an instruction class. "St. Anselm, Correspondence, 1937–1949," SBS.

84 "Letters from Converts," SBS.

85 Farrell, *Parish Catechism*, 45.

86 Moore, "Conversion Narratives," 33.

87 Ibid., 33.

88 See "Feb 9, 1958" and "Nov 23, 1958," OFM, Corpus Christi Parish Bulletins.

89 Mary Dolores Gadpaille, T.O.S.F., *That You May Die Easy* (Chicago: Tyde Publications, 1959), 69.

90 Farrell, *Parish Catechism*, 41.

91 Ibid., 40.

92 Ibid., 93.

93 Ibid., 88–99.

94 Ibid., 124.

95 "The True Meaning of Marriage" (November 1946), OFM, Corpus Christi Parish Bulletins.

96 Asad, *Genealogies of Religion*, 35.

97 Talal Asad, "Comments on Conversion," in *Conversion to Modernities: The Globalization of Christianity*, Peter van der Veer, ed. (New York: Routledge, 1996), 266.
98 Curran, "Missionary Apostolate."
99 Special thanks to Justine Howe for first calling my attention to this contrast between the "One True Church" on the one hand and Black religious plurality on the other.
100 "Letters from Converts," SBS. Another convert story, collected by a Sister at St. Anselm, conveyed this sentiment. "Two weeks ago I made up my mind to become a Catholic. . . . I have a young fellow for a real friend, who is a Catholic, and I like the way he lives; that is why I want to be a Catholic." "Chicago St. Anselm Correspondence, 1937–1949," SBS.
101 "Letters from Converts," SBS.

CHAPTER 3. THE LIVING STATIONS OF THE CROSS

1 Howard, interview with author.
2 This description of the experience of the Living Stations is reconstructed from contemporary newspaper accounts as well as "The Pantomime, 'Living Stations,' presented annually, during Lent, by the Parishioners of Corpus Christi Church, Chicago, Illinois" (unpublished manuscript, undated), OFM, IR00535; "The Living Stations of the Cross," *Extension: The National Catholic Monthly* (Catholic Church Extension Society) (March 1953); *Corpus Christi Parish: A Hundred Years of Faith, 1901–2001* (self-published by parish); Howard, interview with author.
3 Stange, *Bronzeville*, 7, 189. Corpus Christi's parish boundaries were from 45th to 53rd Streets (north-south) and from Wentworth to Cottage Grove Avenues (west-east); Koenig, *History of the Parishes*.
4 Drake and Cayton, *Black Metropolis*, 380.
5 Best, *Passionately Human, No Less Divine*, 2.
6 Ethel Payne, "'Stations of the Cross' at Corpus Christi Church," *Chicago Defender*, March 7, 1953, 9.
7 "The Pantomime," OFM.
8 Ibid.
9 Tiffany Vann Sprecher, Kristi Bain, and Richard Kieckhefer aided me in this devotional history of the stations. See Herbert Thurston, *The Stations of the Cross* (London: Burns and Oates, 1906); Roger Schoenbechler, O.S.B., "The Way of the Cross," *Orate Fratres* 12 (December 1937); Richard Kieckhefer, "Major Currents in Late Medieval Devotion," in *Christian Spirituality: High Middle Ages and Reformation*, Jill Raitt, ed. (New York: Crossroad, 1988), 75–107; Catherine Vincent, "The Way of the Cross," in *Encyclopedia of the Middle Ages*, André Vauchez, ed. (Cambridge: James Clarke and Co.: 2001).
10 For more on the Catholic performance of prayer and how it changed over the twentieth century, see Chinnici, "The Catholic Community at Prayer, 1926–1976," in *Habits of Devotion*, O'Toole, ed., 52–70; James P. McCartin, *Prayers of the Faith-*

ful: The Shifting Spiritual Life of American Catholics (Cambridge, Mass.: Harvard University Press, 2010).

11 "Greater Love Has No Man," *Chicago American*, February 15, 1956, 25.

12 I have reconstructed this imaginative engagement with the stations from the published accounts popular in Catholic magazines in the same years the Living Stations were running. A small sample of this genre of stations-of-the-cross meditations would include Fulton J. Sheen, *Characters of the Passion* (New York: P. J. Kennedy and Sons, 1947); Jule Mary Forster, "Mrs. Flannery Says the Stations," *Catholic Home Journal* (March 1951), 13, 30; C. Houselander, "The Stations of the Cross," *Messenger of the Sacred Heart* (February 1954); Donald F. Miller, "How to Grieve for Your Sins," *Liguorian* (April 1955), 193–200; Delphine Fleury, "14 Steps to Glory," *Extension: A National Catholic Monthly* (November 1956), 21, 46–47; Henry D. Sutton, C.S.S.R., "How to Make the Way of the Cross Privately," *Liguorian* (March 1957); Edwin Dorzweiler, O.F.M., *The Franciscan Way of the Cross* (Patterson, N.J.: St. Anthony Guild Press, 1958).

13 "March 1945," 13–15, OFM, Corpus Christi Parish Bulletins.

14 Orsi, *Between Heaven and Earth*, 21.

15 The *Chicago Tribune* described him as "widely recognized for scholarship in the medieval religious drama and noted for his leadership among Franciscans toward revival of the ancient art"; Rev. John Evans, "Medieval Play Has Revival at Corpus Christi," *Chicago Daily Tribune*, March 13, 1938, W1.

16 "Lent 1944," OFM, Chronicle of the Corpus Christi Church and Friary (1929–1987), IR00525.

17 "March 1946," OFM, Corpus Christi Parish Bulletins.

18 The literature on this Black Chicago Renaissance continues to grow. For more, see Davarian Baldwin, *Chicago's New Negro Movement: Modernity, the Great Migration, and Black Urban Life* (Chapel Hill: University of North Carolina Press, 2007); Richard Hope and Robert A. Courage, *The Muse in Bronzeville: African American Creative Expression in Chicago, 1932–1950* (New Brunswick, N.J.: Rutgers University Press, 2011); Darlene Clark Hine and John McClusky, Jr., ed., *Black Chicago Renaissance* (Champaign: University of Illinois Press, 2012); Elizabeth Schroeder Schlabach, *Along the Streets of Bronzeville: Black Chicago's Literary Landscape* (Champaign: University of Illinois Press, 2013).

19 Green, *Selling the Race*.

20 Ibid., 132.

21 Mary Dolores Gadpaille referred to the parish as "eighty-five percent convert": "Gadpaille to Barth (23 April, 1958)," OFM, Corpus Christi Correspondence.

22 "October 1943," 3, OFM.

23 See Best, *Passionately Human, No Less Divine*, 94–117; Du Bois, *The Souls of Black Folk*, 212.

24 Du Bois, *The Souls of Black Folk*, 212.

25 Best, *Passionately Human, No Less Divine*, 51.

26 Milton Rogovin, "Storefront Churches—Buffalo, N.Y.," in *Aperture* 10.2 (Rochester, N.Y.: Aperture, 1962): 64–85.
27 Ibid., 96.
28 This description of Black Pentecostal practice is drawn from Alexander, *Black Fire*, 28–60. See also Amos Yong and Estrelda Y. Alexander, ed., *Afro-Pentecostalism: Black Pentecostal and Charismatic Christianity in History and Culture* (New York: NYU Press, 2011).
29 Best, *Passionately Human, No Less Divine*, 57, 128.
30 Ibid., 152, 173.
31 Ibid., 189.
32 McDannell, *Picturing Faith*, 245–247.
33 Kathryn Lofton, "The Perpetual Primitive in African American Religious History," in *The New Black Gods*, Curtis and Sigler, ed., 171–191; Evans, *Burden of Black Religion*.
34 For more on Catholic distinctiveness in the twentieth-century United States, see Orsi, "U.S. Catholics between Memory and Modernity."
35 "2,000 Witness Colored Actors in Lenten Rites," *Chicago Daily Tribune*, March 7, 1938, 3; Rev. John Evans, "Medieval Play Has Revival at Corpus Christi," *Chicago Daily Tribune*, March 13, 1938, W1.
36 For more, see Brian James Hallstoos, "Windy City, Holy Land: Willa Saunders Jones and Black Sacred Music and Drama" (Ph.D. dissertation, University of Iowa, 2009).
37 Marc Connelly, *The Green Pastures: A Fable Suggested by Roark Bradford's Southern Sketches, "Ol' Man Adam an' His Chillun"* (New York: Farrar & Rinehart, 1929), xv. For more on *The Green Pastures*, see Curtis J. Evans, "The Religious and Racial Meanings of *The Green Pastures*," *Religion and American Culture: A Journal of Interpretation* 1, no. 18 (Winter 2008): 59–93; and Judith Weisenfeld, *Hollywood Be Thy Name: African American Religion in American Film, 1929–1949* (Berkeley: University of California Press, 2007).
38 Winona L. Fletcher, "Witnessing a 'Miracle': Sixty Years of Heaven Bound at Big Bethel in Atlanta," in *Black American Literature Forum* 25, no. 1 (1991): 85. See also Weisenfeld, *Hollywood Be Thy Name*, 98–99; and Gregory D. Coleman, *We're Heaven Bound! Portrait of a Black Sacred Drama* (Athens: University of Georgia Press, 1992).
39 The *New World* praised the "Oriental costumes, proper to the time of Christ." Agnes T. Ryan, "Corpus Christi Parishioners Present Living Stations during Lent," *New World*, February 28, 1941, 9. Even articles that offered scarce description noted that the costumes and props were "authentic": "Corpus Christi Group to Re-Enact Drama of Passion Weekly," *New World*, February 25, 1938, 10; "Negroes Enact Way of Cross," *New World*, March 13, 1942, 9.
40 Aidan Potter, O.F.M., "The Living Stations," *Franciscan Herald*, May 1938, 335; Ryan, "Corpus Christi Parishioners Present Living Stations," 9; "Vivid Pantomime

of Victorious Death," *Chronicle of the Corpus Christi Church and Friary (1929–1987)*, OFM, IR00525.

41 "Chicago R.C. Church in Lenten Drama," *New York Amsterdam News*, March 10, 1951, 16.

42 "Stations Enacted during Lent at Corpus Christi," and "Revive Old Lenten Drama at St. Joseph's," *New World*, February 17, 1939, 9.

43 For more on the reception (and reproduction) of Oberammergau in the United States, see Sonja E. Spear, "Claiming the Passion: American Fantasies of the Oberammergau Passion Play, 1923–1947," *Church History* 80, no. 4 (December 2011): 832–862.

44 Ryan, "Corpus Christi Parishioners Present Living Stations."

45 "Negroes Enact Way of Cross," *New World*.

46 "Children Inspire Greater Love for Way of the Cross," *New World*, February 27, 1942, 8.

47 Orsi, *Gods of the City*, 4.

48 Baldwin, *Chicago's New Negro Movement*, 157.

49 Fletcher, "Witnessing a 'Miracle,'" 86.

50 Ibid., 87.

51 Potter, "The Living Stations," 335.

52 Ibid., 334.

53 For more on "primitive vitality," see Orsi, *Gods of the City*, 8–11; and Evans, *Burden of Black Religion*, 7–9, 204–205.

54 Potter, "The Living Stations," 332, 335.

55 Evans, "Medieval Play Has Revival."

56 "2,000 Witness Colored Actors in Lenten Rites," 3.

57 Payne, "'Stations of the Cross' at Corpus Christi Church," 9.

58 Sylvester A. Johnson, "The Rise of the Black Ethnics: The Ethnic Turn in African American Religions, 1916–1945," *Religion and American Culture: A Journal of Interpretation* 20, no. 2 (2010): 127. Weisenfeld's *New World A-Coming* similarly studies the ways migration-era religious movements offered alternative "religio-racial identities" for many African Americans.

59 Weisenfeld, *New World A-Coming*, 6.

60 Johnson, "Rise of the Black Ethnics," 141.

61 Louis A. DeCaro, Jr., *Malcolm and the Cross: The Nation of Islam, Malcolm X, and Christianity* (New York: NYU Press, 1998), 105.

62 Fauset, *Black Gods of the Metropolis*, 31.

63 Ibid., 41.

64 Johnson, "Rise of Black Ethnics," 141–142.

65 Weisenfeld, *New World A-Coming*, 90.

66 For more on the distinctive practices of Black Muslims, Black Jews, and other new Black religious movements, see Edward E. Curtis IV, *Islam in Black America: Identity, Liberation, and Difference in African-American Islamic Thought* (Albany: SUNY Press, 2002); Johnson, "Rise of the Black Ethnics"; Dorman, *Chosen People*; Weisenfeld, *New World A-Coming*.

67 E. U. Essien-Udom, *Black Nationalism: The Search for an Identity* (Chicago: University of Chicago Press, 1962), 15, 205–206.
68 Weisenfeld, *New World A-Coming*, 92.
69 Fauset, *Black Gods of the Metropolis*, 33.
70 Ibid., 33, 36–37.
71 Ibid., 48.
72 Ibid., 50.
73 Weisenfeld, *New World A-Coming*, 227.
74 Ibid., 37.
75 Evans, *Burden of Black Religion*, 272.
76 "May 1945," 11, OFM, Corpus Christi Parish Bulletins.
77 Ibid.
78 "January 27, 1957," OFM.
79 "Reverend A. P. Jackson: Tower of Strength," in *Bridges of Memory: Chicago's Second Generation of Black Migration*, Timuel D. Black, Jr. (Evanston, Ill.: Northwestern University Press, 2007), 50.
80 Neary, *Crossing Parish Boundaries*, 60.
81 Father George H. Clements, interview with author (January 30, 2012).
82 "Living Stations," *Extension*, 14.
83 "Gadpaille to Barth (3 April, 1958)," 2–3, OFM.
84 "Gadpaille to Barth" (undated), 1, OFM, Corpus Christi Correspondence.
85 "Letters from Converts," SBS.
86 "Gadpaille to Barth (23 April, 1958)," 2, OFM.
87 Ibid.
88 McKay, "Why I Became Catholic," 32.
89 Nancy M. Davis, "Finding Voice: Revisiting Race and American Catholicism in Detroit," *American Catholic Studies* 114, no. 3 (2003): 50. Ellipsis in the original.
90 "Spoke for His Race," 3.
91 Neary discusses the attraction "Catholicism's universality" held for Black Catholics, in *Crossing Parish Boundaries*, 63–69.

CHAPTER 4. BLACK CATHOLICS AND BLACK POWER

1 Clements, interview with author (January 30, 2012).
2 Ibid.
3 Clements had a controversial career even beyond the issues discussed in this book. He became nationally renowned in the 1980s, for instance, when he became the first Catholic priest in the Chicago area to adopt children. This was depicted in the film *The Father Clements Story* (Lionsgate, 1987).
4 The only published treatments of this particular Father George Clements controversy (surrounding the pastorate of St. Dorothy church) are in McGreevy, *Parish Boundaries*, 225–226; and Lucas, *Black Priest/White Church*, 118–128.
5 Here I am drawing on Michael Eric Dyson's categorization of different modes of Blackness: "incidental," "accidental," and "intentional." See Michael Eric Dyson,

April 4 1968: Martin Luther King, Jr.'s Death and How It Changed America (New York: Basic Civitas Books, 2009), 231–232.

6 For more on the history of the Council itself, see Xavier Rynne, *Vatican Council II* (Maryknoll, N.Y.: Orbis Books, 1999); David G. Schultenover, ed., *Vatican II: Did Anything Happen?* (New York: Continuum, 2007); John W. O'Malley, *What Happened at Vatican II* (Cambridge, Mass.: Belknap Press of Harvard University Press, 2008); Massimo Faggioli, *Vatican II: The Battle for Meaning* (New York: Paulist Press, 2012).

7 See Schultenover, *Vatican II: Did Anything Happen?* Colleen McDannell, *The Spirit of Vatican II: A History of Catholic Reform in America* (New York: Basic Books, 2011); Orsi, *Between Heaven and Earth*, 56.

8 Here I am influenced by The Lived History of Vatican II project, sponsored by Northwestern University and the Cushwa Center for the Study of American Catholicism at the University of Notre Dame.

9 Historian Robert Self notes that from 1957 to 1967, Black freedom struggle precepts changed from "faith in law to faith in direct action; from faith in individualist remedies to faith in collective and community-based remedies; and from faith in American pluralism to faith in Black Nationalism and radicalism." Robert O. Self, "The Black Panther Party in the Long Civil Rights Era," in *In Search of the Black Panther Party: New Perspectives on a Revolutionary Movement*, Jama Lazerow and Yohuru Williams, ed. (Durham, N.C.: Duke University Press, 2006), 36.

10 This definition of Black power as a "constellation" of ideas is drawn from a lecture Thomas Sugrue gave at the 2010 Northwestern University conference, "South Meets North." This fits well with Robert L. Allen's argument in *Black Awakening in Capitalist America: An Analytic History* (New York: Anchor Books, 1970). He argues for the multivalence of "Black power," noting: "The original formulation of Black power as expressed by Carmichael contained not only the seeds of militant Black reformism but also the genesis of revolutionary Black nationalism" (55).

11 Thomas Sugrue identifies Black Power as "a series of experiments, attempts to envision a political alternative to the racial liberalism" prevalent through the postwar era. Sugrue acknowledges, although "it is difficult to reduce black power to its essence," they shared broad ideological commitments to thinking globally and acting locally, a psychological understanding of racism, and a cultural politics of Blackness; Sugrue, *Sweet Land of Liberty*, 354–355. Martha Biondi argues that Black Power emphasized "the creation of Black-controlled institutions and racial solidarity and entailed a vigorous emphasis on culture—both in celebrating African American culture and in seeing it as a catalyst for political action and the forging of a new Black consciousness." They "saw themselves as unmasking U.S. institutions . . . and exposing the whiteness disguised as universalism." Biondi, *The Black Revolution on Campus*, 4.

12 Clements, interview with author (January 30, 2012).

13 "St. Dorothy Church Commemorative: 75th Anniversary" (1991), AAC.

14 Clements, interview with author (January 30, 2012). Biography courtesy of Meg Hall, archivist for the Archdiocese of Chicago.
15 "Fr. George H. Clements," Chicago History Museum Research Center (CHM), Chicago Police Department Red Squad Archive, Box 297, Folder 7 (Red Squad Papers).
16 This narrative of Father George Clements and the Afro-American Patrolmen's League is drawn from the Afro-American Patrolmen's League Records (AAPL) housed in the Chicago History Museum.
17 "Afro American Patrolmen's League," untitled pledge or mission statement, CHM, AAPL, Box 37, Folder 8. See Robert McClory, *The Man Who Beat Clout City* (Chicago: Swallow Press, 1977). Though Clements (and Black Catholics) are notably absent, for more on the AAPL, see Beryl Satter, "Cops, Gangs, and Revolutionaries in 1960s Chicago: What Black Police Can Tell Us about Power," *Journal of Urban History* 42, no. 6 (2015): 1–25.
18 Joshua Bloom and Waldo E. Martin, Jr., *Black against Empire: The History and Politics of the Black Panther Party* (Berkeley: University of California Press, 2013).
19 See Jakobi Williams, *From the Bullet to the Ballot: The Illinois Chapter of the Black Panther Party and Racial Coalition Politics in Chicago* (Chapel Hill: University of North Carolina Press, 2013), 15–51; Taylor Branch, *At Canaan's Edge: America in the King Years, 1965–1968* (New York: Simon and Schuster, 2006), 501–561. This period also witnessed the rise of Black student protests on college campuses in Chicago, most notably Northwestern University and Crane College (later Malcolm X College); see Biondi, *The Black Revolution on Campus*, 79–113. Black Power also served as the roots for Black electoral politics in the 1970s and 1980s; see Manning Marable, "Black Power in Chicago: An Historical Overview of Class Stratification and Electoral Politics in a Black Urban Community," *Review of Radical Political Economics* 17, no. 3 (1985): 157–182.
20 Clements, interview with author (July 9, 2012).
21 Bob Hunter, "Rev. Clements Denies Being 'Black Militant Separatist,'" *Chicago Daily Defender*, August 15, 1968, 3. "White Priest and Nuns Quit in Clash with Negro Cleric," *New York Times*, August 13, 1968, 23.
22 Hunter, "Black Militant Separatist," 3.
23 "Name Negro Pastor, Parish Tells Cody," *Chicago Tribune*, December 16, 1968, 8.
24 Ibid.
25 D. J. R. Bruckner, "Race, Authority Issues Peril Chicago Diocese: Demand That Militant Priest Be Named Pastorate Challenges Cardinal's Power," *Los Angeles Times*, February 3, 1969, A17.
26 Avella, *This Confident Church*, 344; Satter, *Family Properties*, 233 and 317; Mc-Greevy, *Parish Boundaries*, 186–187; Charles Dahm, O.P., *Power and Authority in the Catholic Church: Cardinal Cody in Chicago* (South Bend, Ind.: University of Notre Dame Press, 1981).
27 Patricia Krizmis's *Chicago Tribune* article, "New World Assails Black Groups' Tactics,'" January 12, 1969, noted that only Father Lambert and one other priest from

his ordination class were pastors and that no priests from Clements's ordination class had yet been made pastor.
28. "Name Negro Pastor, Parish Tells Cody."
29. "Father Rollins Lambert Pastor of St. Dorothy," *New World*, December 20, 1968, 3.
30. John McGreevy describes the "logics of the civil rights movement and the Second Vatican Council" as "anti-authoritarian" and discusses the St. Dorothy controversy as part of "the crisis in authority and the collapse of interracialism"; McGreevy, *Parish Boundaries*, 216 and 227.
31. Cardinal Cody invoked the vow of obedience priests take to their bishop upon ordination. Michael D. Wamble, "Black Priests, Black Panthers: Breaking Barriers at Every Turn," *New World*, October 1, 2000.
32. Clements, interview with author (January 30, 2012). See also Lucas, *Black Priest/White Church*, 118–128.
33. "St. Dorothy's New Pastor: Appointment Praised by Parish Council," *New World*, December 27, 1968, 1.
34. "Blacks in Controversy at St. Dorothy," *New World*, January 10, 1969, 1.
35. John T. McGreevy, "Racial Justice and the People of God: American Catholics, Civil Rights, and the Second Vatican Council," *Religion and American Culture: A Journal of Interpretation* 4, no. 2 (1994): 225. Cyprian Davis, O.S.B., and Jamie Phelps, O.P., echo this assessment in *"Stamped with the Image of God": African Americans as God's Image in Black* (Maryknoll, N.Y.: Orbis Books, 2003), 111.
36. McGreevy, *Parish Boundaries*; and Koehlinger, *The New Nuns*.
37. Neary, *Crossing Parish Boundaries*; and Karen Johnson, "Beyond Parish Boundaries: Black Catholics and the Quest for Racial Justice," *Religion and American Culture: A Journal of Interpretation* 25, no. 2 (Summer 2015): 264–300.
38. Biondi, *Black Revolution on Campus*.
39. Sr. M. Martin de Porres Grey, "The Church, Revolution and Black Catholics," *Black Scholar* 2, no. 4 (December 1970): 23. Thank you, Shannen Dee Williams, for directing me to this essay.
40. Lawrence Lucas emphasizes the importance of Chicago in the rise of the Black Catholic Clergy Caucus. See Lucas, *Black Priest/White Church*, 183–184.
41. "A Statement of the Black Catholic Clergy Caucus, 1968," in *"Stamped with the Image of God,"* 111.
42. Ibid., 112.
43. Ibid.
44. Shannen Dee Williams first told me the story of Sister Martin de Porres Grey's exclusion from the founding of the BCCC. She also suggested that, if we are looking for a Catholic Malcolm X, we need look no farther than Sister Grey. Grey (now Dr. Patricia Grey) has since left the sisterhood. Williams has written extensively on Black Catholic sisters, detailing the violence they faced from white sisters as they struggled to desegregate religious orders in the United States. Her forthcoming book will be the first comprehensive study of Black Catholic sisters in the United States. See Shannen Dee Williams, "Subversive Habits: Black Nuns and the Struggle

to Desegregate Catholic America after World War I" (Ph.D. dissertation, Rutgers University, 2013); "The Color of Christ's Brides," in "Forum: Race, White Supremacy, and the Making of American Catholicism," Cressler, ed.; and "Subversive Images and Forgotten Truths," in *American Catholic Studies* 127, no. 3 (Fall 2016).

45 "The Survival of Soul: National Black Sisters' Conference Position Paper, 1969," in *"Stamped with the Image of God,"* 114.

46 Ibid., 115.

47 Faith C. Christmas, "Catholic Issue Still Hot," *Chicago Daily Defender*, January 4, 1969, 1.

48 "Blacks in Controversy." This point echoed a public statement Father Clements and six other Black Chicago priests made earlier that year, which argued that "the Church in the United States has a 'suspicious disdain' of militant Negro elements," and termed it a "great mistake." "7 Negro Priests Criticize Church: Deplore 'Suspicious Disdain' of Militants on Race," *New York Times*, February 18, 1968, 84. Cited in Katrina M. Sanders, "Black Catholic Clergy and the Struggle for Civil Rights: Winds of Change," in *Uncommon Faithfulness: The Black Catholic Experience*, M. Shawn Copeland with LaReine-Marie Mosely, S.N.D., and Albert J. Raboteau, ed. (Maryknoll, N.Y.: Orbis Books, 2009), 91.

49 "Blacks in Controversy."

50 The *New World*, which covered the meeting in depth, also disputed the challenges to Lambert's Blackness. They reminded their readers, for instance, that "Father Lambert had been chosen by the Black priests of America to be chairman of their national Black clergy caucus held in Washington last fall." "Blacks in Controversy."

51 "Blacks in Controversy."

52 Sugrue, *Sweet Land of Liberty*, 354–355.

53 Williams, *From the Bullet to the Ballot*, 109.

54 Quoted in Williams, *From the Bullet to the Ballot*, 109–110.

55 *Sacrosanctum Concilium*, Constitution on the Sacred Liturgy, Paul VI, December 4, 1963.

56 Williams, *From the Bullet to the Ballot*, 110.

57 "Negro Pastor in Chicago Says Cody Is 'Unconsciously Racist,'" *New York Times*, January 11, 1969, 37.

58 Patricia Krizmis, "Black Pastor Charges Cody Is Racist and Threatens to Quit," *Chicago Tribune*, January 11, 1969, 10.

59 Faith C. Christmas, "Controversy in Catholic Church: Furor Growing as Black Pastor Threatens to Quit," *Chicago Defender*, January 13, 1969, 2.

60 "Blacks in Controversy at St. Dorothy," 1.

61 Krizmis, "Black Pastor."

62 Lucas, *Black Priest/White Church*, 120.

63 Ibid., 13.

64 Richard Philbrick, "Jungle Drums Throb at Mass, Irk Cody," *Chicago Tribune*, December 6, 1968, 20; "African Masses Considered," *Chicago Daily Defender*, December 5, 1968, 1.

65 Lucas, *Black Priest/White Church*, 121–122.
66 "St. Dorothy Commemorative" (1991) 22, AAC. Clements, CHM, Red Squad Papers.
67 D. J. R. Bruckner, "Race, Authority Issues Peril Chicago Diocese," *Los Angeles Times*, February 3, 1969, 17.
68 Faith C. Christmas, "New Black Catholic Mass Draws Thousands," *Chicago Defender*, January 13, 1969, 3.
69 Anne Getz, "Rev. Jesse Jackson Joins Black Priest Fight, Challenges Cody," *Chicago Tribune*, January 13, 1969, 6.
70 Clements, CHM, Red Squad Papers.
71 Lucas, *Black Priest/White Church*, 121.
72 Clements, CHM, Red Squad Papers.
73 Faith C. Christmas, "Black Mass Acclaimed: Lambert," *Chicago Defender*, January 15, 1969, 3.
74 "Time to 'Lay It Down' in St. Dorothy Dispute," *New World*, January 17, 1969.
75 P. Armour, "'Quiet' Voice from St. Dorothy," *New World*, January 31, 1969.
76 Elizabeth Johnson, "Views and Opinions: St. Dorothy Member Speaks," *Chicago Defender*, February 8, 1969, 12.
77 L. P., "Mass 'Shocking,'" *New World*, Feb 14, 1969.
78 "January 12, 1969," OFM, Corpus Christi Church Bulletin.
79 "Black Controversy Moves beyond St. Dorothy Issue," *New World*, January 24, 1969.
80 This conspiratorial discourse of outsiders infiltrating and upsetting an otherwise peaceful status quo was not unique or altogether new, but reminiscent of white Mississippians who criticized white and Black activists who attempted to register disenfranchised Black citizen outsiders fomenting rebellion in an otherwise contented population.
81 "Black Controversy."
82 Faith C. Christmas, "'No Threats'—White Priests Support Fr. Clements," *Chicago Defender*, January 22, 1969, 3–4.
83 Mattie Cross, "Reader Says 'No' to Militants," *New World*, January 31, 1969.
84 E. F. H., "Church Has Different Role to Play," *New World*, January 31, 1969.
85 Raboteau, "Minority within a Minority," 136.
86 Singh, *Black Is a Country*, 214.
87 This conception of the relationship between Black Power and the Second Vatican Council has been shaped by conversations with Mary Henold. She argues that for many Catholic women the conversations and debates about the Second Vatican Council were inseparable, unintelligible even, outside of contemporaneous debates about feminism. Mary Henold, Comments at "Presidential Roundtable: The Place of Gender in Catholic Studies," American Catholic Historical Association, Washington, D.C., January 4, 2014. See also Mary Henold, *Catholic and Feminist: The Surprising History of the American Catholic Feminist Movement* (Chapel Hill: University of North Carolina Press, 2008).

88 "Black Militants Crash Meeting," *New World*, January 24, 1969, 1–2.
89 Ibid.
90 Clements, interview with author (July 9, 2012).
91 The notable exception to this is George Augustus Stallings, Jr., who broke from the Roman Catholic Church in 1990 to found the Imani Temple African-American Catholic Congregation. Throughout the 1970s there were debates as to whether African American Catholics should form their own Rite—meaning that they would represent a self-determined Catholic community with its own governance and leadership, separate from but in communion with Rome (akin to the Maronite Church). In the end, though, there was no break from the Roman Church for the vast majority of Black Catholics. For further discussion of this debate about a separate Black Catholic Rite, see Mary E. McGann and Eva Marie Lumas, "The Emergence of African American Catholic Worship," *U.S. Catholic Historian*, 19, no. 2 (Spring 2001): 27–65.
92 Charles D. Burns, S.V.D., "Black Catholics Today," in *The Word in the World: Divine Word Missionaries, '76 Black Apostolate* (Techny, Ill.: Society of the Divine Word, 1976), 19.
93 Mary Roger Thibodeaux, S.B.S., *A Black Nun Looks at Black Power* (New York: Sheed & Ward, 1972), 7.
94 McGreevy, "Racial Justice and the People of God," 223.
95 Ibid., 224.
96 Patricia Krizmis, "Three Negroes Are Selected to Be Pastors," *Chicago Tribune*, June 13, 1969, 15.
97 Kevin Lahart, "Cody 'Deliberate Racist,' Black Priest's Accusation," *Chicago Today*, June 30, 1969, 14. Clipping collected in Clements, Red Squad Papers, CHM.
98 Williams, *From the Bullet to the Ballot*, 19.

CHAPTER 5. BECOMING BLACK CATHOLICS

1 Jeffrey Haas, *Assassination of Fred Hampton: How the FBI and the Chicago Police Murdered a Black Panther* (Chicago: Chicago Review Press, 2009).
2 Clements, interview with author (July 9, 2012).
3 Haas, *Assassination of Fred Hampton*, 96–97.
4 Wamble, "Black Priests, Black Panthers." See also interview with George Clements, conducted by Blackside, Inc., on October 19, 1989, for *Eyes on the Prize II: America at the Racial Crossroads 1965 to 1985*. Washington University Libraries, Film and Media Archive, Henry Hampton Collection; interview with Bobby Rush, conducted on October 20, 1988.
5 Clements's use of "acclamatio populorum" is recounted in a number of sources: Linda Witt, "Chicago's Activist Priest, Father George Clements, Seeks a New Title: Dad," *People Magazine* 14, no. 25, December 22, 1980; Clements, interview with author (July 9, 2012); *The Father Clements Story* (1987). Clements publicly urged the Catholic Church to canonize King even before he took over as pastor of Holy

Angels; see Faith C. Christmas, "Canonize Dr. King, Rev. Clements Urges: Thousands Mark Birthday," *Chicago Daily Defender,* January 16, 1969, 1.
6   Haas, *Assassination of Fred Hampton*, 98.
7   Ibid., 109.
8   Interview with Clements, *Eyes on the Prize II*. African American studies scholar Mark Anthony Neal has reflected specifically on the student proclamation "I Am Fred Hampton" and the significance of the "I Am . . ." construction in Black freedom struggles. See Mark Anthony Neal, "'I Am . . .': Troy Davis, Fred Hampton, and the Black Freedom Movement" (September 24, 2011): newblackman.blogspot.com.
9   "Mural for Holy Angels," *Chicago Daily Defender*, August 1, 1970, 3.
10 For a few examples, see Joseph M. Davis, "The Black Catholic Movement: Where Is the Revolution Today?" (Lecture, 1976), UND, Joseph M. Davis Papers (CDAV), Box 1, Folder 5; Clarence Joseph Rivers, "Toward Unanimity," *Freeing the Spirit: The Magazine of Black Liturgy Published by the National Office for Black Catholics* 1, no. 3 (Summer 1972): 4; Mtumishi Wa Watu Wangu (Michael St. Julien), "From the Reaction of Rebellion to the Action of Revolution," *Freeing the Spirit* (Summer 1972): 56; Joseph M. Davis and Cyprian Lamar Rowe, "The Development of the National Office for Black Catholics," *U.S. Catholic Historian* 7, nos. 2–3, "The Black Catholic Community, 1880–1987" (Spring–Summer 1988): 270, 282.
11 This narrative survey of the Black Catholic movement is based on a number of different sources, many of which I address at greater length below. These sources include Lucas, *Black Priest/White Church*; *Freeing the Spirit* (Summer 1972); *The Word in the World*; Davis and Rowe, "The Development of the National Office for Black Catholics"; Davis and Phelps, *"Stamped with the Image of God,"* 111–130. See also UND, Joseph M. Davis Papers and National Office for Black Catholics Papers.
12 Sister Jamie Phelps first pointed me in this direction during an interview. Sister Jamie Phelps, O.P., interview with author (March 8, 2012). See also Jamie T. Phelps, "The Theology and Process of Inculturation: A Theology of Hope for African American Catholics in the United States," *New Theology Review* 7, no. 1 (February 1994): 5–13.
13 Clements, CHM, Red Squad Papers.
14 Patricia Krizmis, "Black Pride Is Way of Life in Holy Angels School: Holy Angels' Happy Scholars," *Chicago Tribune*, March 7, 1971, 3. The average income of families in the neighborhood continued to decline so that, by the 1990s, it "contains the greatest number of Chicago families in federally supported dwellings. The main sustenance of most of these families, two-thirds of which are headed by single parents, is welfare." Portia H. Shields, "Holy Angels: Pocket of Excellence," in *Growing Up African American in Catholic Schools*, Irvine and Foster, ed., 76.
15 See Krizmis, "Black Pride Is Way of Life"; Sutor, "We're Doing It Ourselves," 27; Sutor, "The Church and Inner City Schools"; Connie Lauerman, "Thriving Inner City School: S.R.O. at Holy Angels Elementary," *Chicago Tribune*, November

18, 1973, 37. The term "inner city" is problematic, to say the least. I use it in this chapter since it was the term used at the time by both Black Catholics themselves and those commenting on Black Catholic communities. Though the term implied geography, it should be understood as a social, racial, and economic signifier. It referred to low-income, predominantly Black communities in urban areas, often used interchangeably with "ghetto." An example of the prevalence of this term among Catholics would be Chicago's Inner-City Priests' Association, comprised of pastors and priests in predominantly Black parishes in the city of Chicago.

16 See Hirsch, *Making the Second Ghetto*; Biondi, *To Stand and Fight*; Self, *American Babylon*; Satter, *Family Properties*; Thomas J. Sugrue, *The Origins of the Urban Crisis: Race and Inequality in Postwar Detroit* (Princeton, N.J.: Princeton University Press, 2005); Keeanga-Yamahtta Taylor, "From American Dream to Predatory Lending: Public/Private Programs to Promote Home Ownership among Low-Income African Americans in the 1970s" (Ph.D. dissertation, Northwestern University, 2013).

17 Self, *American Babylon*, 1.

18 Ibid., 104. See also Keeanga-Yamahtta Taylor, "Back Story to the Neoliberal Moment: Race Taxes and the Political Economy of Black Urban Housing in the 1960s," in "Austerity, Neoliberalism, and Black Communities," Barbara Ransby, ed., *Souls: A Critical Journal of Black Politics, Culture, and Society* 14, nos. 3–4 (2012): 188.

19 See Satter, *Family Properties*, 8, 70; Self, *American Babylon* (2003), 16, 166.

20 Davis and Phelps, *"Stamped with the Image of God,"* 112.

21 Raboteau, "Minority within a Minority," 133.

22 "Black Catholic Blues," *Newsweek* 84 (December 30, 1974), 45.

23 Joseph M. Davis, "Where Is the Revolution Today?" UND.

24 Joseph M. Davis, "The Position of the Catholic Church in the Black Community," *Homiletic and Pastoral Review* LXIX, no. 9 (June 1969), reprinted in *Freeing the Spirit* (Summer 1972): 19.

25 Josephite Conference transcript (July 1971), 218, UND, CDAV, Box 1, Folder 28.

26 "Black Catholic Blues."

27 Robert McClory, "Black Catholics: Church Losing Ground," *National Catholic Reporter* February 4, 1977, 1.

28 Clarence Williams, CPPS, "The Future of the Black Catholic Church," *Freeing the Spirit* 5, no. 4 (1977): 36.

29 Lucas, *Black Priest/White Church*, 188. This conflict among priests was echoed by Charles Burns, S.V.D., who criticized the "revolutionary bombast" of the early movement; Charles Burns, "Black Catholics Today," *The Word in the World*, 20.

30 "Unification of 6 Black Catholic Interest Groups," UND, CDAV, Box 2, Folder 7.

31 Joseph M. Davis, "Reflections on a Central Office for Black Catholicism," *Freeing the Spirit* (Summer 1972), 30–38; Davis and Rowe, "The Development of the National Office for Black Catholics"; Davis and Phelps, ed., *"Stamped with the Image of God"* (2003), 111–130.

32 McGreevy, *Parish Boundaries*, 242–243.
33 Williams, "The Future of the Black Catholic Church," 35.
34 "Black Catholic Schools Hurting," *Chicago Defender*, January 19, 1972, 3.
35 David Sutor, "We're Doing It By Ourselves," *U.S. Catholic* 37 (November 1972), 30.
36 For more sources on the challenges facing Black Catholic schools, see David Sutor, "Special Report: The Church and Inner City Schools: Partners in Education," *New World*, February–March, 1972; Shannen Dee Williams, "Troubling the Waters and Shifting Paradigms: Making the Case for Centering Black Nuns in the Fight for Racial and Educational Justice in Twentieth-Century (Catholic) America," paper presented at the annual meeting of the American Historical Association, Washington, D.C., January 2–4, 2014.
37 "Special Statement: The Crisis of Catholic Education in the Black Community," UND, CDAV, Box 1, Folder 5, ND, 1. Emphasis in the original.
38 Ibid.
39 Ibid., 2.
40 Ibid., 3. Emphasis in the original.
41 "A Statement of the Black Catholic Clergy Caucus, 1968," in *"Stamped with the Image of God,"* 111.
42 Burns, "Catholicism and Black Americans," *The Word in the World*, 9.
43 Joseph M. Davis, "Missionary Mentality," 3, UND, CDAV, Box 1, Folder 41. Emphasis in the original. See Franz Fanon, *Black Skin, White Masks* (Paris: Édition du Sueil, 1952); and Franz Fanon, *The Wretched of the Earth* (Paris: Présence Africaine, 1963).
44 Burns, "Catholicism and Black Americans," *The Word in the World*, 12. Emphasis in the original.
45 Ibid.
46 Davis, "The Missionary Mentality," UND.
47 Lucas, *Black Priest/White Church*, 12.
48 Ibid., 14.
49 Ibid., 70.
50 Ibid., 75.
51 Bryan Massingale has recently called on Catholic theologians broadly and Black Catholic theologians in particular to recover Malcolm X as a theological source and to revive critical Black theological challenges to white supremacy and racism. See Bryan Massingale, "Malcolm X as Neglected 'Classic' for Catholic Theological Reflection," *Origins: CNS Documentary Service* 40, no. 9 (July 8, 2010): 130–144.
52 "Black Catholic Blues." Justin Poché confirms this point in regard to the South in his dissertation, "Religion, Race, and Rights in Catholic Louisiana, 1938–1970," University of Notre Dame, 2007, 322. Edward K. Braxton, a Black Catholic priest from Chicago, also offered this explanation a decade after the *Newsweek* piece. See Braxton, "Black Catholics in America," 75–76.
53 McClory, "Church Losing Ground," 4.
54 Sutor, "We're Doing It by Ourselves," 28.

55 See William Tate, "I'm Going Home: A Journey to Holy Angels," in *Growing Up African American in Catholic Schools*, Irvine and Foster ed., 141–152. See also William F. Tate, "From Inner City to Ivory Tower: Does My Voice Matter in the Academy?" *Urban Education* 29 (1994), 245.
56 Tate, "I'm Going Home: A Journey to Holy Angels," 146–147.
57 Clements, interview with author (January 30, 2012). This is also recounted in *The Father Clements Story* (Lionsgate, 1987).
58 Clements, interview with author (January 30, 2012).
59 "Holy Angels' SOS Gets Nationwide Response," *Chicago Tribune*, September 3, 1970, S3.
60 Streisand backed out at the last moment, but the concert went on without her. Steven Pratt, "Little Angels Sing That Way Even Tho Barbra Wasn't There," *Chicago Tribune*, May 31, 1971, 4. The letter from President Richard Nixon to Father George Clements is in the Women and Leadership Archives, Ann Ida Gannon, BVM, Center for Women and Leadership, Loyola University Chicago (WLA), Suellen Hoy, Ph.D. Papers. This letter is also referenced in the *Chicago Tribune*. See Patricia Krizmis, "Nixon Hails S. Side Parish School Plan," *Chicago Tribune*, March 24, 1971, 18.
61 Father Robert Miller, interview with author. Father Robert Miller, "A Memorial History of Holy Angels Church on the Occasion of Its 125th Jubilee: 6 February 2005," in possession of author. Anonymous School Sisters of St. Francis, "History of Holy Angels Parish and School." Unpublished manuscript, in possession of author.
62 Stokely Carmichael and Charles V. Hamilton, *Black Power: The Politics of Liberation in America* (New York: Penguin Books, 1967): 61. Robert Allen in 1970 and Thomas Sugrue in 2013 both identified this statement by Carmichael and Hamilton as one of the ways Black Power could be put to use to capitalist conservative (rather than Marxist revolutionary) ends. See Allen, *Black Awakening in Capitalist America*; and Sugrue, *Sweet Land of Liberty*, 354–355.
63 Alan Merridew, "Solution to Problems: Priest Tells Blacks: Get Up and Work!" *Chicago Tribune*, November 11, 1973, 26.
64 "2 New Priests Join Holy Angels; Call Church Black Catholic Model," *Chicago Daily Defender*, July 29, 1972, 1; Dorothy A. Drain, "Black Pride Radiates in All Black Parish,"*Chicago Daily Defender*, August 19, 1972, 26.
65 Patricia Krizmis, "Black Pride Is Way of Life," *Chicago Tribune*, March 7, 1971, 3.
66 Williams, "Growth of Black Catholicism in Chicago: Oral History."
67 Haas, *History of Midwest Clergy Conference*.
68 For more on the ways police violence contributed to Black political mobilization, see Donna Jean Murch, *Living for the City: Migration, Education, and the Rise of the Black Panther Party in Oakland, California* (Chapel Hill: University of North Carolina Press, 2010), 119–168; Bloom and Martin, *Black against Empire*, 45–63; Bridgette Baldwin, "In the Shadow of the Gun: The Black Panther Party, the Ninth Amendment, and Discourses of Self-Defense," in *In Search of the Black Panther*

Party, Lazerow and Williams, ed. See also Peniel E. Joseph, *Waiting 'Til the Midnight Hour: A Narrative History of Black Power* (New York: Holt Paperbacks, 2007).
69 Williams, *From the Bullet to the Ballot*, 168.
70 CHM, AAPL, Box 37, Folder 8.
71 Hayden W. Lynch, "Priest Envisions Unarmed Police," *Chicago Daily Defender*, April 29, 1969.
72 Donald Mosby, "Black Priest Hits 'Irish Conspiracy,'" *Chicago Daily Defender*, January 5, 1970, 3.
73 Ibid.
74 "Blacks Plan St. Pat's Day Celebration," *Chicago Tribune*, March 11, 1970.
75 "St. Patrick Protest Draws 75," *Chicago Today*, March 15, 1970.
76 For more on the Afro-American Patrolmen's League generally, see Beryl Satter, "Cops, Gangs, and Revolutionaries," 1–25.
77 "Holy Angels-Monumental Services Are Held," *Chicago Daily Defender*, January 24, 1970, 23.
78 Dorothy A. Drain, "Ecumenical Services at St. John Church-Baptist," *Chicago Defender*, February 23, 1974, 38.
79 "Muslim Ruler Elijah Muhammad Dies: Muslim Leader Muhammad Dies," *Chicago Tribune*, February 26, 1975, 1; "Trace Rise of Prophet," *Chicago Defender*, February 26, 1975, 4.
80 Josephite Conference transcript, UND.
81 Joseph M. Davis, "The Undying Struggle: Restoring Greatness" (1975), UND, CDAV, Box 1, Folder 11; "Religion and Race/Testimony Presented by the National Office for Black Catholics before the Bicentennial Hearings of the National Conference of Catholic Bishops" (1975), and "Religious Education in the Black Community" (1976), UND, CDAV, Box 1, Folder 14.
82 Davis, "Religion and Race," UND. Emphasis in the original.
83 Davis, "Religious Education in the Black Community," UND, CDAV, Box 1, Folder 4.
84 Phelps, interview with author.
85 Martha Biondi argues that Black student protests on campus across the United States in the late 1960s and early 1970s could be identified as the height of the Black freedom struggles. Black seminarians participated in this wider student movement. See Biondi, *Black Revolution on Campus*.
86 See "The Martin Luther King Program in Black Church Studies: A Conversation between Henry H. Mitchell and Clarence Joseph Rivers," *Freeing the Spirit* 2, no. 1 (Fall 1973): 4–17.
87 "The Black Manifesto: The Black National Economic Conference," *New York Times*, July 10, 1969.
88 The 1970s witnessed a flourishing of theological and historical studies about the nature of Black religion and its relationship to Africa and African slavery in the Americas. For examples, see Gayraud S. Wilmore, *Black Religion and Black Radi-*

calism: An Interpretation of the Religious History of African Americans (Maryknoll, N.Y.: Orbis Books, 1973); Eugene D. Genovese, *Roll, Jordan, Roll: The World the Slaves Made* (New York: Vintage Books, 1976); Lawrence W. Levine, *Black Culture and Black Consciousness: Afro-American Folk Thought from Slavery to Freedom* (Oxford: Oxford University Press, 1978); Albert J. Raboteau, *Slave Religion: The "Invisible Institution" in the Antebellum South* (Oxford: Oxford University Press, 1978).

89 "Africans Talk about Church/Liturgy in Africa," *Freeing the Spirit* 1, no. 1 (August 1971): 20.
90 Michael Laguerre, "The Drum and Religious Dance in Christian Liturgy in Haiti," *Freeing the Spirit* 1, no. 2 (Spring 1972): 11, 13.
91 Ibid., 13–14.
92 David Sutor, "Holy Angels School: Unlike Any Other," *New World*, March 10, 1972, 13.
93 John McGreevy notes how Holy Angels "seemed to confirm the value of traditional Catholic educational policies" and how that educational philosophy "became embattled during the 1960s" as liberal Catholics argued that Catholic schools should "abandon parochialism"; McGreevy, *Parish Boundaries*, 243.
94 Sutor notes how priests at another inner-city Catholic school (St. Cyril) considered making religion classes optional, only to have parents insist that they remain mandatory. Sutor pointed out that one reason "why so many parents want their children in the Catholic school is the moral and religious training they receive." See Sutor, "A Need for Good Schools," *New World*, February 25, 1972, 13. Father Paul Smith echoed this sentiment regarding the Holy Angels school community; Sutor, "Holy Angels School," *New World*; Sutor, "We're Doing It by Ourselves," 31.
95 Sutor, "We're Doing It by Ourselves," 28. Patricia Krizmis, "Black Pride Is Way of Life in Holy Angels School: Holy Angels' Happy Scholars," *Chicago Tribune*, March 7, 1971, 3.
96 Jack Slater, "The School That Beat the Odds," *Ebony* 28, no. 7 (May 1973), 64.
97 See Sutor, "We're Doing It by Ourselves," 28; David Sutor, "Holy Angels School," 13; Slater, "The School That Beat the Odds," 64; Suellen Hoy, *Good Hearts*, 100–102.
98 Sister Helen Strueder (interview with Suellen Hoy), WLA, Suellen Hoy Papers; Anonymous, "History of Holy Angels."
99 Father Bob Miller, "History of the Life of Reverend Paul B. Smith."
100 Quote from Hoy, *Good Hearts*, 101. This description of Smith recurs in virtually every record of his life. See Miller, "Life of Rev. Smith"; Anonymous, "History of Holy Angels"; Strueder (interview with Hoy), WLA.
101 Dan Egler, "Holy Angels Sets All-Year School; Even Kids Rejoice," *Chicago Tribune*, May 28, 1972, N3.
102 For more on Sister Hortensia, see Hoy, *Good Hearts*, 98–100.
103 Strueder (interview with Hoy), WLA.
104 Anonymous, "History of Holy Angels."

105 Patricia Krizmis, "Black Pride Is Way of Life in Holy Angels School: Holy Angels' Happy Scholars," *Chicago Tribune*, March 7, 1971, 3
106 Hoy, *Good Hearts*, 101.
107 Slater, "The School that Beat the Odds," *Ebony*, 66. Emphasis in the original.
108 Sutor, "We're Doing It by Ourselves," 28.
109 Ibid., 32.
110 Sutor noted in another article on Holy Angels that the school was "intentionally operated . . . along lines that diverge from popular trends in education"; Sutor, "We're Doing It by Ourselves," 31. See also Hoy, *Good Hearts*, 101. By the 1970s many Catholic educators, along with their secular counterparts, were influenced by the educational philosophy of A. S. Neill, which stressed more student freedom and less coercive adult supervision. See A. S. Neill, *Summerhill: A Radical Approach to Child Rearing* (Oxford: Hart Publishing Company, 1960). Thank you, Casey Beaumier, S.J., for this insight. For more on shifting trends in U.S. Catholic education, see Casey Beaumier, S.J., "For Richer, for Poorer: Jesuit Secondary Education in America and the Challenge of Elitism" (Ph.D. dissertation, Boston College, 2013).
111 Slater, "The School That Beat the Odds," *Ebony*, 72.
112 Casey Banas, "Tough Discipline for Students," *Chicago Tribune*, July 1, 1981, 15.
113 Slater, "The School That Beat the Odds," 70.
114 *Unitatis Redintegratio*, Decree on Ecumenism, November 21, 1964.
115 Sutor, "We're Doing It by Ourselves," 28.
116 Ibid., 30.
117 Ibid., 31.
118 Hoy, *Good Hearts*, 100; Sutor, "We're Doing It by Ourselves," 33.
119 Hoy, *Good Hearts*, 101; Strueder (interview with Hoy), WLA.
120 Amy Koehlinger has addressed at length the changing roles of sisters and nuns in Black communities, as well as the emergence of "Black-thinking sistahs." See "Project Cabrini: Becoming Sistahs," in *The New Nuns*. See also Williams, "Subversive Habits."
121 Daniel P. Moynihan, *The Negro Family: The Case for National Action*, Washington, D.C., Office of Policy Planning and Research, U.S. Department of Labor, 1965. For more on the many debates surrounding the Moynihan Report, see *The Moynihan Report Revisited: Lessons and Reflections after Four Decades (The ANNALS of the American Academy of Political and Social Science Series)* (Thousand Oaks, Calif.: Sage Publications, 2009); and James T. Patterson, *Freedom Is Not Enough: The Moynihan Report and America's Struggle over Black Family Life—From LBJ to Obama* (New York: Basic Books, 2010).
122 Two prominent examples would be: Angela Y. Davis, *Women, Race, and Class* (New York: Vintage Books, 1983); and Paula J. Giddings, *When and Where I Enter: The Impact of Black Women on Race and Sex in America* (New York: HarperCollins, 1984). For an analysis of masculinity in the Moynihan Report, see Steve Estes, "Chapter 5: The Moynihan Report," in *I Am a Man: Race, Manhood, and the Civil*

Rights Movement (Chapel Hill: University of North Carolina Press, 2005), 107–130. For more on gender, sexuality, and the civil rights era generally, see McGuire, *At the Dark End of the Street*.

123 Steve Estes deals comprehensively with masculinity in the long civil rights era. See Estes, *I Am a Man* (2005). This masculinist argument was part and parcel of arguments for self-sufficiency and self-help central to organizations like the Nation of Islam, a major influence on the nascent Black Power movement. Father George Clements directly connected self-help and the Black Muslims. See Merridew, "Solution to Problems."
124 *Holy Angels School Rules and Regulations, 1974–1975*, WLA, Suellen Hoy Papers.
125 Casey Banas, "Tough Discipline for Students," *Chicago Tribune*, July 1, 1981, 15.
126 Davis, "Central Office for Black Catholics," *Freeing the Spirit*, 34. See also Clarence Joseph Rivers, "Thank God We Ain't What We Was: The State of the Liturgy in the Black Catholic Community," *U.S. Catholic Historian* 5, no. 1, "The Black Catholic Experience" (1986): 81.
127 Lucas, *Black Priest/White Church*, 69–70, 181.
128 Ibid., 206.
129 Ibid., 207.
130 Lucas referred to Catholic communities that resisted Black nationalism as "culture-white white churches, and white-culture Negro churches"; Lucas, *Black Priest/White Church*, 67. The generational argument is made in Davis, "The Position of the Catholic Church in the Black Community" (1969): 19; Williams, "The Future of the Black Catholic Church," 36.
131 *Freeing the Spirit* 1, no. 1 (August 1971). Emphasis in the original.
132 Joseph M. Davis, "Why a Black Catholic Organization?" UND, CDAV, Box 1, Folder 15.
133 National Office for Black Catholics, "Black Perspectives on Evangelization of the Modern World (1974)," collected in *"Stamped in the Image of God,"* Davis and Phelps, ed., 121.
134 Ibid., 123.
135 Clarence Jos. Rivers, "Thank God We Ain't What We Was: The State of Liturgy in the Black Catholic Community," *Freeing the Spirit* 6, no. 2 (Spring 1979): 28–32.
136 "The National Office for Black Catholics, 1970–1973," UND, CDAV, Box 1, Folder 31.
137 "Letter from Joseph M. Davis to Msgr. John Egan, December 7, 1976"; and "Proposal for a Summer Course on Liturgy and Liturgical Practice in the Black Community," UND, National Office for Black Catholics Papers (NOBC).
138 "Proposal for a Summer Course on Liturgy and Liturgical Practice in the Black Community," UND, NOBC.
139 "What We Have Seen and Heard," 4.
140 Ibid., 8–9.
141 Ibid., 9.
142 Ibid., 10.

143 Ibid., 8.
144 Ibid., 30.
145 Ibid., 31.
146 *Lead Me, Guide Me: The African American Catholic Hymnal* (Chicago: G.I.A. Publications, 1987).

CONCLUSION

1 Quoted in Robert McClory, *Radical Disciple: Father Pfleger, St. Sabina Church, and the Fight for Social Justice* (Chicago: Lawrence Hill Books, 2010), 6.
2 McClory, *Radical Disciple*, xv.
3 Ibid., 41–42.
4 "Saint Sabina Academy," accessed on September 15, 2016, saintsabina.org.
5 I borrow this turn of phrase from M. Shawn Copeland, ed., *Uncommon Faithfulness*.

BIBLIOGRAPHY

PRIMARY SOURCES

Archives
Archdiocese of Chicago Joseph Cardinal Bernardin Archives and Records Center (AAC)
Celano Archives of the Sisters of St. Francis, Dubuque, Iowa (OSF)
Chicago History Museum Research Center (CHM)
Franciscan Province of the Sacred Heart Archives (OFM)
Loyola University Chicago Archives (LUC)
Northwestern University Archives (NU)
Robert Meyers Archives, Chicago Province of Society of the Divine Word (SVD)
Sisters of the Blessed Sacrament Archives, Bensalem, Pa. (SBS)
University of Notre Dame Archives, South Bend, Ind. (UND)
Vivian G. Harsh Research Collection of Afro-American History, Chicago Public Library (CPL)
Women and Leadership Archives, Ann Ida Gannon, BVM Center for Women and Leadership, Loyola University Chicago (WLA)

Chicago Parish Archives
Corpus Christi Catholic Church
Holy Angels Catholic Church
St. Elizabeth Catholic Church
St. Malachy Catholic Church

Author Interviews
Dr. Sheila Adams, August 30, 2012
Richard Andrus, S.V.D., January 30, 2012
Cheryl Cattledge, November 13, 2012
Rev. George H. Clements, January 30 and July 9, 2012
Adrienne Curry, October 11, 2011
Dr. Timone Davis, September 4, 2012
Rev. Matthew Eyerman, November 4, 2011
Most Rev. Wilton D. Gregory, June 6, 2012
Mary Howard, December 11, 2011
Dr. Kimberly Lymore, September 11, 2012

Rev. Robert Miller, October 21, 2011
Maurice Nutt, C.S.S.R., April 8, 2013
Parishioners at St. Malachy, December 4, 2011
Jamie Phelps, O.P., March 8, 2012
Rev. Freddy Washington, October 26, 2011
Dr. C. Vanessa White, August 16, 2012
Delores Williams, October 12, 2011
Marita Zeller, S.S.S.F., December 18, 2012

Other Interviews
Msgr. Daniel Cantwell, Rev. Steven Avella Oral History Project, AAC.
George Clements, conducted by Blackside, Inc. on October 19, 1989, for *Eyes on the Prize II: America at the Racial Crossroads 1965 to 1985*. Washington University Libraries, Film and Media Archive, Henry Hampton Collection.
Rev. Martin "Doc" Farrell, Rev. Steven Avella Oral History Project, AAC.
Rev. Rollins Lambert, Rev. Steven Avella Oral History Project, AAC.
Bobby Rush, October 20, 1988, *Eyes on the Prize II*. Washington University Libraries, Film and Media Archive, Henry Hampton Collection.
Sister Helen Strueder, S.S.S.F., Suellen Hoy Papers, WLA.
Clarence Earl Williams, C.P.P.S., "The Growth of Black Catholicism in Chicago since World War II: An Oral History" (July 2, 1976), tapes in possession of Dr. Larry Murphy, Garrett Evangelical Seminary (Evanston, Ill.).

Published Works
Adams, Elizabeth Laura. "The Finding of a Soul." *Sentinel of the Blessed Sacrament* (February 1930): 97–101.
Anonymous. "Reflections of a Negro Convert." *Interracial Review* 9, no. 12 (December 1936): 183.
Braxton, Edward K. "Black Catholics in America: Authentically Black, Truly Catholic." *Commonweal* 112 (February 8, 1985): 73–77.
Carmichael, Stokely, and Charles V. Hamilton. *Black Power: The Politics of Liberation in America*. New York: Penguin Books, 1967.
Connelly, Marc. *The Green Pastures: A Fable Suggested by Roark Bradford's Southern Sketches "Ol' Man Adam an' His Chillun."* New York: Farrar & Rinehart, 1929.
Curran, Patrick. "Missionary Apostolate among the Non-Catholic Negroes in Chicago." *Christ to the World* 5 (1960).
Ellis, John Tracy. *Documents in American Catholic History*. Milwaukee, Wis.: Bruce Publishing Company, 1962.
Fanon, Franz. *Black Skin, White Masks*. Paris: Édition du Sueil, 1952.
———. *The Wretched of the Earth*. Paris: Présence Africaine, 1963.
Farrell, Martin W. *The Parish Catechism*. Chicago: United Book Service, 1954.
Fey, Harold E. "Can Catholicism Win America? A Series of Eight Articles Reprinted from *The Christian Century*." (1945).

Gadpaille, Mary Dolores, T.O.S.F. *That You May Die Easy*. Chicago: Tyde Publications, 1959.
Gillard, John T., S.S.J. *The Catholic Church and the American Negro*. Baltimore, Md.: St. Joseph's Society Press, 1929.
———. S.S.J. *Colored Catholics in the United States*. Baltimore, Md.: Josephite Press, 1941.
Grey, Sr. M. Martin de Porres. "The Church, Revolution and Black Catholics." *Black Scholar* 2, no. 4 (December 1970): 20–26.
Haas, O.F.M., Capistran J. *History of the Midwest Clergy Conference on Negro Welfare*. 1963.
King, Martin Luther, Jr. *Stride toward Freedom: The Montgomery Story*. Boston: Beacon Press, 1958.
Lead Me, Guide Me: The African American Catholic Hymnal. Chicago: G.I.A. Publications, 1987.
Lucas, Lawrence. *Black Priest/White Church: Catholics and Racism*. New York: Random House, 1970.
Moynihan, Daniel P. *The Negro Family: The Case for National Action*. Washington, D.C.: Office of Policy Planning and Research, U.S. Department of Labor, 1965.
Mundelein, Most Rev. George William. *Two Crowded Years: Being Selected Speeches, Pastorals, and Letters Issued in the First Twenty-Four Months of Episcopate*. Chicago: Extension Press, 1918.
O'Brien, Rev. John A., ed. *The White Harvest: A Symposium on Methods of Convert Making*. New York: Longmans, Green and Co., 1927.
Sheen, Fulton J. *Characters of the Passion*. New York: P. J. Kennedy and Sons, 1947.
Shuster, George, and Robert M. Kearns, S.S.J. *Statistical Profile of Black Catholics*. Washington, D.C.: Josephite Pastoral Center, 1976.
Tarry, Ellen. *The Third Door: The Autobiography of an American Negro Woman*. Westport, Conn.: Negro Universities Press, 1955.
Thibodeaux, S.B.S., Mary Roger. *A Black Nun Looks at Black Power*. New York: Sheed & Ward, 1972.
Three Afro-American Catholic Congresses. Cincinnati, Ohio: American Catholic Tribune, 1898.
Thurston, Herbert. *The Stations of the Cross*. London: Burns and Oates, 1906.
"What We Have Seen and Heard: A Pastoral Letter on Evangelization from the Black Bishops of the United States" (September 9, 1984).
Williams, C.P.P.S., Clarence. "The Black Catholic and the Urban Experience." Detroit, Mich.: Academy of the Afro-World Community, 1976.
The Word in the World: Divine Word Missionaries, '76 Black Apostolate. Techny, Ill.: Society of the Divine Word, 1976.

SECONDARY SOURCES

Books
Alexander, Estrelda Y. *Black Fire: One Hundred Years of African American Pentecostalism*. Downers Grove, Ill.: IVP Academic, 2011.

Allen, Robert L. *Black Awakening in Capitalist America: An Analytic History*. New York: Anchor Books, 1970.
Anderson, R. Bentley, S.J. *Black, White, and Catholic: New Orleans Interracialism, 1947–1956* Nashville, Tenn.: Vanderbilt University Press, 2008.
Appleby, R. Scott, and Kathleen Sprows Cummings, ed. *Catholics in the American Century: Recasting Narratives of U.S. History*. Ithaca, N.Y.: Cornell University Press, 2012.
Asad, Talal. *Genealogies of Religion: Discipline and Reasons of Power in Christianity and Islam*. Baltimore, Md.: John Hopkins University Press, 1993.
Austin, Flannery, O. P., ed. *Vatican Council II: The Basic Sixteen Documents*. New York: Costello Publishing Company, 1996.
Avella, Steven M. *This Confident Church: Catholic Leadership and Life in Chicago, 1940–1965*. South Bend, Ind.: University of Notre Dame Press, 1992.
Baldwin, Davarian. *Chicago's New Negro Movement: Modernity, the Great Migration, and Black Urban Life*. Chapel Hill: University of North Carolina Press, 2007.
Bell, Catherine. *Ritual Theory, Ritual Practice*. Oxford: Oxford University Press, 1992.
Best, Wallace D. *Passionately Human, No Less Divine: Religion and Culture in Black Chicago, 1915–1952*. Princeton, N.J.: Princeton University Press, 2005.
Biondi, Martha. *To Stand and Fight: The Struggle for Civil Rights in Postwar New York City*. Cambridge, Mass.: Harvard University Press: 2003.
———. *The Black Revolution on Campus*. Berkeley: University of California Press, 2012.
Black, Jr., Timuel D. *Bridges of Memory: Chicago's Second Generation of Black Migration*. Evanston, Ill.: Northwestern University Press, 2007.
Blatnica, Dorothy Ann, V.S.C. *"At the Altar of Their God": African American Catholics in Cleveland, 1922–1961*. New York: Garland Publishing, 1995.
Bloom, Joshua, and Waldo E. Martin. *Black against Empire: The History and Politics of the Black Panther Party*. Berkeley: University of California Press, 2013.
Blum, Edward J., and Paul Harvey. *The Color of Christ: The Son of God and the Saga of Race*. Chapel Hill: University of North Carolina Press, 2012.
Bonner, Jeremy, Mary Beth Fraser Connolly, and Christopher Denny, ed. *Empowering the People of God: Catholic Action before and after Vatican II*. New York: Fordham University Press, 2014.
Boyle, Kevin. *Arc of Justice: A Saga of Race, Civil Rights, and Murder in the Jazz Age*. New York: Holt Paperbacks, 2004.
Branch, Taylor. *At Canaan's Edge: America in the King Years, 1965–1968*. New York: Simon and Schuster, 2006.
Brandewie, Ernest. *In the Light of the Word: Divine Word Missionaries of North America*. Maryknoll, N.Y.: Orbis Books, 2000.
Buetow, Harold A. *Of Singular Benefit: The Story of Catholic Education in the United States*. New York: MacMillan, 1970.

Cobb, Jr., Charles E. *This Nonviolent Stuff'll Get You Killed: How Guns Made the Civil Rights Movement Possible*. Durham, N.C.: Duke University Press, 2015.

Cohen, Lizabeth. *Making a New Deal: Industrial Workers in Chicago, 1919–1939*. Cambridge: Cambridge University Press: 1990.

Coleman, Gregory D. *We're Heaven Bound! Portrait of a Black Sacred Drama*. Athens: University of Georgia Press, 1992.

Comaroff, Jean, and John Comaroff. *Of Revelation and Revolution: Christianity, Colonialism, and Consciousness in South Africa*, Vol. 1. Chicago: University of Chicago Press, 1991.

Cone, James H. *The Cross and the Lynching Tree*. Maryknoll, N.Y.: Orbis Books, 2011.

Copeland, M. Shawn, with LaReine-Marie Mosely, S.N.D., and Albert J. Raboteau, ed. *Uncommon Faithfulness: The Black Catholic Experience*. Maryknoll, N.Y.: Orbis Books, 2009.

Countryman, Matthew J. *Up South: Civil Rights and Black Power in Philadelphia*. Philadelphia: University of Pennsylvania Press, 2007.

Cox, Harvey. *Fire from Heaven: The Rise of Pentecostal Spirituality and the Reshaping of Religion in the Twenty-First Century*. Reading, Mass.: Addison-Wesley, 1995.

Curtis IV, Edward E. *Islam in Black America: Identity, Liberation, and Difference in African-American Islamic Thought*. Albany: SUNY Press, 2002.

Curtis IV, Edward E., and Danielle Brune Sigler, ed. *The New Black Gods: Arthur Huff Fauset and the Study of African American Religions*. Bloomington: Indiana University Press, 2009.

Dahm, Charles, O.P. *Power and Authority in the Catholic Church: Cardinal Cody in Chicago*. South Bend, Ind.: University of Notre Dame Press, 1981.

Davis, Angela Y. *Women, Race, and Class*. New York: Vintage Books, 1983.

Davis, Cyprian. *The History of Black Catholics in the United States*. New York: Crossroad Publishing Company, 1995.

Davis, Cyprian, O.S.B., and Jamie Phelps, O.P. *"Stamped with the Image of God": African Americans as God's Image in Black*. Maryknoll, N.Y.: Orbis Books, 2003.

DeCaro, Jr., Louis A. *Malcolm and the Cross: The Nation of Islam, Malcolm X, and Christianity*. New York: NYU Press, 1998.

Dillard, Angela D. *Faith in the City: Preaching Radical Social Change in Detroit*. Ann Arbor, Mich.: University of Michigan Press, 2007.

Doody, Colleen. *Detroit's Cold War: The Origins of Postwar Conservatism*. Champaign: University of Illinois Press, 2013.

Dorman, Jacob S. *Chosen People: The Rise of American Black Israelite Religions*. Oxford: Oxford University Press, 2013.

Drake, St. Clair, and Horace R. Cayton. *Black Metropolis: A Study of Negro Life in a Northern City*. Chicago: University of Chicago Press, 1945.

Dries, Angelyn, O.S.F. *The Missionary Movement in American Catholic History*. Maryknoll, N.Y.: Orbis Books, 1998.

Du Bois, W. E. B. *The Souls of Black Folk*. New York: Signet Classic, [1903] 1995.

Dyson, Michael Eric. *April 4 1968: Martin Luther King, Jr.'s Death and How It Changed America*. New York: Basic Civitas Books, 2009.
Essien-Udom, E. U. *Black Nationalism: The Search for an Identity*. Chicago: University of Chicago Press, 1962.
Estes, Steve. *I Am a Man: Race, Manhood, and the Civil Rights Movement*. Chapel Hill: University of North Carolina Press, 2005.
Evans, Curtis J. *The Burden of Black Religion*. Oxford: Oxford University Press, 2008.
Faggioli, Massimo. *Vatican II: The Battle for Meaning*. New York: Paulist Press, 2012.
Fauset, Arthur Huff. *Black Gods of the Metropolis: Negro Religious Cults of the Urban North*. Philadelphia: University of Pennsylvania Press, 1944.
Fisher, James T., and Margaret M. McGuinness, ed. *The Catholic Studies Reader*. New York: Fordham University Press, 2011.
Frederick, Marla F. *Between Sundays: Black Women and Everyday Struggles of Faith*. Berkeley: University of California Press, 2003.
Gamm, Gerald. *Urban Exodus: Why the Jews Left Boston and the Catholics Stayed*. Cambridge, Mass.: Harvard University Press, 2001.
Genovese, Eugene D. *Roll, Jordan, Roll: The World the Slaves Made*. New York: Vintage Press, 1976.
Giddings, Paula J. *When and Where I Enter: The Impact of Black Women on Race and Sex in America*. New York: HarperCollins, 1984.
Giggie, John M. *After Redemption: Jim Crow and the Transformation of African American Religion in the Delta, 1875–1915*. Oxford: Oxford University Press, 2005.
Glaude Jr., Eddie S. *Exodus! Religion, Race, and Nation in Nineteenth-Century Black America*. Chicago: University of Chicago Press, 2000.
Greeley, Andrew M. *The American Catholic: A Social Portrait*. New York: Basic Books, 1977.
———. *The Catholic Imagination*. Berkeley: University of California Press, 2000.
Green, Adam. *Selling the Race: Community, Culture, and Black Chicago, 1940–1955*. Chicago: University of Chicago Press, 2009.
Gregory, James N. *The Southern Diaspora: How the Great Migrations of Black and White Southerners Transformed America*. Chapel Hill: University of North Carolina Press, 2005.
Grossman, James R. *Land of Hope: Chicago, Black Southerners, and the Great Migration*. Chicago: University of Chicago Press, 1989.
Haas, Jeffrey. *Assassination of Fred Hampton: How the FBI and the Chicago Police Murdered a Black Panther*. Chicago: Chicago Review Press, 2009.
Hayes, Diana L., and Cyprian Davis, ed. *Taking Down Our Harps: Black Catholics in the United States*. Maryknoll, N.Y.: Orbis Books, 1998.
Henold, Mary. *Catholic and Feminist: The Surprising History of the American Catholic Feminist Movement*. Chapel Hill: University of North Carolina Press, 2008.
Heywood, Linda M., and John K. Thornton. *Central Africans, Atlantic Creoles, and the Foundation of the Americas, 1585–1660*. Cambridge: Cambridge University Press, 2007.

Higginbotham, Evelyn Brooks. *Righteous Discontent: The Women's Movement in the Black Baptist Church, 1880–1920*. Cambridge, Mass.: Harvard University Press, 1993.
Hine, Darlene Clark, and John McClusky, Jr., ed. *Black Chicago Renaissance*. Champaign: University of Illinois Press, 2012.
Hirsch, Arnold R. *Making the Second Ghetto: Race and Housing in Chicago, 1940–1960*. Chicago: University of Chicago Press, 1983.
Hope, Richard, and Robert A. Courage. *The Muse in Bronzeville: African American Creative Expression in Chicago, 1932–1950*. New Brunswick, N.J.: Rutgers University Press, 2011.
Hoy, Suellen. *Good Hearts: Catholic Sisters in Chicago's Past*. Champaign: University of Illinois Press, 2006.
Irvine, Jacqueline Jordan, and Michèle Foster, ed. *Growing Up African American in Catholic Schools*. New York: Teachers College Press, 1996.
James, William. *The Varieties of Religious Experience, a Study in Human Nature*. New York, London: Longmans, Green, and Co., 1902.
Johnson, Clifton H., ed. *God Struck Me Dead: Voices of Ex-Slaves*. William Bradford Collection Edition. Cleveland, Ohio: Pilgrim Press, 1993.
Johnson, Sylvester A. *The Myth of Ham in Nineteenth-Century American Christianity: Race, Heathens, and the People of God*. New York: Palgrave Macmillan, 2004.
———. *African American Religions, 1500–2000: Colonialism, Democracy, and Freedom*. Cambridge: Cambridge University Press, 2015.
Joseph, Peniel E. *Waiting 'Til the Midnight Hour: A Narrative History of Black Power*. New York: Holt Paperbacks, 2007.
Kelly, Timothy. *The Transformation of American Catholicism: The Pittsburgh Laity and the Second Vatican Council, 1950–1972*. South Bend, Ind.: University of Notre Dame Press, 2009.
Koehlinger, Amy L. *The New Nuns: Racial Justice and Religious Reform in the 1960s* Cambridge, Mass.: Harvard University Press, 2007.
Koenig, Harry C. *A History of the Parishes of the Archdiocese of Chicago. Published in Observance of the Centenary of the Archdiocese*, 2 vols. Chicago: Archdiocese of Chicago, 1980.
Lazerow, Jama, and Yohuru Williams, ed. *In Search of the Black Panther Party: New Perspectives on a Revolutionary Movement*. Durham, N.C.: Duke University Press, 2006.
Lemann, Nicholas. *The Promised Land: The Great Black Migration and How It Changed America*. New York: Alfred A. Knopf, 1991.
Levine, Lawrence W. *Black Culture and Black Consciousness: Afro-American Folk Thought from Slavery to Freedom*. Oxford: Oxford University Press, 1978.
Lynch, Patricia, S.B.S. *Sharing the Bread in Service: Sisters of the Blessed Sacrament, 1891–1991*. Bensalem, Pa.: Sisters of the Blessed Sacrament, 1998.
Maffly-Kipp, Laurie F. *Setting Down the Sacred Past: African-American Race Histories*. Cambridge, Mass.: Harvard University Press, 2010.
Matovina, Timothy. *Latino Catholicism: Transformation in America's Largest Church*. Princeton, N.J.: Princeton University Press, 2011.

McCartin, James P. *Prayers of the Faithful: The Shifting Spiritual Life of American Catholics.* Cambridge, Mass.: Harvard University Press, 2010.

McClory, Robert. *The Man Who Beat Clout City.* Chicago: Swallow Press, 1977.

———. *Radical Disciple: Father Pfleger, St. Sabina Church, and the Fight for Social Justice.* Chicago: Lawrence Hill Books, 2010.

McDannell, Colleen. *Picturing Faith: Photography and the Great Depression.* New Haven, Conn.: Yale University Press, 2004.

———. *The Spirit of Vatican II: A History of Catholic Reform in America.* New York: Basic Books, 2011.

McGreevy, John T. *Parish Boundaries: The Catholic Encounter with Race in the Twentieth-Century Urban North.* Chicago: University of Chicago Press, 1996.

———. *Catholicism and American Freedom: A History.* New York: W. W. Norton, 2003.

McGuinness, Margaret M. *Called to Serve: A History of Nuns in America.* New York: NYU Press, 2013.

McGuire, Danielle L. *At the Dark End of the Street: Black Women, Rape, and Resistance—A New History of the Civil Rights Movement from Rosa Parks to the Rise of Black Power.* New York: Vintage Books, 2011.

McKay, Claude. *The Passion of Claude McKay: Selected Poetry and Prose, 1912–1948,* Wayne F. Cooper, ed. New York: Schocken Books, 1973.

———. *Complete Poems,* William J. Maxwell, ed. Champaign: University of Illinois Press, 2008.

McMahon, Eileen M. *What Parish Are You From? A Chicago Irish Community and Race Relations.* Lexington: University Press of Kentucky, 1996.

Mitchell, Koritha. *Living with Lynching: African American Lynching Plays, Performance, and Citizenship, 1890–1930.* Champaign: University of Illinois Press, 2012.

Murch, Donna Jean. *Living for the City: Migration, Education, and the Rise of the Black Panther Party in Oakland, California.* Chapel Hill: University of North Carolina Press, 2010.

Nabhan-Warren, Kristy. *The Cursillo Movement in America: Catholics, Protestants, and Fourth-Day Spirituality.* Chapel Hill: University of North Carolina Press, 2013.

Neary, Timothy B. *Crossing Parish Boundaries: Race, Sports, and Catholic Youth in Chicago, 1914–1954.* Chicago: University of Chicago Press, 2016.

Neckerman, Kathryn M. *Schools Betrayed: Roots of Failure in Inner-City Education.* Chicago: University of Chicago Press, 2007.

Neill, A. S. *Summerhill: A Radical Approach to Child Rearing.* Oxford: Hart Publishing Company, 1960.

Nickels, Marilyn Wenzke. *Black Catholic Protest and the Federated Colored Catholics, 1917–1933: Three Perspectives on Racial Justice.* New York: Garland, 1988.

Ochs, Stephen. *Desegregating the Altar: The Josephites and the Struggle for Black Priests, 1871–1960.* Baton Rouge: Louisiana State University Press, 1993.

O'Malley, John W. *What Happened at Vatican II.* Cambridge, Mass.: Belknap Press of Harvard University Press, 2008.

Orsi, Robert A. *Thank You, St. Jude: Women's Devotions to the Patron Saint of Hopeless Causes.* New Haven, Conn.: Yale University Press, 1996.

———. *Between Heaven and Earth: The Religious Worlds People Make and the Scholars Who Study Them*. Princeton, N.J.: Princeton University Press, 2005.
———. *History and Presence*. Cambridge, Mass.: Belknap Press of Harvard University Press, 2016.
Orsi, Robert A., ed. *Gods of the City: Religion and the American Urban Landscape*. Bloomington, Ind.: Indiana University Press, 1999.
O'Toole, James M., ed. *Habits of Devotion: Catholic Religious Practices in Twentieth Century America*. Ithaca, N.Y.: Cornell University Press, 2004.
———. *The Faithful: A History of Catholics in America*. Cambridge, Mass.: Belknap Press of Harvard University Press, 2008.
Otto, Rudolf. *The Idea of the Holy: An Inquiry into the Non-Rational Factor in the Idea of the Divine and Its Relation to the Rational*. London: Oxford University Press, 1923.
Pasquier, Michael. *Fathers on the Frontier: French Missionaries and the Roman Catholic Priesthood in the United States, 1789–1870*. Oxford: Oxford University Press, 2010.
Patterson, James T. *Freedom Is Not Enough: The Moynihan Report and America's Struggle over Black Family Life—From LBJ to Obama*. New York: Basic Books, 2010.
Pimblott, Kerry. *Faith in Black Power: Religion, Race, and Resistance in Cairo, Illinois*. Lexington: University of Kentucky Press, 2017.
Pinn, Anthony B. *Varieties of African American Religious Experience*. Minneapolis, Minn.: Augsburg Fortress Publishers, 1998.
Raboteau, Albert J. *Slave Religion: The "Invisible Institution" in the Antebellum South*. Oxford: Oxford University Press, 1978.
———. *A Fire in the Bones: Reflections on African-American Religious History*. Boston: Beacon Press, 1995.
Rambo, Lewis R., and Charles E. Farhadian. *The Oxford Handbook of Religious Conversion*. Oxford: Oxford University Press, 2014.
Ransby, Barbara. *Ella Baker and the Black Freedom Movement: A Radical Democratic Vision*. Chapel Hill: University of North Carolina Press, 2006.
Robbins, Joel. *Becoming Sinners: Christianity and Moral Torment in a Papua New Guinea Society*. Berkeley: University of California Press, 2004.
Robert, Dana L. *Christian Mission: How Christianity Became a World Religion*. Oxford: Wiley-Blackwell, 2009.
Rynne, Xavier. *Vatican Council II*. Maryknoll, N.Y.: Orbis Books, 1999.
Sanders, James W. *Education of an Urban Minority: Catholics in Chicago, 1833–1965*. Oxford: Oxford University Press, 1977.
Satter, Beryl. *Family Properties: How the Struggle over Race and Real Estate Transformed Chicago and Urban America*. New York: Metropolitan Books, 2009.
Savage, Barbara Dianne. *Your Spirits Walk beside Us: The Politics of Black Religion*. Cambridge, Mass.: Belknap Press of Harvard University Press, 2008.
Schlabach, Elizabeth Schroeder. *Along the Streets of Bronzeville: Black Chicago's Literary Landscape*. Champaign: University of Illinois Press, 2013.
Schultenover, David G., ed. *Vatican II: Did Anything Happen?* New York: Continuum, 2007.

Seitz, John C. *No Closure: Catholic Practice and Boston's Parish Shutdowns.* Cambridge, Mass.: Harvard University Press, 2011.
Self, Robert O. *American Babylon: Race and the Struggle for Postwar Oakland.* Princeton, N.J.: Princeton University Press, 2003.
Seligman, Adam B., Robert P. Weller, Michael J. Puett, and Bennett Simon. *Ritual and Its Consequences: An Essay on the Limits of Sincerity.* Oxford: Oxford University Press, 2008.
Singh, Nikhil Pal. *Black Is a Country: Race and the Unfinished Struggle for Democracy.* Cambridge, Mass.: Harvard University Press, 2004.
Smith, Anthony Burke. *The Look of Catholics: Portrayals in Popular Culture from the Great Depression to the Cold War.* Lawrence: University Press of Kansas, 2010.
Smith, Jonathan Z. *The Map Is Not the Territory: Studies in the History of Religions.* Chicago: University of Chicago Press, 1993.
Southern, David W. *John LaFarge and the Limits of Catholic Interracialism, 1911–1963.* Baton Rouge: Louisiana State University Press, 1996.
Spear, Allan H. *Black Chicago: The Making of a Negro Ghetto, 1890–1920.* Chicago: University of Chicago Press, 1967.
Sponsler, Claire. *Ritual Imports: Performing Medieval Drama in America.* Ithaca, N.Y.: Cornell University Press, 2004.
Stange, Maren. *Bronzeville: Black Chicago in Pictures, 1941–1943.* New York: New Press, 2003.
Stephens, Randall J. *The Fire Spreads: Holiness and Pentecostalism in the American South.* Cambridge, Mass.: Harvard University Press, 2008.
Sugrue, Thomas J. *The Origins of the Urban Crisis: Race and Inequality in Postwar Detroit.* Princeton, N.J.: Princeton University Press, 2005.
———. *Sweet Land of Liberty: The Forgotten Struggle for Civil Rights in the North.* New York: Random House, 2008.
Tuttle, Jr., William M. *Race Riot: Chicago in the Red Summer of 1919.* Champaign: University of Illinois Press, 1970.
Tweed, Thomas. *America's Church: The National Shrine and Catholic Presence in the Nation's Capital.* Oxford: Oxford University Press, 2011.
Tyson, Timothy B. *Radio Free Dixie: Robert F. Williams and the Roots of Black Power.* Chapel Hill: University of North Carolina Press, 2001.
Walls, Andrew F. *The Missionary Movement in Christian History: Studies in the Transmission of Faith.* Maryknoll, N.Y.: Orbis Books, 1996.
Walton, Jonathan L. *Watch This! The Ethics and Aesthetics of Black Televangelism.* New York: NYU Press, 2009.
Weisenfeld, Judith. *Hollywood Be Thy Name: African American Religion in American Film, 1929–1949.* Berkeley: University of California Press, 2007.
———. *New World A-Coming: Black Religion and Racial Identity during the Great Migration.* New York: NYU Press, 2016.
Williams, Jakobi. *From the Bullet to the Ballot: The Illinois Chapter of the Black Panther Party and Racial Coalition Politics in Chicago.* Chapel Hill: University of North Carolina Press, 2013.

Wills, Garry. *Bare Ruined Choirs: Doubt, Prophecy, and Radical Religion*. Garden City, N.Y.: Doubleday, 1971.
Wilmore, Gayraud S. *Black Religion and Black Radicalism: An Interpretation of the Religious History of African Americans*. Maryknoll, N.Y.: Orbis Books, 1973.
Wood, Amy Louise. *Lynching and Spectacle: Witnessing Racial Violence in America, 1890–1940*. Chapel Hill: University of North Carolina Press, 2011.
Woodward, C. Vann. *The Strange Career of Jim Crow*, 2nd rev. ed. Oxford: Oxford University Press, 1966.
Yong, Amos, and Estrelda Y. Alexander, ed. *Afro-Pentecostalism: Black Pentecostal and Charismatic Christianity in History and Culture*. New York: NYU Press, 2011.

Articles and Book Chapters

Alston, Jon P., Letitia T. Alston, and Emory Warrick. "Black Catholics: Social and Cultural Characteristics." *Journal of Black Studies* 2, no. 2 (December 1971): 245–255.
Asad, Talal. "Comments on Conversion." In *Conversion to Modernities: The Globalization of Christianity*, Peter van der Veer, ed. New York: Routledge, 1996.
———. "Thinking about Religion, Belief, and Politics." In *The Cambridge Companion to Religious Studies*, Robert A. Orsi, ed. Cambridge: Cambridge University Press, 2012.
Best, Wallace D. "'The Right Achieved and the Wrong Way Conquered': J. H. Jackson, Martin Luther King, Jr., and the Conflict over Civil Rights." *Religion and American Culture: A Journal of Interpretation* 16, no. 2 (2006): 195–226.
Collins, Daniel F. "Black Conversion to Catholicism: Its Implications for the Negro Church." *Journal for the Scientific Study of Religion* 10, no. 3 (Autumn 1971): 208–218.
Cooley, Will. "Moving On Out: Black Pioneering in Chicago, 1915–1950." *Journal of Urban History* 36, no. 4 (July 2010): 485–506.
Copeland, M. Shawn. "Tradition and Traditions of African American Catholicism." *Theological Studies* 61 (2000): 632–655.
Cressler, Matthew J., ed. "Forum: Race, White Supremacy, and the Making of American Catholicism." *American Catholic Studies* 127, no. 3 (Fall 2016): 1–33.
Davis, Cyprian. "The Holy See and American Black Catholics: A Forgotten Chapter in the History of the American Church." *U.S. Catholic Historian* 7, no. 2–3 (Spring/Summer 1988): 157–181.
Davis, Nancy M. "Finding Voice: Revisiting Race and American Catholicism in Detroit." *American Catholic Studies* 114, no. 3 (2003): 39–58.
Dunch, Ryan. "Beyond Cultural Imperialism: Cultural Theory, Christian Missions, and Global Modernity." *History and Theory* 41, no. 3 (October 2002).
Evans, Curtis J. "The Religious and Racial Meanings of *The Green Pastures*." *Religion and American Culture: A Journal of Interpretation* 1, no. 18 (Winter 2008): 59–93.
Feagin, Joe R. "Black Catholics in the United States: An Exploratory Analysis." *Sociological Analysis* 29, no. 4 (1968): 246–254.
Fletcher, Winona L. "Witnessing a 'Miracle': Sixty Years of Heaven Bound at Big Bethel in Atlanta." *Black American Literature Forum* 25, no. 1 (1991): 83–92.

Giggie, John M. "'When Jesus Handed Me a Ticket': Images of Railroad Travel and Spiritual Transformations, 1865–1917." In *Visual Culture of American Religions*, David Morgan and Sally M. Promey, ed. Berkeley: University of California Press, 2000.

———. "The Mississippi River and the Transformation of Black Religion in the Delta, 1877–1915." In *Gods of the Mississippi*, Michael Pasquier, ed. Bloomington, Ind.: Indiana University Press, 2013.

Hall, Jacquelyn Dowd. "The Long Civil Rights Movement and the Political Uses of the Past." *Journal of American History* 91, no. 4 (March 2005): 1233–1263.

Hunt, Larry. "Black Catholicism and Secular Status: Integration, Conversion, and Consolidation." *Social Science Quarterly* 77, no. 4 (1996): 842–859.

Hunt, Larry L., and Janet G. Hunt. "Black Catholicism and the Spirit of Weber." *Sociological Quarterly* 17, no. 3 (Summer 1976): 369–377.

Hutton, Leon. "Catholicity and Civility: John Francis Noll and the Origins of 'Our Sunday Visitor.'" *U.S. Catholic Historian* 15, no. 3 (Summer 1997): 1–22.

Johnson, Karen. "Beyond Parish Boundaries: Black Catholics and the Quest for Racial Justice." *Religion and American Culture: A Journal of Interpretation* 25, no. 2 (Summer 2015): 264–300.

Johnson, Sylvester A. "The Rise of the Black Ethnics: The Ethnic Turn in African American Religions, 1916–1945." *Religion and American Culture: A Journal of Interpretation* 20, no. 2 (2010): 125–163.

Kieckhefer, Richard. "Major Currents in Late Medieval Devotion." In *Christian Spirituality: High Middle Ages and Reformation*, Jill Raitt, ed. New York: Crossroad, 1988.

Kollman, Paul. "The Promise of Mission History for U.S. Catholic History." *U.S. Catholic Historian* 24, no. 3 (Summer 2006): 1–18.

Lofland, John, and Rodney Stark. "Becoming a World-Saver: A Theory of Conversion to a Deviant Perspective." *American Sociological Review* 30 (1965): 862–875.

Marable, Manning. "Black Power in Chicago: An Historical Overview of Class Stratification and Electoral Politics in a Black Urban Community." *Review of Radical Political Economics* 17, no. 3 (1985): 157–182.

Massingale, Bryan. "Malcolm X as Neglected 'Classic' for Catholic Theological Reflection." *Origins: CNS Documentary Service* 40, no. 9 (July 8, 2010): 130–144.

———. "Malcolm X and the Limits of 'Authentically Black and Truly Catholic': A Research Project on Black Radicalism and Black Catholic Faith." *Journal of the Black Catholic Theological Symposium* 5 (2011): 7–23.

McGann, Mary E., and Eva Marie Lumas. "The Emergence of African American Catholic Worship." *U.S. Catholic Historian* 19, no. 2 (Spring 2001): 27–65.

McGreevy, John T. "Racial Justice and the People of God: American Catholics, Civil Rights, and the Second Vatican Council." *Religion and American Culture: A Journal of Interpretation* 4, no. 2 (1994): 221–254.

Moore, Cecilia A. "African American Catholic Conversion." *Sacred Rock* (Summer 1999): 1–6.

———. "Keeping Harlem Catholic: African American Catholics in Harlem, 1920–1960." *American Catholic Studies* 114, no. 3 (2003): 3–21.

———. "Conversion Narratives: The Dual Experiences and Voices of African American Catholic Converts." *U.S. Catholic Historian* 28, no. 1 (Winter 2010): 27–40.

———. "Writing Black Catholic Lives: Black Catholic Biographies and Autobiographies." *U.S. Catholic Historian* 29, no. 3 (Summer 2011): 43–58.

Neal, Mark Anthony. "'I Am . . .': Troy Davis, Fred Hampton, and the Black Freedom Movement." (September 24, 2011): newblackman.blogspot.com.

Neary, Timothy B. "Black-Belt Catholic Space: African-American Parishes in Interwar Chicago." *U.S. Catholic Historian* 18, no. 4 (Fall 2000): 76–91.

Nelsen, Hart M., and Lynda Dickson. "Attitudes of Black Catholics and Protestants: Evidence for Religious Identity." *Sociological Analysis* 33, no. 3 (Autumn 1972): 152–165.

Noll, Mark. "The New History of Missions." *Books and Culture* 30, no. 2 (2004): 30.

Orsi, Robert A. "U.S. Catholics between Memory and Modernity: How Catholics Are American." In *Catholics in the American Century: Recasting Narratives of U.S. History*, R. Scott Appleby and Kathleen Sprows Cummings, ed. Ithaca, N.Y.: Cornell University Press, 2012.

Pasquier, Michael. "'Though Their Skin Remains Brown, I Hope Their Souls Will Soon Be White': Slavery, French Missionaries, and the Roman Catholic Priesthood in the American South, 1789–1865." *Church History* 77, no. 2 (June 2008): 337–370.

Phelps, Jamie T. "The Theology and Process of Inculturation: A Theology of Hope for African American Catholics in the United States." *New Theology Review* 7, no. 1 (February 1994): 5–13.

Powers, Richard Gid. "American Catholics and Catholic Americans: The Rise and Fall of Catholic Anti-Communism." *U.S. Catholic Historian* 22, no. 4 (Fall 2004): 17–35.

Rogovin, Milton. "Storefront Churches—Buffalo, N.Y." In *Aperture* 10, no. 2. Rochester, N.Y.: Aperture, Inc. (1962): 64–85.

Sanders, Katrina M. "Black Catholic Clergy and the Struggle for Civil Rights: Winds of Change." In *Uncommon Faithfulness: The Black Catholic Experience*, M. Shawn Copeland, with LaReine-Marie Mosely, S.N.D., and Albert J. Raboteau, ed. (Maryknoll, N.Y.: Orbis Books, 2009).

Satter, Beryl. "Cops, Gangs, and Revolutionaries in 1960s Chicago: What Black Police Can Tell Us about Power." *Journal of Urban History* 42, no. 6 (2015): 1–25.

Spear, Sonja E. "Claiming the Passion: American Fantasies of the Oberammergau Passion Play, 1923–1947." *Church History* 80, no. 4 (December 2011): 832–862.

"Special Issue: The Black Catholic Community, 1880–1987." *U.S. Catholic Historian* 7, nos. 2–3 (Spring–Summer 1988).

"Special Issue: African American Spirituality and Liturgical Renewal." *U.S. Catholic Historian*, 19, no. 2 (Spring 2001).

Tate, William F. "From Inner City to Ivory Tower: Does My Voice Matter in the Academy?" *Urban Education* 29 (1994).

Taylor, Keeanga-Yamahtta. "Back Story to the Neoliberal Moment: Race Taxes and the Political Economy of Black Urban Housing in the 1960s." In "Austerity, Neoliberalism, and Black Communities," Barbara Ransby, ed. *Souls: A Critical Journal of Black Politics, Culture, and Society* 14, nos. 3–4 (2012).

Vader, Anthony J. "Mission to Black America." *Chicago Studies* 23 (August 1984): 169–181.

Vincent, Catherine. "The Way of the Cross." In *Encyclopedia of the Middle Ages*, André Vauchez, ed. Cambridge: James Clarke and Co., 2001.

Williams, Shannen Dee. "The Color of Christ's Brides." In "Forum: Race, White Supremacy, and the Making of American Catholicism," Matthew J. Cressler, ed. *American Catholic Studies* 127, no. 3 (Fall 2016).

———. "Subversive Images and Forgotten Truths." *American Catholic Studies* 127, no. 3 (Fall 2016).

Dissertations

Beaumier, Casey, S.J. "For Richer, For Poorer: Jesuit Secondary Education in America and the Challenge of Elitism." Ph.D. dissertation, Boston College, 2013.

Hallstoos, Brian James. "Windy City, Holy Land: Willa Saunders Jones and Black Sacred Music and Drama." Ph.D dissertation, University of Iowa, 2009.

Johnson, Karen. "The Universal Church in the Segregated City: Catholic Interracialism in Chicago, 1928–1963." Ph.D. dissertation, University of Illinois at Chicago, 2012.

Poché, Justin. "Religion, Race, and Rights in Catholic Louisiana, 1938–1970." Ph.D. dissertation, University of Notre Dame, 2007.

Rath, Julia Wally. "Faith, Hope, and Education: African American Parents of Children in Catholic Schools and Their Social and Religious Accommodation to Catholicism." Ph.D. dissertation, University of Chicago, 1995.

Sobczyk, Mary Clarice, O.S.F. "A Survey of Catholic Education for the Negro of Five Parishes in Chicago." Ph.D. dissertation, De Paul University, 1954.

Taylor, Keeanga-Yamahtta. "From American Dream to Predatory Lending: Public/Private Programs to Promote Home Ownership among Low-Income African Americans in the 1970s." Ph.D. dissertation, Northwestern University, 2013.

Williams, Shannen Dee. "Subversive Habits: Black Nuns and the Struggle to Desegregate Catholic America after World War I." Ph.D. dissertation, Rutgers University, 2013.

INDEX

Adams, Elizabeth Laura, 217n63
Adrian Dominican sisters, 17
Africa/Africans, 1, 7, 9, 31–33, 39–40, 104, 173–176, 234n88
African Americans: academic study of, 10, 129, 176, 181; and the Great Migrations, 3–6, 12, 16, 19, 21–28, 30, 39, 48, 93, 96, 102–103, 111, 198; as "heathens," 16, 22, 28–33, 40, 46, 48, 163; non-religious, 139; Protestants, 4, 7, 22, 24, 46, 51, 57, 60, 100, 108–109, 139, 141, 164, 173, 175–176, 184, 188, 198; and self-definition, 119–120, 124, 147; and self-determination, 5, 14, 17, 116, 119–120, 123–124, 130–132, 137, 140, 145, 147–151, 153, 156, 162, 165–170, 178–179, 189, 193, 199. *See also* Black Catholicism; Black Catholics; Black Hebrews; Black Muslims; Black Power; civil rights movement; Moorish Americans
African Methodist Episcopal Church, 4, 96, 98
Afro-American Catholic Congresses, 205n36
Afro-American Firemen's League, 137, 139, 150
Afro-American Patrolmen's League (AAPL), 121–122, 133, 137, 139, 150–153, 170–171
Afro-American Youth Organization, 139
aggiornamento, 118–120
Agnella, Sister Mary, 124
Alabama, 21, 64, 122

Ali, Noble Drew, 104. *See also* Moorish Science Temple of America
All Nations Pentecostal church, 95
Alvez, Joshua, 132, 134
America (periodical), 58
Archdiocese of Chicago, 14, 17, 30, 52–53, 56, 64, 121, 125–128, 132–134, 137, 144–145, 148, 166, 179
Arizti, Fernando, 197
ARK of St. Sabina, 195
Armstrong, Louis, 86, 92
Asad, Talal, 61, 80
Auburn Gresham (neighborhood), 195–196
Avella, Steven, 53

Baldwin, Davarian, 99, 101
Baltimore, 6, 20, 38, 117, 158, 180
Baltimore Catechism, 42, 49, 72
Baptists, 1, 17, 23–25, 47, 53, 76, 78, 82, 95–97, 109, 112, 125, 140–141, 144, 169, 171–175
Barth, Father Pius, 110, 113
Belafonte, Harry, 197
Best, Wallace D., 24, 87, 93–94
Big Bethel AME Church (Atlanta), 98, 100
Biondi, Martha, 129, 224n11, 234n85
Black, Timuel, 109
Black Belt (Chicago), 19–20, 25–27, 32, 35, 40, 49, 54, 95, 196
Black Catholic Clergy Caucus (BCCC), 130–132, 137, 144, 154–155, 158–159, 162, 226n44, 227n50

Black Catholicism, 1–6, 9–10, 16–17, 117, 128–129, 154–155, 158–159, 196, 200–201; and Black Power, 5–7, 13–15, 17, 115, 117, 128–139, 142, 147–151, 154–156, 164–165, 169–170, 178–187, 189, 199–201; and missionary Catholicism, 174, 187–193, 199; and Vatican II, 118–120, 134–139, 143–147, 149–150, 164, 190, 205n36, 228n87

Black Catholic Movement, 17, 131, 151, 152–168, 173–175, 178, 184, 187–192, 197, 199–200

Black Catholics: and Black Power, 5–7, 13–15, 17, 115, 117, 128–139, 142, 147–151, 154–156, 164–165, 169–170, 178–187, 189, 199–201; and slavery, 7, 9, 38, 51, 121, 191, 210n66; converts, 4–7, 16, 23, 27–48, 77, 79–82, 87, 96–97, 106, 164, 189; decline of, in Chicago, 156–160, 162, 164; divisions among, 5, 124, 134–135, 142, 187–189; growth of, in Chicago, 16, 20–21, 40, 158

Black Chicago Renaissance (New Negro movement), 92–93, 99

"Black Church," 1, 4, 9–10, 15–16, 77, 96–97, 104, 154, 171, 175–178, 189–191, 199, 205n30

Black Consortium, 137, 139

Black Gods of the Metropolis: Negro Religious Cults of the Urban North (Fauset), 46, 103–105

Black Hebrews, 16, 82, 86, 103–107, 112, 114, 198–199

Black Lay Catholic Caucus, 169–170

Black Liberation flag, 141, 182

"Black Manifesto," 175

Black Metropolis: A Study of Negro Life in a Northern City (Drake and Cayton), 62, 86, 216n46

Black Moors. *See* Moorish Americans

Black Muslims, 8, 16, 25, 86, 105–107, 112, 139, 168, 173, 184, 198, 237n123. *See also* Malcolm X; Muhammad, Honorable Elijah; Nation of Islam

Black national anthem, 182

Black National Economic Conference, 175

Blackness, 1, 8, 15–16, 98, 103, 133–143, 147, 164, 173–175, 178, 189–191, 200, 223n5, 224n11, 227n50

A Black Nun Looks at Black Power (Thibodeaux), 149

Black Panthers, 5, 14, 17, 116, 119, 121–123, 128, 133–139, 151–153, 163, 182, 199

"Black Perspectives on Evangelization in the Modern World" (pastoral letter), 190

Black Power, 3, 9, 91, 119, 121–123, 127, 162–163, 173, 224n10–11, 225n19, 233n62, 237n123; Black Catholic critics of, 142, 187–189; and Black Catholicism, the rise of, 5–7, 13–15, 17, 115, 117, 128–139, 142, 147–151, 154–156, 164–165, 169–170, 178–187, 189, 199–201, 203n9; and self-definition, 119–120, 124, 147; and self-determination, 5, 14, 17, 116, 119–120, 123–124, 130–132, 137, 140, 145, 147–151, 153, 156, 162, 165–170, 178–179, 189, 193, 199; and Vatican II, 118–120, 134–139, 143–147, 149–150, 164, 190, 205n36, 228n87; transition from Civil Rights to, 13–14, 120, 122, 128–129, 150, 170, 199, 224n9

Black Power: The Politics of Liberation (Carmichael and Hamilton), 131, 168, 170, 233n62

Black Priest/White Church: Catholics and Racism (Lucas), 8, 138, 163, 188, 215n29

"Black religion," 6, 15, 23–24, 43, 46–47, 57, 82, 86–87, 93–98, 100–102, 138, 175, 191, 198, 234n88; and Black Spirituality, 1, 4, 9, 15, 96, 174, 192

Black Theology, 164

Black Unity Masses, 14, 135–151

Bontemps, Arna, 92

Boston, 110

Boyd, Louis, 153
Boyo, Father Chris Edema, 176
Brandewie, Ernest, 31
Braxton, Edward, 2, 232n52
Brazil, 7
Brigham, Father Kenneth, 132, 150
Bronzeville (neighborhood), 8, 27, 32, 35, 40–42, 53, 62, 83, 86, 93, 97, 108–109, 121, 197, 216n46
Brooks, Gwendolyn, 92
Brown v. Board of Education, 11, 13, 129
Buetow, Harold A., 63, 68
Burns, Charles, 162, 231n29

Cabeza de Vaca, Alvar Nuñes, 7
Carmichael, Stokely, 13, 119, 130–131, 168, 170, 199, 224n10, 233n62
Carmon, Father Dominic, 150–151
Catholic Action movement, 28
Catholic Charities, 195
The Catholic Church and the American Negro (Gillard), 47
Catholic Interracial Council, 11–13, 45, 129, 133–134, 137
Catholics/Catholicism, 2, 16, 25, 57, 62, 114, 125, 129, 143, 148–149, 155–156, 160, 163–165, 174, 178, 183–185, 199–201, 205n36, 216n47; conversion of African Americans, 4–7, 16, 23, 27–48, 77, 79–82, 87, 96–97, 106, 164, 189; historiography of, 10–16, 129; Irish, 11, 20–21, 25, 33, 53, 92, 122, 167, 170–171, 174–175, 195–196, 199; Italian, 11, 19, 167, 174, 199; liturgy/mass, 1–2, 15, 43–44, 69, 118, 136, 138–143, 147, 150, 164–165, 176–177, 187, 190–192, 197, 200, 227; and marriage, 75–79; as the "One True Church," 35, 48–49, 51, 59–60, 74, 77, 80–81, 97, 107, 111–112, 117, 146, 154, 156, 164, 183, 193, 219n99; Polish, 25, 143, 167, 174, 199; white Catholics, 4–5, 7–9, 11–13, 16, 21, 25–27, 32–34, 38–39, 45–46, 52–58, 62, 96, 115, 116–117, 121–124, 129–130, 132–135, 139, 143, 145–151, 154–165, 168–171, 173–181, 184–193, 196–200, 208n30, 215n29, 226n44. *See also* Black Catholicism; Black Catholics; Catholic schools; Second Vatican Council
Catholic schools, 5, 10, 15–20, 25, 27, 33–42, 48, 51–81, 117, 121, 123–126, 140–141, 148, 153, 156, 160–162, 166–168, 171, 175, 178–187, 193, 195–197, 216n46, 235nn93–94, 236n110
The Catholic World, 58
Cayton, Horace, 62, 86, 216n46
Cherry, Prophet F. S., 104–105
Chicago, 6, 17, 20, 23, 26–27, 54–55, 92, 108, 117, 120, 144, 148, 152, 156–157, 164, 167, 170–171, 195–196, 199; as a Catholic Metropolis, 6, 25, 31, 195; as the "Black Metropolis," 6, 8, 16, 23, 26, 82, 86–87, 92–97, 111–112, 117; Black migration to, 6, 16, 19, 21–27, 79; Black population of, 19–20, 27, 158; Black Power in, 6, 14, 17, 120–123, 135–138, 150–151, 178–187; Black Renaissance in, 92–93, 99; as a foreign mission field, 16, 21–22, 29–48, 52–53; religious landscape of, 25, 44, 82, 95, 168; segregation in, 23, 156–159. *See also names of specific neighborhoods, churches, and schools*
Chicago American, 89
Chicago Conference on Laymen, 137, 139
Chicago Defender, 23, 29, 102, 143, 209n42
Chicago Freedom Movement (CFM), 120, 197
Chicago Plan, 52, 56, 58, 63, 71, 75, 86, 179, 183
Chicago Police Department (CPD), 122–123, 135, 140, 152, 170–171; "Red Squad" (CPD Tactical Unit), 135, 140–141
Chicago race riot of 1919, 8, 26
Chicago Tribune, 102, 140, 157, 220n15
Chinguku, Father Alkuin, 176
Church of God, 104

256 | INDEX

civil rights movement, 10–14, 119, 122–123, 129, 140, 150, 166, 173, 198–199, 205n30, 226n30; transition to Black Power from, 13–14, 120, 122, 128–129, 150, 170, 199, 224n9
Cleage, Albert, 175
Clements, Father George H., 17, 109, 116–117, 121–151, 152–153, 156–157, 161, 165–173, 179–186, 188, 195, 197, 223n3, 227n48, 237n123
Cobb, Rev. Clarence, 95
Cody, Cardinal John P., 116, 125–128, 132, 137–140, 148, 150–151, 165–166
Cold War, 10, 65
Colgate Rochester Divinity School, 175
Commandment Keepers Ethiopian Hebrew Congregation of the Living God, 103, 112
Commission for Catholic Missions among the Colored People and the Indians, 39
Committee for One Society, 137
Commonweal, 58
Concerned Black Catholics (CBC), 116, 132–142, 145–150, 155
Concerned Transit Workers, 137, 139
Cone, James, 175
Connelly, Mark, 97–98
conversion, 3, 8, 16, 29–30, 35–37, 40–45, 51–81, 86, 111, 116, 154–156, 158, 163, 198, 214n27; concept of, 51–52, 57–61, 79–82, 213n3, 215nn28–30
Convert Makers of America (CMOA), 28
Co-Ordinating Council on Community Organization, 122
Copeland, M. Shawn, 12, 238n5
Corpus Christi (parish), 20–21, 26, 32–34, 38, 52–55, 78, 93, 96, 121, 144–145, 196, 198, 219n3; and Living Stations of the Cross, 69, 83, 86–91, 98–99, 101–102, 107–114, 117, 185, 219n2
Corpus Christi School, 68, 121
Council of Trent, 118

Cousins, William, 137
Crane College/Malcolm X College, 225n19
Curia, 118
Curran, Father Patrick, 56, 212n118, 214n21

Daley, Richard J., 122, 130
Davis, Angela, 13, 130, 182
Davis, Cyprian, 7, 9–10, 211n78
Davis, Brother Joseph M., 158, 162, 174, 187, 189, 192
Davis, Nancy M., 114
DePaul University, 71, 181
Detroit, 6, 23, 114, 130
devotionalism, 16, 87, 111, 115, 117, 188, 218n81
devotion moderna, 31
Dillard, Angela, 14
Dorsey, Thomas A., 92
Douglass, Frederick, 166
Drake, St. Clair, 62, 86, 216n46
Drexel, Mother Katharine, 33, 59, 210n61
Du Bois, W. E. B., 93–96
Dunch, Ryan, 34

Ebony, 29, 74, 114, 179
Eckert, Father Joseph, 32, 39–45, 50, 52–55
education, 29, 38, 42, 51–52, 56–57, 62–64, 71–72, 77, 156, 161, 179–180, 182, 186–187, 216n46–47, 235n93, 236n110. See also Catholic schools
Elsen, Father Vincent, 144
Englewood (neighborhood), 17
Esteban/Estevanico (Moroccan slave), 7
evangelical Christianity, 4–5, 7, 15–16, 82, 86–87, 104–107, 111–113, 164, 188, 197
Evans, Curtis, 15, 43, 107
Evans, Rev. John, 101
Evers, Medgar, 154
Extension (periodical), 109–110

Faith Community of St. Sabina, 195–198
Falsani, Cathleen, 196
Fanon, Franz, 9, 162–163

Farrakhan, Minister Louis, 197
Farrell, Father Martin, 52–55, 58, 60, 72–73, 77–79, 86, 197, 214n13
Father Divine, 112
Fauset, Arthur Huff, 46, 102, 104–106, 212n17
Feast of Corpus Christi, 107–108
Feast of St. Peter Claver, 1, 191
Feast of the Immaculate Conception, 65
Feast of the Seven Dolors, 2, 110
Federal Bureau of Investigation, 152
Federal Housing Administration, 157
Federated Colored Catholics, 205n36
Feeney, Rev. Daniel, 63
First Church of the Deliverance Spiritualist, 47, 95
First Vatican Council, 118
Fletcher, Winona, 98, 100
Fochtmann, Father David, 87, 101
For God So Loved the World (painting), 197
Fort Mose, 7
Forty Hours of Devotion, 107
Foster, Michèle, 64, 216n46
Franciscan friars, 20, 33, 87, 89, 91, 113
Franciscan Herald, 100
Franciscan Province of the Sacred Heart, 33, 110
Freeing the Spirit, 176, 189–190
Freeman, Eldridge, 179–180

Gadpaille, Mary Dolores, 2–5, 8–9, 78, 110–114, 198, 220n21
Garfield Boulevard Improvement Association, 53
Garvey, Marcus, 131
Gaudium et Spes, 150
Genealogies of Religion (Asad), 80
George, Cardinal Francis, 197–198
Getz, Anne, 140
Giggie, John, 23
Gillard, John T., 47
Grand Boulevard (neighborhood), 157, 165, 183

Gravissimum Educationis, 161
Great Migrations, 3–6, 12, 16, 19, 21–28, 30, 39, 48, 93, 96, 102–103, 111, 198
Greeley, Andrew, 43
Green, Adam, 92–93
The Green Pastures (Connelly), 97–98
Gregory, Archbishop Wilton D., 17–18, 39, 192–193, 211n81
Grey, Sister Martin DePorres, 130–131, 173, 192
Grossman, James, 23
Growing Up African American in Catholic Schools (Irvine and Foster), 64

Haiti, 7, 176, 178
Hall, Jacquelyn Dowd, 11
Hamilton, Charles, 131, 168, 170, 233n62
Hampton, Fred, 14, 123, 133–134, 152–154, 230n8
Harding, Vincent, 176
Harlem, 29, 138, 163, 214n13
Harlem Renaissance, 29, 92, 114
Hatch, John, 133
"heathen," 16, 22, 28–33, 40, 46, 48, 163
Heaven Bound (play), 98, 100–101
Heywood, Linda, 7
Higginbotham, Evelyn Brooks, 24
Holiness-Pentecostalism, 1, 24–25, 44, 47, 82, 86, 93, 95, 104–106, 112
Holy Angels (parish), 17, 54, 71, 150–151, 152–157, 161, 165–173, 178–187, 195–196, 198, 200
Holy Angels School, 71, 166, 235nn93–94, 236n110
Horne, Lena, 86
Hortensia, Sister, 181
Howard, Mary, 19, 84, 198
Hoy, Suellen, 33–34, 59

Imani Temple African-American Catholic Congregation, 229n91
immigrants/immigration, 4, 10, 33–36, 92, 97, 108, 117, 157, 167, 181, 204n25

Inner City Priests Conference (ICPC), 137, 148
Interdenominational Ministers Alliance, 173
interracialism, 11–14, 45, 129–130, 198–200, 212n110, 226n30
Interracial Review, 58
Ireland, 34, 181
Irvine, Jacqueline Jordan, 64, 68, 70
Islam, 46, 103–105, 112, 168, 173, 184. *See also* Black Muslims; Nation of Islam
Italy, 34, 64

Jackson, Mahalia, 182
Jackson, Rev. A. P., 109
Jackson, Rev. Jesse, 125, 139–140, 173
Jackson, Rosemary, 169
Jackson State College, 154
Jamaica, 114, 176
Janssen, Father Arnold, 31
Jim Crow, 13, 19, 22, 186
Johnson, Karen, 13, 129
Johnson, Monsignor George, 63
Johnson, Sylvester, 7, 32, 103–104
Jones, Willa Saunders, 97
Josephite Fathers, 39, 47, 158, 173
Jubilee, 58

Kallay, Jane Sophia. *See* Therese, Sister Mary Francis
Kentucky, 21, 121
Kentucky Holy Land, 121
King, Coretta Scott, 197
King, Martin Luther, Jr., 12–14, 120–122, 125, 129–131, 136; as a saint, 136–137, 140, 152, 154, 165–166, 197; assassination of, 116, 121, 129–130, 154, 199
King, Rev. D. E., 171

LaChapelle, Father James, 150, 188
LaFarge, Father John, 45
Laguerre, Michael, 176–178

Lambert, Father Rollins, 126–128, 130–140, 142, 144, 148, 150–151, 169, 225n27, 227n50
Lead Me, Guide Me: The African American Catholic Hymnal, 192–193
Levine, Lawrence, 176
Life, 109
Life is Worth Living (television show), 109
Living Stations of the Cross, 83–92, 97, 106–107, 113–115, 117, 121, 185, 188, 219n2, 220n12; news coverage of, 97–102, 109–110, 221n39; and Protestant passion plays, 97–101
Long, Charles, 176
Los Angeles Times, 140
Louisiana, 20, 98, 180, 211n71
Loyola College (Baltimore), 180
Lucas, Father Lawrence, 8, 138–139, 141, 149, 151, 159, 163, 188–189, 192, 215n29, 226n40, 237n130
Lyke, Bishop James P., 17–18, 192–193
Lymore, Kimberly M., 197

Malcolm X, 8–9, 13–14, 104, 130–131, 154, 163, 192, 226n44, 232n51. *See also* Black Muslims; Nation of Islam
March on Washington for Jobs and Freedom, 122
Martin Luther King Laymen's League, 137
Martin Luther King Program in Black Church Studies, 175–176
Maryland, 20, 121, 180
Massingale, Bryan, 12, 203n9, 232n51
Matthew, Rabbi Wentworth, 104, 106
McClory, Robert, 159, 164
McDannell, Colleen, 26, 96
McDermott, John, 164
McGreevy, John, 11–13, 25–26, 56, 129, 150, 160, 216n47, 226n30, 235n93
McGuiness, Margaret, 59
McKay, Claude, 29, 114
Menéndez, Francisco, 7

Methodists, 1, 4, 8, 25, 47, 53, 96, 171. *See also* African Methodist Episcopal Church
Mexico, 7, 34, 64
Meyer, Cardinal Albert, 125
Midwest Clergy Conference on Negro Welfare (MCCNW), 45–47, 56, 169
Milwaukee, 6, 56, 181
missions/missionaries, 5–6, 12, 16–18, 27–28, 50, 93, 115, 154–156, 162–164, 169, 174, 176, 197–200, 212n118, 214n13; and Black Power, 178–187; and Catholic schools, 52–61, 71, 75, 81, 117; and Chicago as a foreign mission field, 16, 21–22, 29–48, 52–53; and cultural imperialism, 154–156, 210n66; and the rise of Black Catholicism, 187–193
Mississippi Delta, 23–24
Mitchell, Rev. Dr. Henry H., 175–176
Mitchell, Thomas, 133–135, 138
Mooney, Father Michael, 144
Moore, Cecilia, 58, 77, 214n27
Moorish Americans, 86, 104–107, 112, 114, 199
Moorish Science Temple of America (MST), 103–106, 112
Motley, Archibald John Jr., 92
Moynihan, Daniel Patrick, 186–187
Moynihan Report. See *The Negro Family: The Case for National Action*
Muhammad, Honorable Elijah, 104, 131, 167–168, 173
Mundelein, Cardinal George, 27

National Black Sisters' Conference (NBSC), 131–132, 154, 159, 173
National Catholic Conference on Interracial Justice, 164
National Catholic Educational Association, 63
National Catholic Reporter, 159, 164
National Conference of Catholic Bishops (NCCB), 159
National Convention of Black Lay Catholics, 159
National Eucharistic Congress, 28
National Office for Black Catholics (NOBC), 158–161, 176, 189–191
Nation of Islam (NOI), 103–105, 112, 168, 173, 184, 237n123. *See also* Black Muslims; Malcolm X; Muhammad, Honorable Elijah
Native Americans, 20, 29, 33–34, 39
Neary, Timothy, 13, 26, 62, 109, 129, 216n46
"Negro Apostolate," 45–46, 163
The Negro Family: The Case for National Action (Moynihan), 186–187
New Jersey, 29
New Negro movement. See Black Chicago Renaissance
New Orleans, 6, 19–21, 28, 117, 121
Newsweek, 159, 164
Newton, Huey P., 123
New World (newspaper), 28, 99, 127, 143, 145–146, 152, 179, 221n39, 227n50
New York Amsterdam News, 98
New York City, 6, 23, 186
Nixon, Richard, 167, 233n60
Noll, Bishop John, 28
nonviolence, 14, 130–131
Northwestern University, 224n10, 225n19
Nutt, Maurice, 12

Oakland (Chicago neighborhood), 167
Oberammergau, Germany, 87, 113
Olivet Baptist church, 95
Operation Breadbasket, 125, 137, 140, 150
Order of Friars Minor. See Franciscan friars
Orsi, Robert, 32, 63–64, 68–69, 91, 99
Osia, Father J. Kunirum, 176
O'Toole, James, 59
Our Lady of Perpetual Help, 150
Our Lady's Sodality, 66

Parish Boundaries: The Catholic Encounter with Race in the Twentieth Century Urban North (McGreevy), 11, 25, 235n93

The Parish Catechism: Written Especially for Instructing Non-Catholic People in the Basic Teachings of Religion (Farrell), 60, 72–73, 79

Parish Gleanings (Corpus Christi parish bulletin), 91

Parks, Rosa, 14

parochial schools. *See* Catholic schools

Peace Mission Movement, 112

Pentecostalism. *See* Holiness-Pentecostalism

Perry, Theresa, 173

Pfleger, Father Michael L., 196–198

Phelps, Sister Jamie, 12, 174–175, 192, 230n12

Philadelphia, 33, 104

Pimblott, Kerry, 14

Pope Clement XII, 88

Pope John XXIII, 118

Pope Paul VI, 1

Pope Pius XII, 29, 65

Porter, Father Herman, 130

Potter, Father Aidan, 100–101

Presbyterians, 49, 78

"Progressives" (Black Baptist reformers), 24

Protestant Reformation, 51, 114, 118

Quigley Preparatory Seminary, 121

Raboteau, Albert, 10, 146, 176

Rainbow Coalition, 123

"religion," 4, 6, 11–14, 25, 32, 51, 60–61, 77, 80–81, 105, 199, 213n3. *See also* "Black religion"; conversion

"religio-racial movements," 86, 102–103, 105–106, 112, 114

Revolutionary Action Movement, 122

Richards, Father Joseph, 52–58, 71, 86, 181, 197, 214n13

Ritual and its Consequences (Seligman, et al), 60

Rivers, Father Clarence Joseph, 187, 190

Robinson, Renault "Reggie," 122, 153, 171

Rockford, Illinois, 130

Rogovin, Milton, 94–95

Roman, Sister Mary, 68–70,

"romantic racialism," 43

Rummel, Archbishop Joseph, 28–29

Rush, Bobby, 123, 152–153

"sacred slumming," 99–101

Sacrosanctum Concilium, 136

San Francisco State University, 123

Satter, Beryl, 8

Scanlan, Father Gerald, 122, 124–126, 128

Scott, William Edouard, 92

School Sisters of St. Francis, 181, 184

Seale, Bobby, 123

Second Plenary Council of Baltimore, 38

Second Vatican Council, 5, 17, 77, 91, 117–120, 126, 134–139, 143, 147, 149–150, 161, 164–165, 179, 183–184, 190, 205n36, 226n30, 228n87

segregation, 8, 12–13, 19, 23, 45; in Catholic churches, 12, 30, 52, 114, 156–159, 180, 226n44; in Chicago housing, 156–159; in schools, 62, 64

Self, Robert O., 157, 224n9

self-formation, 34, 63–74, 77, 80–81

Selma, Alabama, 122

Sertum Laetitiae, 29

Shea, John Gilmary, 28

Sheen, Bishop Fulton, 109, 113

Shrine of St. Martin Luther King Jr., 152, 165–166

Singh, Nikhil Pal, 14

Sisters of Charity of the Blessed Virgin Mary, 123

Sisters of St. Francis, 33–34, 121, 181, 184

Sisters of the Blessed Sacrament for Indians and Colored People (SBS), 20, 33, 35–39, 52, 65, 67

Slater, Jack, 179
slavery/slaves, 7, 9, 32, 38, 51, 93, 95, 103–104, 107, 121, 131, 157, 176, 186, 191, 210n66, 234n88
Smith, Elder Lucy, 95
Smith, Father Paul, 161, 165, 180–186, 235n94
Smith, J. Z., 10
Sobczyk, Sister Mary Clarice, 71–73, 218n78
Society of the Divine Word (SVD), 30–32, 35, 39–40, 53
The Song of Bernadette (film), 76, 218n78
The Souls of Black Folk (Du Bois), 95
Southern Christian Leadership Conference, 120, 125
South Side (Chicago), 8, 17, 19, 21, 25, 29, 32–35, 39–40, 48, 52–54, 76, 84, 87, 92–93, 113, 116, 122–123, 126, 132, 145, 152, 156, 161, 165, 167, 171, 178, 188, 193, 195–199
Spiritualists, 25, 47, 95
Stallings, George Augustus, 229n91
St. Anselm (parish), 26–27, 35–36, 40, 52, 65, 218n83
St. Bernadette, 76
St. Carthage School, 17, 39
St. Charles Borromeo (Harlem parish), 214n13
St. Cyprian of Carthage, 31
St. Dorothy (parish), 117, 122–127, 132–133, 136–147, 153, 226n30. *See also* Black Unity Masses; Concerned Black Catholics
St. Dorothy Parish Council, 133, 137
St. Dorothy School, 123–124, 126
St. Edmund's Episcopal Church, 96
St. Elizabeth (parish), 26, 35–36, 40, 50, 52–56, 58, 150, 188
St. Elizabeth School, 65
St. James (parish), 54, 126–127, 132, 135–136, 138, 141
St. John Church-Baptist, 173

St. Jude, 76, 218n80
St. Malachy (parish), 53–54, 57, 198, 215n30
St. Martin (parish), 132–133, 135
St. Mary of the Lake Seminary, 53, 121
St. Monica (parish), 30, 40, 50
St. Monica School, 42
Stono Rebellion, 7
storefront churches, 25, 48, 82, 87, 94–95, 106
St. Philip Lutheran Church, 171
Streisand, Barbara, 167, 233n60
Strueder, Sister Helen, 181–195
St. Sabina Academy, 195, 197
St. Sabina Elders Village, 195
St. Sabina Employment Resource Center, 195
St. Sabina (parish), 195–198
Student Nonviolent Coordinating Committee, 119
Sugrue, Thomas, 134, 224n11, 233n62
Sutor, David (journalist), 165, 178–179, 193, 235n94, 235n110

Tarry, Ellen, 60, 70
That You May Die Easy (Gadpaille), 76
Therese, Sister Mary Frances, 36–37, 58–59, 75, 81, 111
Thibodeaux, Sister Mary Roger, 149
Third Order of St. Francis, 110
Third Plenary Council of Baltimore, 38
Thornton, John K., 7
Tolton, Father Augustus, 9, 114
The Torch, 58
Tre Ore service, 42, 109
Turner, Thomas Wyatt, 205n36
Turner, Victor, 99

Uganda, 1
ultramontanism, 216n47
Unitatis Redintegratio, 183
University of Chicago, 133
University of Scranton, 180
U.S. Catholic, 165

Vatican II. *See* Second Vatican Council
Verda, Sister Mary, 71
via crucis. See Way of the Cross
Visitation (parish), 53
Vodou, 178
Voting Rights Act of 1965, 11

Walker, Margaret, 92
"Wall of Black Saints," 153–154
Walls, Pedro, 132–134
Way of the Cross, 2, 43, 83, 88, 90–91, 99, 101, 110. *See also* Living Stations of the Cross
Weisenfeld, Judith, 102–103, 105–106
Wentworth Gardens (housing project), 17

West, Cornel, 197
"What We Have Seen and Heard" (pastoral letter), 1, 10, 191
whiteness, 57, 156, 163, 178, 188, 200, 224n11. *See also* Blackness
Whites Concerned about the Black Community, 135
Williams, Father Clarence, 151, 159–160
Williams, Jakobi, 170
Williams, Mary Lou, 190
Williams, Shannen Dee, 38, 226n44
Wilmore, Gayraud, 176
World War I, 21–22
World War II, 21–22
Wright, Rev. Jeremiah, 197
Wright, Richard, 92

ABOUT THE AUTHOR

Matthew J. Cressler is Assistant Professor of Religious Studies at the College of Charleston.